T0161447

FORWARD FROM
THIS MOMENT

||||||||||||||||||||||||||||||||||||||||||||||||||||||||||||||||

FORWARD FROM THIS MOMENT

LEONARD PITTS, JR.

A Bolden Book

AGATE

CHICAGO

Library of Congress Cataloging-in-Publication Data

Pitts, Leonard.
Forward from this moment : selected columns, 1994/2009 / Leonard Pitts, Jr.
    p. cm.
Summary: "A collection of columns from nationally-syndicated, Pulitzer Prize-winning journalist, Leonard Pitts, Jr"--Provided by publisher.
Includes index.
ISBN-13: 978-1-932841-50-3 (hardcover)
ISBN-10: 1-932841-50-4 (hardcover)
ISBN-13: 978-1-932841-32-9 (pbk.)
ISBN-10: 1-932841-32-6 (pbk.)
I. Title.
PS3616.I92F67 2009
814'.6--dc22
                        2009012637

Trade paperback edition: 10 11 12 13   10 9 8 7 6 5 4 3

Bolden Books is an imprint of Agate Publishing. Agate books are available in bulk at discount prices. For more information, go to agatepublishing.com.

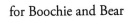

for Boochie and Bear

CONTENTS

FOREWORD

Some books are labors of love. This one is a labor of guilt.

For years now, not a week has passed without someone asking me The Question: Is there a collection of your works available?

It is, make no mistake, one of the most flattering questions you can hear as a newspaper columnist, suggesting as it does that something you have done in this most disposable of media merits permanence, has touched someone sufficiently to earn space on their library shelf.

All that notwithstanding, the answer to the question has always been no. Whereupon the disappointed person would tell me in a vaguely accusatory voice that I'd better get on the stick, because various columns of mine were affixed all over his or her refrigerator, and space was filling up rapidly. That's where the guilt comes in; one doesn't like to think he is responsible for the cluttering and defacement of peoples' Whirlpools and Frigidaires.

So I am pleased to be able to say the answer to the question is finally yes. There is a collection available, and, indeed, you hold it in your hands.

I've divided the book into three sections. The first, Waiting for Someday to Come, contains columns about family. The second, White Men Can't Jump (And Other Stupid Myths), includes columns exploring race, gender, sexual orientation, culture, religion and other fault lines of American culture. The third, Forward from This Moment, contains ruminations on a wide variety of subjects, everything from Sept. 11 and its aftermath to the nature of God. Also, Magic Johnson and Britney Spears.

I began writing columns for the *Miami Herald* in 1992, back when I was still the paper's pop music critic. Though they had hired me the year before to do music reviews and chase rock stars around backstage, the *Herald* also encouraged me to write occasionally about other topics, such as a riot in my hometown of Los Angeles and Magic Johnson's blockbuster announcement that he was infected with HIV.

By 1994, after a cumulative 18 years as a music journalist, I was beginning to feel truly burned out on pop. It is said that the average lifespan of a successful pop act is five years, which means I was working on my fourth lifetime. So I went to my boss and told him I'd had it; if they made me review another Michael Bolton CD, I would not be responsible for my actions afterward.

Thankfully, they didn't call my bluff. Instead, the *Herald* reassigned me as a general interest columnist—i.e., they pay me to write about whatever happens to be on my mind at any given time. And no, I can't believe it either. I wake up every morning expecting that this will surely be the day they come to their senses and send me off to cover sewer commission meetings or something.

But so far, it hasn't happened. Indeed, over the years, I have been guided, goaded, prodded, challenged and cheered on in writing my column by a procession of talented editors—Steve Sonsky, Ileana Oroza, Lynn Medford, Emily Hathaway, Elissa Vanaver, John Barry, Shelley Acoca—and this seems as good a place as any to thank them. I am also grateful to my intrepid agent, Janell Walden-Agyeman, for her unflagging work to bring this about. Special thanks, too, to Miami Herald Executive Editor Anders Gyllenhaal for permission to reprint these columns. And finally, before I get out of gratitude mode, let me also express my love and appreciation to my lovely and gracious wife, Marilyn, and to our kids (Markise, Monique, Marlon, Bryan, Onjel) and grandkid (Eric) for their generosity and patience in allowing me to mine our lives for truths to share on deadline.

I have always found it difficult to answer when people ask me what I write about. Other columnists can say they write about politics or the economy. If such a pithy description exists for my column, I have yet to find it. The best I can do is to crib a line I once saw in some promotional material: it said that mine is a column about "the politics of the human condition."

I have always liked that description and would like to believe it's true. Because above and beyond the economy, above and beyond politics, the thing that shapes a country and a people, that determines what sort of lives we live, is this whole issue of how we treat one another, and how we get along in this country: black and white and Jew and Gentile and Muslim and Mexican and woman and man and gay and straight and whomever and whomever. Figuring out what's right, and finding the courage to do it, are steps one and two in the process of becoming a truly good human being.

That's the process I've spent the last 14 years trying to chronicle, and I'd like to offer my last thanks to you, dear reader, for being so generous with your criticism and your praise of my attempts. I hope you enjoy this book.

Now, go clean off your fridge.

Leonard Pitts, Jr.
Bowie, Maryland
March, 2009

PART ONE:

WAITING FOR SOMEDAY TO COME

JULY 2, 1993

SENDING A MAN OFF TO COLLEGE

Fifteen years ago, I had my first date with the woman I eventually married. As the car pulled away from the curb, her little son ran behind it, crying frantically. "Mommy, where are you going? Mommy, can I go, too?"

Last Tuesday morning at 2 my wife and I took that kid—our son—to a Greyhound station and waited with him for the bus that would take him off to college.

He was, he told us, scared, nervous, excited and happy. "You're supposed to be," I replied. "Life is passages and milestones, and you're about to embark on one of the biggest."

But I felt the same butterflies he did. At a time when black boys are wasting their precious lives by the thousands, Markise is going to college. They haven't invented the words to describe how great that makes me feel.

So we stood there with him, his mother and I, in the balmy darkness of the morning and tried to remember the things we'd meant to say. But it came out as "Do you have your ticket? Are you sure you have enough money? Call as soon as you get there."

"I'll be all right," he assured us—though more for his own courage, I suspect, than ours.

"I know," I said. I embraced my son, who is almost as tall as I am. "You're special," I told him. "I love you."

He is and I do, but oh, you wouldn't have known it from some of the arguments we've had over the years. He'd probably tell you that no matter how big or small a particular infraction was, I stubbornly cast it in terms of its impact on his future and the sort of grown-up he would be. "There are more than enough 30-year-old boys out there," I said. "It's a waste of time to grow up to be a boy. I want you to grow up to be a man."

God, I was probably a tiresome scold, as I preached it with a Southern Baptist intensity: Be a man. A real man has integrity, I said. A man respects himself and others. A man takes responsibility for his actions. A man, my son, uses his head. I wanted him to learn a lesson that has seemingly eluded many of his contemporaries: That a man does the right thing not because it will make him popular, not because it is easier or will put money in his pocket. He does the right thing because it is the right thing.

My son often answered all that high-minded preaching with impertinent sarcasm. The kid can be a royal pain in the posterior when he puts his mind to it.

Why does he do that? I once asked my wife. Why does he answer everything with a wisecrack? Because, replied my wife, you do.

That stopped me cold. What could I say? She's right. It was frightening—and humbling—to realize that this child, who shares no blood with me, nevertheless resembles me so much. Arguing with him was like arguing with myself.

Be a man, I kept telling him, and if I sometimes sounded like a broken record, it's only because I wanted so desperately for him to hear me. Wanted him to understand how special and rare a thing it is these days, to be a man. Wanted him to understand that it is not a thing that comes with a certain car or a certain salary or a certain age. It is a knowing that comes from within.

Be careful of the choices you make, I always told him. One day you'll be a 30-year-old man living according to the decisions made by a teenager. You never know if they hear these things. But then, a couple of weeks ago, my son and some friends were supposed to go out for the evening. At the last minute, Markise pulled out. He had a suspicion, he said, that the guy who was driving—a guy he didn't know all that well—had stolen the car.

It turned out he was right. The boy was arrested two days later.

"I can't afford to get mixed up in something like that," Markise told us. "I'm going to college to be a lawyer."

And, of course, he did go. When he unpacked his duffel bag, he found a couple of things he wasn't expecting: a Bible from his mother and a book of poetry from me with a bookmark stuck in at page 116—Rudyard Kipling's "If."

Maybe you remember it from school: "If you can fill the unforgiving minute with 60 seconds' worth of distance run, yours is the Earth and everything that's in it. And—which is more—you'll be a man, my son!" He'll read it and think I'm being a Baptist preacher again. And maybe I am. But I have no apologies. I know and fear the alternatives.

That morning, my wife and I followed his bus down the street until it turned onto I-95. We watched until it was just red taillights blinking in the distance, and then we drove on in silence.

A couple of miles later I took my wife's hand. "We done good, kid," I told her.

Forgive me my pride. But, you see, last week, I sent a man off to school.

FEBRUARY 7, 1994

MONSTERS THAT LURK IN FANTASY, REALITY

We have a monster problem at my house.

Monsters under the bed, monsters reaching out of the darkness, monsters bouncing around off the walls. Monsters everywhere. And poor Onjel, 3 years old and about as many feet tall, has no choice but to run for her life. She scurries through the house in her Barney pajamas in the dead of night and doesn't stop till she reaches the security of Mommy and Daddy's bed.

I've been doing battle with these monsters for years, and I must say, they're hardier than even your average cockroach. I go into that room with my bat ready or my Nerf gun cocked, and make a great show of routing 'em out of the closet or the underside of the bed. I thrash them to within an inch of their miserable lives, then send 'em packing and assure my daughter that her room is now monster-free.

And yet they always come back. Child after child, year after year, the monsters return as faithfully as a puppy until finally a child reaches an age where she's not the smallest thing in the world. After that, the demons fade away.

Probably I should be tired of monster-bashing. But Onjel is my last child, which means these are my last monsters. And so I treasure this most uniquely paternal of duties the way you do the final notes of a favorite song or the last ticking seconds of a fiery sunset. Tell me if you can, what else a man can do that requires so little effort but makes him such a hero in his daughter's eyes?

Onjel's monsters are monsters of innocence, you see, gargoyles from an imagination as yet untouched by the incidental meanness of life. Her monsters have horns, bug eyes and slavering jaws, but they slink from the light. You can hug them away.

For all the fear they inspire in her, they inspire in me only the need to seize the time and cherish the day. Because soon, these monsters will fade and be replaced by the real ones—beasts in suits and dresses, brutes that drive nice cars or have puppy dogs, demons that laugh and smile.

Monsters, in other words, that look like everyone else.

Life would sure be a heck of a lot easier if the dark hearts of this world looked like Onjel thinks they do. That way you could see them coming. They'd have goat hooves for feet, a single bloodshot eye, and white froth dripping from their lips, and you'd know that it might be prudent to cross to the other side when you see them coming at you on the street.

But life's not like that and the real monsters, the vilest miscreants, are invisible. Because they look not unlike ourselves.

It's a tough concept for a child to grasp.

I didn't realize how tough until I chanced to catch an Oprah show a few weeks ago. She had sent a camera crew to a park on the pretext of asking mothers what they had told their children about strangers. As the mothers talked in the foreground, the camera's eye zoomed past them to where their children were playing in the sandbox. And then a man—engaged by Winfrey for just that purpose—approached the sandbox. He was an unremarkable, unthreatening man, well-dressed, who seemed genuinely distressed that his puppy was missing and asked the children's help in finding it. Time and again, the children linked their tiny hands with his and went to help him look.

The mothers would be chattering with happy assurance about how their child knew better than to talk to strangers. Then the camera crew would point behind her where the dumbfounded woman would see her child being led out of the park—by a stranger. More than one mother wept.

In hindsight, it's not at all difficult to understand why the kids were so easily lured away. The man didn't look like a stranger.

Onjel says the monsters that haunt her room are green. I suppose that'd be a dead giveaway should she ever encounter one on the street.

But she won't. Her monsters haunt the dark places in her room and her dreams. Her monsters hide from the righteous wrath of her Nerf-gun-toting dad. Her monsters are relatively easy to deal with.

But one day too soon, she'll be released into a world where the monsters are harder to discern and where so many things can happen. So many bad things. And so, each day, when I watch her walk off to school, I'll feel this tiny twinge of apprehension. And each day, when she returns safely, there'll be this small rush of relief.

My daughter and I aren't all that different when you get right down to it. The monsters are keeping me awake, too.

NOVEMBER 28, 1994

DON'T GIVE UP SANTA TO THE GRINCHES OF THE WORLD

I was 9 years old when one of my teachers took it upon herself to disabuse me of my belief in Santa Claus.

I never saw my mother angrier at anyone who wasn't my dad.

Mom spent an inordinate amount of time and energy making real for us the myths of childhood, and she regarded my teacher's disclosure as an infringement on parental prerogative. As I recall, she got on the phone and told her that in no uncertain terms.

Me, I was stricken. I had been unwillingly exposed to terrible knowledge, had been dragged before my time across the border into some awful, adult place.

And so I did a strange thing. I unheard what I'd been told, unlearned what I now knew, willed myself back to innocence.

I reclaimed Santa Claus and never again let go.

I mention this because it's at this time every year that the self-appointed experts come scuttling Grinch-like from their holes to do battle with Santa. They argue with ponderous solemnity that jolly old St. Nick represents a clear and present danger to the psyche of the American child.

Last week, Dr. Robert R. Butterworth, a Los Angeles psychologist, issued a statement that parents who foster a child's faith in Santa Claus risk earning that child's anger and mistrust.

"Make-believe behavior is an important part of socialization and cognitive growth, but when childhood fantasies collide with the common belief of their peers, these fantasies can lead to emotional distress," says Butterworth.

Humbug, says I.

I can't help but believe folks like the good doctor go through a lot of effort to make complex something that's so blissfully simple. What a shame that some of us are so serious, literal and imagination-starved that we're threatened by Santa Claus. And that others just don't get it. I get depressed when I wander the aisles of the local toy emporium and see parents Christmas shopping alongside their children. I'm sure it's more efficient, but for crying out loud, where's the fun in it? Where's the excitement, the wondering, the days of anticipation that creep by like eons? Where's the twilight spent scanning the sky, the eating early and fast, the jumping into bed with all your clothes on and then waiting, waiting ... waiting wide awake, tingling, beckoning sleep that refuses to come?

Where, in a word, is the magic? And childhood must be magic, especially in an era when headlines are full of sad and dreamless youngsters, baby-faced killers and baby-faced victims.

Children believe in magic. They expect ultimate good, have faith in things unseen, trust that problems will work out just fine and that we'll all live happily ever after.

It is the thing about them we sometimes forget. We dress them as miniature adults, teach them to worship at the altar of hipper-than-thou, ring them about with dire warnings about uncles who touch, strangers who threaten, diseases that stalk, preach to them a gospel of on-your-guard, in-your-face reality ... But they are still children, man. Fantasy is their natural medium, magic their birthright. As a child, I had magic in the very heart of urban decay. No miracle on 34th Street, mind you, but quite a few on 79th.

I'll never forget lying in bed, too-awake, one Christmas Eve, and hearing something hit the roof. It was, I was certain, the prancing and pawing of each little hoof.

So I sprang from my bed to see what was the matter, ran out to the living room ... and caught my mom and dad in mid-assembly on a bicycle. My father looked up like the proverbial deer caught in the headlights and said something profound, like "Duh." Mom, bless her heart, calmly explained that Santa Claus had just that moment left all these goodies. He was right outside feeding his reindeer, but if he heard me stirring around, he'd return and confiscate all he had given.

I was a vapor trail. Dove in the bed and lay there trembling, eyes squeezed tight, snoring as hard as I could.

And no, the memory occasions no anger, mistrust or mental distress. Just a fond smile and a certain sense of wistful longing. Even now, lying awake on a Christmas Eve, I can't help listening for a thump against the roof.

I believe in Santa Claus.

DECEMBER 13, 1995

THE GHOST OF CHRISTMAS PAST: WHEN TOYS WERE TOYS

There comes a moment, deep in every major toy hunt, when you catch yourself saying things adults just do not ordinarily say. Like: "Excuse me, do you know your Zords?"

Take it as a sign of what this season does to some of us that the toy store stock clerk of whom I asked the question didn't punch me in the nose or say, "Sir, I think that's rather personal." Instead he replied, in an affable voice, "Yes. What do you need?" There followed a perfectly polite discussion of the merits and availability of various Zords. For those of you without small children, your basic Zords come in a frightening variety that includes, but is not limited to: Falconzord, Ninja Megazord, Frog Ninjazord, Ape Ninjazord, Ninja Ultrazord and Shogun Ultrazord.

I suspect I've just done more to encourage birth control than anyone this side of Planned Parenthood.

Once upon a time, toys were a lot simpler. Take the Christmas I wanted a toy bus. I said, "Mom, tell Santa Claus I want a toy bus." Christmas morning, there it was.

What a difference a generation makes. A child of the '90s, after all, would request the Super Destructo Mega-Ninja Bus with working headlights, authentic engine sounds and a special button which, when pressed, transforms the whole megillah into a fire-breathing Tyrannosaur. It's enough to make one long for days of yore. A pox upon the toy makers. Do they think we're made of money and time?

You're probably thinking to yourself, "This sounds like the raving of a man who's come up empty after searching two counties for a black Baby Sip and Slurp doll." But I'd say to you, "Ha! Do you know where I can get one?"

I hate this doll so much I can't even keep its name straight. Or maybe I subconsciously refuse to say it right because I'm sick of saying it at all. "Excuse me, do you have a black Baby Slurp and Burp?"

"…Baby Sit and Spit?"

"…Baby Slip and Fall?"

"…Baby Ski and Pee?"

It strikes me that I'm going through an awful lot of trouble for a hunk of plastic that, by Dec. 28, will be naked, hairless and blind in one eye. But that's what many of us do this time of year, isn't it? Each year brings at least one hot toy, one Holy Grail item for which Santa's helpers search in mounting panic, schlepping breathless and vacant-eyed from store to store like tabloid reporters chasing Elvis sightings, except that one has a better chance of actually finding Elvis.

Holy Grail toys, on the other hand, always sell out by August—and the next shipment is never due before February.

I speak from experience here. Your humble correspondent is a veteran of the Great Cabbage Patch Wars, where ordinary adults engaged in bare-knuckle brawls in toy store aisles for the right to be overcharged for ugly little goblin-faced dolls. And don't even get me started on the toy that I will henceforth and forever know as Those Damned Power Rangers.

Two years ago, I'm calling toy stores up, down and across the Florida peninsula asking, "Do you have Those Damned Power

Rangers?" Then I start trying stores in states where I have friends or family. Nada. Finally, I begin to call stores in states next to states where I have friends or family. They finally pried the phone from my hand when I got off the line with a store in Anchorage. For the record, I don't know a living soul who knows a living soul within 500 miles of Alaska.

Never did find Those Damn Power Rangers, either—the one blot on an otherwise spotless record. But that year taught us an unforgettable lesson about the magic of Christmas. Because when the special morning came and our son found no Power Rangers under the tree, he still turned big brown eyes upon us and gave us a look that said, with touching, unmistakable poignancy: You people are absolutely worthless.

Which is, of course, why we jump through the toy makers' hoop this time of year. Trust me: you never want to see that look.

Speaking of which, you'll have to excuse me now. Looks like we've got a line on Baby Surf and Turf. If we hustle, we can just make the plane in time.

JANUARY 26, 1996

A MAN'S WISHES FOR HIS DAUGHTER AND GRANDCHILD

Dear Eric:

Hello, grandson. I'm sorry that greeting doesn't come naturally to me yet. You see, you're a bit of a shock. Your mother, 18 and unmarried, kept it secret from us that you were on the way. She did not, she said, want to "hurt" or "disappoint" us.

She hid her body in oversize clothes, denied pregnancy indignantly and repeatedly. Her mother suspected she was pregnant anyway, but me, I accepted her denials. I wanted to believe her.

Raising a child is quite a thing, Eric. You want so much for them, want it with a purity and a selflessness that shock your jaded soul. You want them to have more than you did, reach higher than you could, to be better than you are.

You don't necessarily want things like that for your friends or your siblings, but you want them for your child—a truth, I guess, that your mother will now learn.

But the thing is, she's our child, and we wanted so much for her. Still do, I suppose.

Maybe, during one of your 2 a.m. lung testings, you chanced to catch the movie *Parenthood* on cable. There's a scene in which Steve Martin, coaching a youth league baseball team, pushes his son to play a position the son doesn't want. Well, the kid drops a pop fly, which costs his team the game and earns him everyone's scorn. Martin fantasizes that years later the kid is shooting people from a bell tower, screaming, "Dad, you shouldn't have made me play second base!"

As far as I'm concerned, it wasn't much of an exaggeration. When you're a parent, you fear your own ineptitude. You fear that you will ruin a young life by saying or doing the wrong thing, or just not being equal to the task. You fear that your 18-year-old daughter will come home pregnant.

And when it happens, you fear that you screwed up. Even though intellect informs you with irrefutable logic that you've done everything you could as a parent, your heart insists with a fervor that you have failed. It yells that you could have said something, done something, somehow changed something. You'll never figure out what the something is, but not knowing won't silence the clangor of your heart.

It's like I told you, Eric: You want so much for your kids. Possibility renews itself through children. You see things in their eyes—a reflection of far horizons, a shadow of discarded dreams coming back for another chance.

As a parent, you are the guardian of all that. It's hard to imagine a more daunting responsibility.

Of course, I don't blame you, Eric. You are the most blameless of creatures. But I have silences with your mother now, wounded places that have yet to begin to heal.

I can't say it enough, Eric. You *want* for your children. Want with an unrelenting ferocity that leaves you aching and numbed. Which brings us, I guess, to you.

I don't know you yet. You are an awkward fit in my arms, an uncertainty wedged into my life. And I don't mind telling you, I'm ill at ease with the absurd new role you've thrust me into.

Grandpa? Ugh.

I don't know you, but I do know this: Holding you, I feel it stirring again—that desperate sense of wanting, without regard to self. You struggle, you gurgle, you watch the world with eyes that have yet to see meanness and pain, and wanting is just automatic.

Wondering, too. Who are you, child? A teacher or preacher? Entertainer or explorer? Will you sink the winning shot? Win the Nobel Prize? Or will you, just possibly, change the whole world?

These are questions that must wait a lifetime for answers. But their mere asking has power to lift downcast eyes and spirits.

Don't get me wrong, kid. I expect that the silences in our home will remain deep and the wounded places tender and raw for a long time to come. And yet those questions buoy me. Even your young aunt and uncles see it. They gaze down at you with such luminous eyes, wondering who you are.

Perhaps they see in you what I do: possibility renewed, a future unmortgaged, a second chance.

And a hope. That someday, the wounded places will be healed and the deep silences overflow with joy.

JUNE 6, 1996

A CRY WE NEED TO HEED: 'LOOK AT ME, DAD'

The other morning I drove to McDonald's, bought two breakfasts and took them to a nearby elementary school. There I waited in a hallway with 15 or 20 other men.

We were a motley bunch, and I sensed our collective unease, as if without wives and significant others to lean on we were skittish and abashed in this place of children. Finally, the door to Ms. Stubbs' kindergarten class swung open.

One by one, she sent the children out to lead their fathers in. When my little girl spotted me, she forgot to wait for her teacher's prompting. Onjel ran and wrapped her arms around my waist.

I folded myself into a chair far below me and watched as the kids literally sang our praises. Each child recited the reason his or her dad was special ("He plays with me," said Onjel), and they gave us drawings and pencil holders.

Later we sat outside beneath a shade tree and I had breakfast with my favorite girl.

Ms. Stubbs also organizes an annual tea for mothers. She says the kids love that, but nothing compares with the day the dads come. It's a red-letter morn, a V.I.P. affair. The kids are extra excited. As she and I spoke on the playground, it wasn't hard to see what she meant. The air was filled with the screams of kids on monkey bars and swings.

"Dad, look!" they cried. "Look at me, Dad!"

There was something poignant about the way they performed for us, beseeched our attention. It was a reminder that we fathers are so often absent from the lives of our offspring. Not just the physical absence produced by divorce and desertion, but the emotional absence that can happen even when Dad is there. So many things claw at our attention—jobs, cars, wives, bills, sports—that our children sometimes become small voices, distantly heard.

But that's a rationalization, isn't it? Many things claw at women for attention as well, and yet, speaking generally, they remain more engaged in the lives of the children than we.

Yes, I know there are exceptions. But one feminist movement later, dads are still, at least in most two-parent households, likely to be the auxiliary parent. In trying to be anything else, a man strains against the weight of acculturation and, perhaps, even biology itself. A family counselor once told me men can be intimidating to children through no effort or fault of their own. She said we do it with our size, our physicality, the rumble of our voices.

Which may be true, but it's also a convenient excuse.

Of course, it's not like we've had many prototypes to learn from. On the one hand there is the media-promoted model of harmless, bumbling incompetence. That's hard on a man's dignity.

Then there's the traditional model, all aloofness and unknowability. Dad as snowy alpine peak. That's hard on a man's heart.

And a child's love.

Somewhere between those polar opposites lies a place I'm trying to reach. That I am not the only one may, perhaps, be imputed from the fact that every father with a child in Ms. Stubbs' class showed up for the breakfast. Except one, that is, and he sent two grandfathers in his place.

It was a great thing to see. A yard full of dads and daughters, sires and sons. Made me realize that getting to that place between the extremes doesn't entail some vaguely beneficent ideal of making time in my life for the kids. Rather, it requires undertaking the harder task of leaving my concerns behind to spend time in their lives, with them. To see the places where they play and learn and to show them by my presence that those things matter to me. Because how to get our attention is, it seems to me, the central question a child faces in the relationship with a father.

"Dad, look!" cried the children, swinging, sliding and climbing all across the yard. "Look at me, Dad!"

As my favorite girl scaled the bars, I made a point of watching her without being asked.

SEPTEMBER 19, 1996

IN CLEANUP GAME, BOYS PLAY DIRTY

Told the boys to clean up their room. There followed the usual whining, wheedling and cries of pain, but once I was finished, the project got under way.

Look, I'm no Felix Unger, but I've always believed there comes a point when you have to take a stand against dirt, preferably before the Health Department gets involved. My boys, unfortunately, do not share this belief. They're convinced that if you just stall long enough, magic trash fairies will spirit your garbage away to the land of Ever Clean.

What else am I to make of kids who put empty tubes of toothpaste back on the bathroom counter? Never mind that the Incredible Hulk with a hydraulic press couldn't squeeze out even one more micron of paste.

It wouldn't be so bad if I felt the boys operated from some misguided sense of frugality. But they operate from a very well-guided sense of sloth, desperate not to accidentally, inadvertently—you know how these things happen—do any work around the house.

You think I jest, don't you? Consider this: While allegedly cleaning up the kitchen, a kid encounters a platter on which rests the remains of the meal—a quarter of a hotdog, let's say. So he chucks the meat and washes the platter, right?

Silly person! Of course not! Washing the dish is work, whereas designating that little morsel of meat a leftover provides a convenient dodge for said work. So my kid puts the platter in the fridge, as if thinking that in two or three days, someone's going to look inside and say to themselves, Boy, I hope there's a dried up, stinky little scrap of hotdog in here. That would really hit the spot!

You see, the object of the game is to avoid cleaning up the mess by moving it around—as if the garbage would enjoy a change of scenery. This hit me full force the other day as I sat in my favorite chair to read. On the floor next to said chair is a wicker basket for magazines. Well, actually, the magazines were somewhere beneath old newspapers, T-shirts, toys, a ski mask, and everything else the boys have been asked to remove from the dining room table for the last month.

You know and I know that this simply means they have to do the same work twice. I keep explaining that to them, but they don't get it. I've never seen anyone expend so much effort to avoid expending effort.

So tidying up the room has become a ritualized affair, the highest expression of their art. It goes like this: I tell them to clean up. They pretend they're going to do it and I pretend to believe them. An hour later, I find them having a heated discussion of whose job it is to pick up the candy wrapper on the floor.

An hour after that, I go back and the argument has escalated to a full-scale war of glowering eyes and poked-out lips. They make motions like they're picking up stuff, but the room is getting no cleaner.

Half an hour later they're in my face, tattling on each other over misdeeds that go back to the womb. I make threatening sounds and gesture toward the belt. They rush back to that landfill, vowing to get along long enough to make it clean.

They finally finish at dinner. Well, "finish" is a relative term. Let's just say they present a room that a normal person wouldn't mind sleeping in if he had no other choice on a sub-zero night. And all the gas station bathrooms were taken.

Mind you, this is a 90-minute job that they've been doing all day. You know what that means, don't you? I'm raising future plumbers here.

Their object, of course, is to make the experience so unpleasant for me that I'll think twice before asking them to do it again. And they've succeeded: Next time, I'll clean up the room myself and move them out to the garage.

Nah, I'm just blowing off steam. There's no way I could clean up that room. I don't even own a flamethrower.

OCTOBER 31, 1996

PARENTS ARE NEVER FREE OF FEAR— OR OF LOVE

I am at my desk when my wife rushes in, breathless with alarm. Our son has been hurt. Head injury while playing basketball at school. Ambulance taking him to the emergency room.

Everything drops. I am up and moving at once. One thought and one only: Get there.

I am driving too fast on a winding road, rain misting against the windshield. I am rushing across the grass, plunging into the emergency room, interrogating nurses. But he's not even there yet. I am pacing, looking down the long driveway, willing the lights of the ambulance to appear. Behind me, the theme music from *The Price Is Right* is a tinny distraction and I marvel that some part of my brain hears television, some part is not consumed with fear. In the distance red lights flash against a sky the color of a dusty nickel.

I am in the ambulance bay, waiting for the vehicle doors to open and the paramedic is trying to steel me, telling me that the tubes, neck brace and back board I will see are just precautionary. I nod. He and his partner lift the stretcher out and of course, no words could ever have prepared me for my middle son looking like that.

My voice rings false cheer as I call to him. "Marlon! Hey, Marlon!" Marlon looks through me. He is dazed and not fully aware of his surroundings.

I am at his bedside. Minutes have passed and he is becoming lucid. His eyes are focused and he knows me. I test him with Lakers questions because that team is bond between us.

Starting center in 1988? Small forward in 1979? His answers are slow, but correct.

Half an hour later, he doesn't remember talking to me.

Watching him, I am recalling what happened just a few days ago, when my wife and I flew home to L.A. for a visit with family. Sitting in my sister's living room, I went into my standard kids-are-driving-me-crazy routine. Nothing you haven't said yourself if you've been a parent for any length of time. Just standard complaints about dishes that aren't washed, bedrooms that are unclean, behavior that frustrates.

Twelve years, I told my sister. That's when my youngest turns 18. That's when my "sentence" is up and I go free. We all laughed.

But of course, parents never go free, do they? That's the lesson I am learning here for the umpteenth time.

I am holding my son's hand and reflecting that not so long ago, I could close my fingers over his and make them disappear. Now he is all arms and legs, all go! go! go! and it seems unnatural that his blue jeans and Air Jordans lie atop this bed, unmoving. And, God, whatever happened to the time?

I reproach God because it's not fair, really. Seems unjust that you love anything as much as you do a child. The love makes you helpless hostage to their careless lives, their reckless whims. The love means you can't be serene unless they allow it, can't unclench until they navigate the day safely and return home. And when disaster strikes as inevitably it must, the love can damn near kill you.

I am listening to my son tell his mother how he got hurt. Going for a layup, came down on someone's shirt, slipped and slammed head-first into the wall. "How much is it going to cost me to have the wall fixed?" I crack, because at times like this, dads joke. Marlon grins at father wit, but wants me to bear the most important thing in mind: "I made the shot," he says.

I am back home, watching my sleeping son. I kneel and wake him to make sure I can. He is cranky and has a headache but seems otherwise OK, so I go upstairs, sit at my desk and raise a window. A feeble sun has split open the gray. A welcome breeze rustles the curtains. Outside, I hear the school bus wheeze to a stop, depositing my youngest son safely on the curb.

It is a good day.

NOVEMBER 28, 1996

CRIME ISN'T LIMITED TO 'CERTAIN ASPECTS OF SOCIETY'

Police say it happened like this: Early that morning, Amy Grossberg gave birth in a motel room in Newark, Del. Her boyfriend, Brian Peterson, took the baby and stuffed it into a garbage bag, pulled the drawstrings tight and dumped it in a trash bin. The temperature outside was below freezing, but police who found the baby later that day say it wasn't the cold that killed. Rather, it was the skull fractures.

Friends of the two 18-year-old college freshmen and accused murderers say they are the "nicest kids" you could ever meet. Indeed, a high school yearbook photo presents them as smiling, apple-cheeked and wholesome, two sweet-faced white kids from the upper crust. Peterson's attorney, looking for empathy, has referred to his client as a "baby" himself.

And so, people profess to be shocked. As Grossberg's attorney, Charles Oberly III, recently explained it: "Maybe we expect criminality to occur in certain aspects of society."

"Certain aspects," he said. What loaded, coded words. They lend antiseptic innocence to an odious statement, sit atop his meaning like a room deodorizer on a dung heap. "Certain aspects." A neat, lawyerly way of referring to black people, brown people and, yes, poor and uneducated people of whatever race or ethnicity.

We expect criminality from them, he says. As if the abomination his client is alleged to have committed might be less incomprehensible had it originated where se habla espanol. Or where the brothers gather. Or where white people live in trailers.

The audacity of the assumption leaves me struggling with an anger that looms above the heinous crime. An anger that makes me want to scream at people who are shocked because they thought things like this don't happen to people like those in places like that.

"...We expect criminality...in certain aspects..." the attorney said. It's been a long time since I heard a statement of such bare-knuckles classism, and so a declaration of the obvious seems necessary: we should not "expect" this kind of barbarism from anyone.

And yet, the lawyer has a point, doesn't he? That's the sad part.

Let the unthinkable happen in certain neighborhoods, among certain people, and our response is conditioned and predictable. We cluck pieties, speak words of remorse and move on, essentially unfazed.

Let the same things happen in middle or upper class neighborhoods, in places where they wrap themselves in the delusion of seclusion, and all hell breaks loose. I remember when I lived in Los Angeles, how media kicked into overdrive and police started barricading streets after a gang shooting left one woman dead in the tony Westwood district. Those of us who lived in communities where it was not unknown for gang violence to pick off half a dozen in a single weekend with barely a nod of notice from media and police could only marvel at the disparity.

What do you think it says to a child that some expect terrible things from people like her? How long do you think it takes her to assimilate that expectation—to learn to accept criminality and failure as her natural element?

Not long enough. Not nearly.

I am insulted that anyone is surprised that the rich, the beautiful or the white could be capable of murder. After the Billionaire Boys Club and O.J. Simpson, after John DuPont and the "rough sex" murder case where a rich preppy admitted to strangling his girlfriend, how can we continue to believe that the rich are somehow different, higher, intrinsically better than we?

Money is not a badge of morality, but a barometer of financial standing. It can only magnify what we are—not change it.

And if a rich person is an amoral, psychopathic piece of man-trash who prizes expediency above human life, then what, really, is the difference between him and some grubby, illiterate, thrill-killing drifter?

So I am profoundly unmoved by the call to feel empathy for murder suspects Brian Peterson and Amy Grossberg on the basis that they were sweet, beautiful, wealthy or white.

For whatever it's worth, that baby was, too.

MAY 24, 1997

APPROACHING FOOTSTEPS SIGNAL BEGINNING AND END

I was walking along minding my own business when my son hit me.

This was not unexpected. Indeed, two seconds before, the kid had announced his intention with perfect equanimity. "I'm going to beat you up," he said.

"Take your best shot," said I. Whereupon he gave me two jabs that thudded solidly into my upper left arm. I immediately punched him back, then grabbed him in a headlock and administered a few noogies for good measure. He laughed, I laughed, and he moved on. Meantime, I drifted back to where my wife was pushing the baby stroller.

"I can't move my arm," I whispered.

"What?" she said.

"I was fooling around with Bryan and he punched me and now I can't use my arm."

She started laughing. "It's not funny," I hissed. "I can't even feel my fingers."

Marilyn, because she is an angel of mercy, laughed harder. And I wondered aloud, "When did he start hitting so hard?"

It is the latest in a series of similar questions I find myself asking about my two youngest boys: "When did they grow so tall? When did their voices get so deep? When did girls become so important to them?"

I studied my 12-year-old son while massaging my aching shoulder. We were on the boardwalk in Atlantic City, and he was watching sea gulls glide by above us. He was so big. More and more, the boys who used to look up to me now look me dead in the eyes. It's proud-making. And unsettling.

"He probably just hit a nerve," said Marilyn in belated consolation.

Which was true in more ways than one.

Indeed, he hit the same nerve his 14-year-old brother hit last time we played basketball. Used to be, my size and strength were more than a match for Marlon's quickness and skill. Used to be, I could swat his shots like errant mosquitoes. Used to be.

This time, the boy dusted me. Wasn't even close. I tell myself I had an off day—and maybe I did. Or maybe the future is coming like a semi with bad brakes.

Children are God's wake-up call, His reminder that the moment is finite and nobody makes it to forever. Children, after all, have but one mission: to render you obsolete.

Which is why I've watched with amusement the debate over the 63-year-old woman who became a mother and the 77-year-old actor who fathered a child. We've questioned whether they are too old for the task they've undertaken, questioned the sexist way some of us commend the man but condemn the woman.

But the thing we haven't questioned is this: Can either of them take a punch that lands like mortality on the flesh of the upper arm?

Probably not.

But then, that'd be true even if they were 30 years younger.

People often ask me if I let my kids preview columns that are written about them. The answer is yes, always. Except for this one. This one they won't see. This one I'm going to scissor out of the paper and hide, because of the confession I'm about to make: They're catching up to me.

I tell them they're not, but they are. I'm running as fast as I can, but they're. running faster. And pretty soon, I'll have no place left to run.

"Take that bass out of your voice when you talk to me!" I bark. And they laugh like, Oh, Dad is so funny.

But who's joking?

You'd think I would be cool with this, having been through it once before. I have a son who's 23, and we've spent years doing this same dance, redefining a relationship that once seemed fixed and secure. So you'd think I'd have it down pat, would have anticipated this upheaval and prepared accordingly.

And intellectually, I did.

But guess what? This doesn't have a lot to do with intellect. This has to do with that jolt of recognition that comes when a 12-year-old is able to sock your shoulder and make it hurt and you realize he's closing in on you.

If the knowledge brings disbelief, it also brings a certain misty-eyed pride. You want to drape an arm around him and say, "You're becoming a man, my son."

Which is just what I'm going to do. Soon as I'm able to lift my arm again.

JUNE 11, 1998

FAMILIAR SPRING RITUAL SUMMONS NEW HOPE

The girls are more beautiful than girls have ever been, lithe and graceful in long white robes.

And the boys are handsome and clear-eyed, their blue robes lending them dignity boys don't often have.

I am in a place I've not been for 24 years. Backstage among high-school seniors ready for graduation. The ceremony begins in minutes and I'm searching for my stepdaughter, trying to deliver the cap and gown she didn't receive, thanks to a clerical snafu.

If you had told me before that I'd be doing this, I would have laughed out loud. Raising the daughter in question has been like trying to disarm a ticking bomb. She's been the proverbial problem child, brought more pain into the house than her four siblings combined. The estrangement she's created by a lifetime of ill-considered words and shortsighted deeds has been long, painful and deep.

So much so that there was a time I thought she would never make it to this day. Or that I would not choose to meet her here if she did.

But there she is, and here I am.

Don't make too much of it. It would be the worst, most saccharine lie to say that a few bars of "Pomp and Circumstance" can magically seal fissures that took years to develop. Not close. Not a chance. But all the same, this ritual of spring is not without its power, is it?

The air is vivid with excited murmurs and nervous laughter and I stand among these no-longer-children, not-quite-adults trying to remember when or if I was ever as young. When or if I stood so anxiously at one of life's borderlines, waiting to cross into a place I had never been before.

As a child, I was fascinated by borders, the idea that this side of an invisible line was one place, but the other side was somewhere wholly different. Traveling across the country at 11, I remember trying to stay awake so as not to miss it when we crossed the state lines.

Needless to say, I was a little disappointed. As we passed from state to state, California to Arizona to New Mexico to Texas, I kept expecting an instant ... something. Waiting to feel different, looking for some sign in the sky to acknowledge that we had come abruptly into a new place.

Doesn't work that way though, does it? Trees on one side of the border seemed to look pretty much like trees on the other. A change had come, but its effects were not immediately to be seen.

The same, I think, is true of these rituals we use like borders to mark off one part of life from another. So I imagine that a new graduate will wake up the morning after the ceremony disappointed to discover that he's pretty much the same person he was before.

He'll understand soon enough. Nothing is different, yet everything is.

I don't know who decided that graduations—and for that matter, weddings—were to be held in June, but the symbolism of it is irresistible because June itself is a border: spring to summer. From the season of new birth, redemption and renewal into that of heat, immediacy and opportunity.

And is it too much to pray that a daughter who has been nobody's picnic, who has spurned second chances by the dozen, will understand this and cross over from a childhood of trouble? There is, of course, no way of knowing.

In the end, there is only hope. Always and only ... hope.

The orchestra strikes up the stately strains of the graduation march and lines of girls-to-women and boys-to-men begin wending past me to take their seats. There is a distant thunder of applause.

My daughter, cap and gown delivered, is one of the last in line. As she passes me, she lifts her hand and gives a luminous grin. All things seem possible.

Then she is gone, filing out with the other girls, walking softly toward the border.

JULY 18, 1998

TEENS' CHANGES CAN BE CRUEL TIME FOR PARENTS

So we're down the street at a neighbor's backyard barbecue a couple of weeks ago when my wife is asked to leave. It's our son who does the asking.

Seems there are girls around and, well, you know how it is: No self-respecting guy can make a move on the babes if his mother is watching. So Mom, would you mind going home? Before someone sees us talking and thinks we're related? Thanks, Mom.

Mr. Sensitivity even seals the deal with a kiss on the cheek.

Behind him, Marilyn looks as if her mouth just sprung a hinge. Needless to say, Marlon has since been treated to several vivid retellings of the 23½ hours of labor it took to bring him into the world.

Some days the boy is amazingly perceptive. Other days, you swear that if you put your ear next to his, you'd hear the ocean.

There is, of course, a simple explanation for that: He's a teenager. Third member of that alien race we've hosted in our home. I wish I could report that it gets easier, but it doesn't. All that happens is you learn the terrain a little better. For instance, having just passed through the Rebel Without a Cause stage, we're now deep into the Parents Just Don't Understand stage. This is the one where you go overnight from the adored mom or dad to the unbearable dolt who embarrasses his kid by any number of thoughtless actions.

Like existing, for instance.

Not that there aren't advantages. Lately, I find that if I want Marlon to do something, I have only to threaten to come within 20 yards of him in public. Especially if I imply that I might try to speak to him in his own language: "Yo, homeboy. Wassup? Chillin'? Word."

Just a hint of that, and I get the lawn mowed any time I want. Front and back.

Know what, though? I'd gladly cut the grass myself just to get through the day without being treated like a human zit.

Not that I don't understand. Change is an adolescent's birthright. Heck, it's his job description.

But pity the poor parents. Change is not easy for us. It's abrupt and cruel, has neither pity for memories nor regard for sentiment. It just comes, and demands to be dealt with.

We're doing the best we can, but Marlon's at that age where he's a different person every time I see him. His very face seems but a trick of the light. He grins while trying to sweet-talk his mom and he looks like the quintessential boy, then he turns his head to a certain angle and you see the dawning shadow of a man.

We should be better prepared for this, I guess. After all, children begin breaking away almost from birth. My grandson, all of 2 years old, recently figured out how to unlock the front door. Twice now, the neighbors have found Eric toddling merrily down the street and brought him home. Don't say it: We've already bought a doorknob guard.

Like Eric, Marlon's going to overestimate his own abilities. Going to wander off in directions we didn't expect and can't protect him from. And all we can do is hope we've taught the right lessons and that if he gets in trouble, he'll be able to find his way home.

As I wait with eagerness to meet the man he becomes, it dawns on me that I'm really going to miss the boy he was. Going to miss talking pop music and basketball and comic books with him. There's always been a neon streak of kid in me and that guy really brought it out. Really did.

Now he's impatient to be gone, and me, I'm just treasuring the waning days.

Poor Marlon doesn't understand why he sometimes catches me watching him. Just watching. Won't understand for years to come.

He throws an arm around my neck and assures me it will ever be thus and he's never going to leave. Then he turns his head to a certain angle.

And it's like he's already gone.

OCTOBER 22, 1998

FOR EACH THRILL OF VICTORY, A CHILD IS CRYING IN DEFEAT

I was hollering for my daughter to knock this other kid's block off.

Yikes. The column is barely two paragraphs old and already I have to explain myself.

See, I had taken my 8-year-old, who has a purple belt in karate, to a tournament where she was to compete. Your humble correspondent had never been to a karate competition before and was appalled by the naked barbarity he saw.

I mean, those parents were truly frightening:

"Kill her, Michelle!"

"Eat his eyes, Tommy!"

OK, so I exaggerate a tiny bit. But the parents were, shall we say, exuberant in their support.

Onjel competed in two categories, the first of which was forms. Forms is when you do a bunch of karate moves in a specific order, kicking and punching your way across the mat in a ritual whose intricacies and nuances I could not explain at gunpoint. Naturally, this minor deficiency did not stop me from standing off to the side shouting encouragement, nor from concluding that, because she maintained a really serious expression while doing her moves, Onjel deserved first prize.

The judges, obviously on the payroll of the Vast Rightwing Conspiracy, did not agree. In fact, after first, second and third place awards had been handed out, they gave my daughter and some of the other kids these dinky little "Thanks for showing up—sorry, you weren't good enough" trophies. Actually, "trophy" is an exaggeration. "Paperweight" is more like it.

"Congratulations," I said, smiling at her as she came off the floor. But Onjel was already crying. Cascade of tears, quivering bottom lip, the whole bit. I patted her and shushed her and, like any good American, began wondering if there was somebody I could sue.

Hey, what can I tell you? A little girl's tears fall like acid on her father's heart.

A lot of boys and girls were crying that day. They'd step into competition dreaming of getting one of those big trophies you had to wheel out on a dolly—and come back with a paperweight. And they'd just start bawling.

When I got my daughter quieted down a little, I tried to explain a few things to her. Everybody gets a turn to win, and everybody has to take a turn losing, I said. That's just the way it is. The chance of getting beaten is what makes competing such a rush, winning such a glorious high. There can be no thrill of victory where there is no threat of defeat.

The fact that all of this was absolutely true impressed my bitterly disappointed little girl not at all, of course. She handed me the paperweight. Said she didn't even want to see it.

And though I knew I had given her good words and that someday, she would come to value them, I also knew that if this girl didn't take a trophy home that day, I was in for a very long drive home. Which is why, when the sparring competition—Onjel's second and last—rolled around, I got down on the floor with other parents fearing long drives to their homes, and desperately willed my daughter to please, please remove this other little girl's heavily-padded head.

Her teacher, Master Victor, was yelling out all sorts of highly-technical karate instructions: "Keep your hands up! Hook kick! Sidestep!"

And I added some of my own: "Get her! Get her!"

Under the rules, you needed five points for victory. It was close all the way. First, Onjel's down, one to nothing, then she's up two to one, then she's down, three to two ... and then she wins. Takes second place overall in her age group.

Amazing what a big ol' trophy will do to banish the blues. Onjel wouldn't relinquish that thing the rest of the day, took it with her everywhere she went. And as I watched that beaming face, my mind traveled back, a little guiltily, to my last glimpse of the kid my daughter had beaten to claim the prize.

After the match, that girl climbed into the bleachers to sit in her mother's arms. She didn't say a word.

She was crying.

MARCH 27, 1999

NO RESPECT FOR CHAIRMAN OF THE HOUSE

I want to tell you about my new chair.

Bought it the other day when we remodeled my home office—a recliner that sits in front of the television, attended by a floor lamp that casts a mellow pool of light perfect for reading.

The thing is huge—made to accommodate a man twice my size. Which is just what I'll become if I spend too much time relaxing there. But The Chair is hard to resist. So plush you could lose yourself in it and they'd need a search party to find you. Even massages your back while you sit with eyes closed, thinking deep thoughts.

I admit it: I'm in love with this chair. Problem is, I'm not the only one. Ever since I bought The Chair, my office gets more visitors than the men's room at a bar. I mean, the thing should have a waiting list.

There's the toddler bouncing on it like a trampoline. The eight-year-old sinking into it like quicksand. The teenagers sprawling across it, arms and legs sticking out like tree limbs from a pond. I'm yelling, "Get outta da chair!" like Archie Bunker on the day the subway breaks down in Harlem, and they're looking at me like, "Did you say something, Dad? Couldn't hear you over the massager."

Then there's my wife. The other day, she comes in, just as pretty as you please, and grabs a sit-down in The Chair.

Now, I'm not the territorial type. Not particularly possessive. It's just a piece of furniture, after all. And this is the woman I've been with for 21 years. The woman who helped me redecorate the office. The woman who found and ordered my new recliner.

Nevertheless, I start shooting brain waves at her: Get ... out ... of ... The ... Chair.

Maybe it's a man thing.

OK, so maybe it's a mental-health thing, too, but I prefer to think of it as a man thing.

The Chair is where a man goes to hide. And if you say, "Hide from what?" you reveal something. Namely, that you have no kids.

Because if you did, you wouldn't have to ask.

Diary of a dad seeking a few minutes of peace on a typical night: Oops, can't go to the kitchen, because there's a kid in there doing dishes while listening to the latest CD by Scary Thugs With Potty Mouths. Can't hit the family room because another kid's in there watching the latest video by Women In Short Dresses Who Have No Talent. The dining room? The daughter is on the phone, urgently talking to a kid she hasn't seen in, like, 14 whole minutes. Your very own bedroom? That's where the grandkid is hitting the same note on a toy piano over and over again—tink tink tink tink tink—and the sound is such a torture that the CIA could use it to break enemy spies.

Then, just to liven things up, one kid gives another kid a funny look, prompting whiny cries for the nearest available parent to come resolve a conflict that reminds you of the one in the Middle East, except the one in the Middle East is less complicated and not quite as long-standing.

So what's a parent to do? Hide, that's what. But where?

My wife takes bubble baths we're allowed to interrupt only if the house is burning down. Woman spends more time in the water than a mackerel. She goes in there with the lights low, candles burning, quiet music on the radio and sometimes we don't see her again for days.

Meantime, I'm left stranded with the bad music and the feuding kids and the tink tink tink tink tink.

Or at least I was. Now I've got The Chair. Now I've got a sanctuary of my own.

And these guys think they're going to take it from me? Not on your life. I'm reminded of what Winston Churchill said in defense of his chair: "We shall fight in the fields and in the streets, we shall fight in the hills. We shall never surrender."

I would have more to say, but it's time for my medication. Then I think I'll go sit down.

SEPTEMBER 30, 1999

KIDS SHOULDN'T KISS OFF 'OLD PEOPLE'

We were walking past the meat counter, en route to a jug of milk, when my son hit me with one of Those Questions.

If you're a parent, the term needs no definition. If not, suffice it to say that Those Questions invariably come out of nowhere. Right when you're distracted, cogitating upon no subject deeper than groceries, the kid suddenly pipes up with some unpredictable inquiry that shocks you back into the moment.

Which is how we come by today's topic. Here in this space, where we routinely wrestle great and significant questions of human existence, let us pause to consider what a 14-year-old asked me last week with earnest curiosity.

"Do old people kiss?"

Excuse me?

But I'd heard him right. Indeed, as I stood there making astonished faces, he elaborated on the question. He did not, he explained, mean the occasional peck on the cheek. No, what he wanted to know was—geez, there's no delicate way to do this, is there?—do old people ever play tonsil hockey? Suck face? You know, really lean into it and ... kiss?

I stammered something about passion knowing no age limit. Snow on the roof, fire in the furnace and all that.

He, of course, laughed like I'd just gotten off a good one.

As it happens, we were passing the cookie aisle, where a gray-haired couple was shopping. I suggested half-jokingly that we take the question to them. Took half a step in that direction. The boy panicked and pulled me back.

I glanced at the couple as he dragged me away. They stood close, she nestling in the shadow of him, as they read the label on some package. I thought it made a nice picture. I doubt my kid even noticed.

Why should he? He's of an age where sex is a giggly mystery and love barely a blip on the horizon. More to the point, he's of an age where the lives of old people are barely imaginable. They might as well be extraterrestrial for all he can picture of their world.

Which says a lot about how our lives have changed. There was a time, not so long ago, when their world and his might have intersected. There was connection between generations—Grandma lived in the back room, or Grandpa was around to show you how to throw the curve ball, just like he once did for your mom.

We moved more slowly then. There was time to catch yourself in the moment.

Now that era becomes a half-mythic memory gone yellow at the edges, a blast from the past that has begun cracking at the seams, soon to turn to dust and be blown away by the gale force of modern living. We are simply too busy, too harried. Too distant.

My son, for example, has no elder relatives closer than about a thousand miles.

But if the distance between generations can be measured in miles, it can also often be measured in simple emotion.

Either way, though, the result is the same. We catch each other only in passing. We miss each other's lives.

Do old people kiss? My kid asks, and his tone is the same as if he were asking how fish sleep. As if old people were such a mystery one would have to read *National Geographic* to learn about them.

Do old people kiss, he wonders, and I keep thinking of that couple in the store.

Kind of wishing I had stopped them. That I'd found a way to ask and they'd found a way to answer, to tell a 14-year-old stories he needs to hear and never has. Maybe about waiting on the home front while love went off to war. Maybe about buying a first home in some cookie cutter of a subdivision. Maybe about money troubles and rebellious kids. Maybe about thinning hair and creaking joints. Maybe about sharing an ice cream in the harsh shadows of a dying sun. Maybe about loving one another through it all, come what may.

Do old people kiss?

I like to think they'd have told him yes. Maybe even shown him, right there in the cookie aisle.

And that he might have learned.

That age ravages only flesh. But the spirit, defiant, endures.

NOVEMBER 18, 1999

DON'T LOSE OUT ON YOUR KIDS' CHILDHOOD

There's a man in my backyard building a child's swing set. I watch it take shape, thinking how surprised my daughter will be when she gets home from school. Feeling guilty, too. Hoping this doesn't come too late.

The old swing lies in the grass, a heap of disassembled metal awaiting a ride on the garbage truck. Seeing it always reminds me of the day the real estate man brought us here for the first time. It was me, my wife, Marilyn, and Onjel, who had just turned 4. Still small enough to ride her daddy's hip.

When we stepped out into the backyard that first time, she gave this squeal of delight and bounded right over to the swing, a shiny metal construct painted bright red. "It's just what I always wanted!" she kept crying. "Just what I always wanted."

If we'd had any doubts before, that pretty much killed them. It would be a few days before we made it official, but for all intents and purposes, that was the moment this house became our home.

The old swing fell into disrepair a few years ago, paint fading, rust eating through critical joints. I told Onjel it wasn't safe to play on anymore. Told her I'd replace it soon.

But I didn't. Summer came and went, came and went again and there it sat, ugly and unusable. I meant to replace the thing. Swear I did. But I meant it in the way you mean to paint the trim or clean the attic—in the way of all those projects you keep putting off because other things place more pressing demands on your money or time.

Then one day I looked at my daughter and didn't recognize her. Still a little girl, only 9 years old. But you can see the clock ticking on childhood. Too big now to ride her father's hip. And I realized the day is coming soon when she'll also be too big for Barbie dolls or Curious George. And swing sets. Too big for swing sets, too.

So I got on the phone with a company that makes the things. Ordered one with all the bells and whistles. It's way too much, but still not quite enough.

The workman finishes his work and takes my money. I go to pick up my daughter from school. As we're pulling out of the parking lot,

I tell her casually, "You're in trouble with Mom. You left some junk in the backyard and she says when you get home you better go straight out there and pick it up." I'm thinking what a clever fib this is and how Marilyn is waiting in the backyard with the camera at this very moment to capture the look of surprise and joy.

Onjel replies emphatically. "Uh uh. You got me a new swing set."

Who me? Swing set?

Sigh. It wasn't so long ago that she was a whole lot easier to fool.

So of course we go into the backyard and of course she gives a happy shout and rushes off to climb and explore. The new swing set is made of wood. It has a seesaw, a rope ladder and a little house that an adult must bend double to enter. This is, Onjel keeps saying, the "coolest" swing on the block.

Marilyn wants me to have the credit. This was Daddy's idea, she says. Daddy bought it. Tell Daddy thank you. Onjel responds to all of this by giving me a fast hug and then is gone to explore some more.

I'm left standing there, wishing I had done this sooner, thinking how cruel it is that time rushes past a man before he can even get his bearings in life—that change is such an unforgiving master. Bad enough it takes his hair. It also takes his little girl.

Which is when my little girl comes back. She wraps her arms around my waist, puts her cheek to my belly and says solemnly, "Thank you, Daddy."

I'm confused. "Did Mommy tell you to do that?" I ask.

She says no. This is from her.

The clock is ticking. My daughter holds me tight.

JULY 15, 2000

SUDDENLY, MY SON'S 18—AND I'M FRANTIC

A few words for my son on the occasion of his 18th birthday.

Dear Marlon:

You can't be 18. It has not been 18 years since the nurse wheeled you out of the delivery room and we met for the first time. Maybe it's been five years, maybe as many as 10. But 18? My God, no way.

Remember how we rejoiced last month when the Lakers won the title? Remember how we whooped at the television as the final buzzer sounded? Remember how happy we were?

When you were born, I was happier than that.

Now 18 years have passed and sometimes you catch me studying your face. You get this quizzical expression and you say, Dad, why are you staring at me? There are lots of reasons.

I'm staring because it amazes me that something as handsome, charming and smart as you ever came out of me.

I'm staring with a prayer because I know that you're a cocky kid, and the world you're moving into can be capricious and cruel.

And I'm staring because I know our time together is short and growing shorter. The day is coming soon when I'll no longer be a part of your everyday life. There will be college and work, some girl who steals your heart, some career that keeps you busy. So knowing that my opportunities to teach and influence you will soon peter out to Sunday dinners and holidays, I find myself frantically wondering if I've covered all the bases, told you all the things I wanted you to know. And wondering, too, if you ever truly listened.

Did you understand what I meant when I said you shouldn't satisfy a short-term desire at the expense of a long-term goal?

Were you listening when I explained that the man who calculates his worth by money alone will always be poor where it counts the most?

Did you take it to heart when I told you to respect women, do more than the minimum required and always have a backup plan?

Or did you just roll your eyes and say, "There goes Dad again."

Life is difficult, son. Getting ahead is often a series of false starts and blind alleys. Progress and setback frequently walk hand in hand. So a man is required to be tough, to have it in him to come back against long odds.

But Marlon, I think it's also important—maybe more important in the long run—that a man be good. That he have fundamental decency.

That's not a trait we celebrate much. The era in which you've come of age is consumed with material virtue, with the notion that you're a good person because you have things. Truth is, son, you're a good person when you treat people the way you'd want them to treat you. When you come to understand that the world didn't begin and doesn't end with you. When you struggle everyday for the wisdom to know what's right and the courage to do it.

Have I taught you those things? Have I shown them to you in the way I've conducted my own affairs?

I hope I have, but it's all gone by so fast that it's hard to know for sure. Last week, you were a toddler eating cereal in front of the television, riveted by the adventures of He-Man. Day before yesterday, you were a preteen vowing that there'd never come a day you'd want to kiss some icky girl.

Now you're 18, and it makes me painfully conscious of how finite is the time, how narrow the window of opportunity to teach a girl to be a woman or a boy, a man. Painfully conscious, too, of my own limitations.

It occurs to me that a better man might have spent more time playing ball with you in the driveway. Might have read you to sleep more often. A better man might have been able to demonstrate a crossover dribble or shown how you throw the perfect curve.

But I promise you: No man could be more proud. No man could love you more.

AUGUST 3, 2000

IN DISPOSABLE SOCIETY, OLD FAITHFUL DOESN'T STAND A CHANCE

Ode to my television.

We bought it in 1986, a 26-inch RCA Colortrak. Paid $600 at Circuit City. Over the years, the set has been reliable as sunrise—brought us sitcoms, soap operas and made-for-TV movies every time, without fail. Once kept me up half the night for an *I Love Lucy* marathon. I remember the morning after Hurricane Andrew, we found it lying under a collapsed ceiling in a puddle of water. When electricity was restored, we plugged it in, not expecting much. But it worked—still works—as well as it ever did.

My children hate this.

For years, they've been campaigning for a new television, largely on the basis that the old one is, well ... old. Last week, one of the 15-year-old's friends started ragging on the set. The wooden cabinet is warped and cracked from Andrew; you need a degree in engineering to hook a video game to the ancient works in the back. The kid takes this in and starts laughing.

Next thing I know, I'm being dragged like a mule through the TV department of the local electronics emporium. All the kids are in on it. Even the wife is in on it, and this is surprising, given that she is the cheapest woman alive. But there she is, gazing speculatively at the wall of shiny new televisions.

I have to admit, it is intoxicating. This one has something called an "S" video outlet, and that one over there is HDTV, and the other one lets you watch two channels at once. I'm sorely tempted.

But I also remember old faithful at home and it makes me feel not unlike a guy who's about to cheat on a devoted, albeit unexciting, wife. I've had that television since Reagan was in office. Doesn't that count for something?

I mean, I'm not in the habit of composing paeans to major appliances, but have you noticed how absolutely nothing you buy these days is built to last? The CD player I got for Christmas didn't live to see the next Yuletide; my printer is failing after only three years. I drove a spanking new van off the lot, had to tow it back before the first oil change. It's as if new things come out of the box falling apart.

And, automobiles aside, you can forget about getting your stuff fixed. The TV in my bedroom went out a few months back. I called a repair shop, and they asked how old the set was. Seven years, I said. Might as well have said it dated from the Paleolithic Era. We don't work on anything that old, said the guy. He told me, sight unseen, that my television was not worth repairing.

No matter what you try to get fixed lately, that's what they say: Get a new one. The old one's not worth it.

I won't stretch this theme any further. But if you choose to see in it a metaphor for the disposable society, feel free. If you think it speaks to our tendency to toss the old away without a backward glance, that's up to you. If it leaves you questioning our forward rush, our reflexive worship of all things young and new, our inability to value long service, I won't argue the point.

Heck, I'd be a hypocrite if I did. Because for what it's worth, I'm resigned to the fact that I'll probably end up buying a new television before long. After all, I'm not immune to the exhortations of family. Nor to the seductions of an "S" video outlet—whatever that may be.

We've got this room out back that we're turning into a playroom for my grandson. I figure we'll put the old TV out there so he can watch *The Lion King* his usual 48 times in a row without the older kids threatening to hakuna his matata.

And maybe once in awhile, I'll go out there and pass the time of day with a friend who was always faithful, always served me well, whose only real sin was getting old.

Doggone it. I promised myself I wasn't going to cry.

AUGUST 5, 2000

LITTLE BOY TEACHES ME HARD LESSONS

An old joke: "If you want to give God a really good laugh, tell Him your plans."

The way I figure it, I must have the Almighty rolling on the floor by now. See, I've never been short of plans. I planned to have my last child off to college in a few short years. After which, I planned to travel, planned to play, planned to walk around the house in boxer shorts whenever the mood struck.

I didn't plan to be raising a little boy with autism.

He's not even my child. Rather, he's the 4-going-on-5-year-old son of my 23-year-old stepdaughter. She, in turn, is my life's great heartbreak, an unstable young woman financially and emotionally incapable of raising her child. And since she won't identify the father, guess who has custody?

Then, about a year ago, the other shoe falls—we learn that our grandson is autistic. I've been struggling with it ever since. Whining, really. It's not fair, I moan. Don't I have a say in what happens in my own life?

I had plans, God!

Stop it, laughs God, hammering the floor, You're killing me!

I've gradually come to believe there must be a larger point to this. Lessons to be learned. In struggling with God and autism, I struggle with myself. My selfishness. My lack of faith.

Maybe you've read the serenity prayer. It says: "God grant me the serenity to accept the things I cannot change, the courage to change the things I can, and the wisdom to know the difference."

So easy to say. But it's hard to be serene when the steering wheel of your life has been yanked from your hands.

Autism, the dictionary says, is an "abnormal introversion and egocentricity." In other words, it means the autistic person lives alone in a world of his own. His ability to interact, to even acknowledge others, is limited. There's no known cure, though, thankfully, my grandson's case has been characterized as mild.

Even so, he can carry on only fragmentary conversations. Sometimes, you'd swear he's just ignoring you. He finds it hard to follow simple instructions. He's still in diapers.

There's no way of knowing to what degree those things will change. No way of knowing if he'll someday be capable of living on his own.

He's a happy little boy, though, and right now, that's all that matters. He sings the *Power Rangers* theme song. He loves Chicken Mc-Nuggets and broccoli—pronounced "brocky." He beams when he shows "Paw-Paw" drawings he made in school. He learns new things all the time.

And he teaches, too. Indeed, though he has no way of knowing, Paw-Paw is his No. 1 student.

An autistic child demands patience—a virtue, the cliché says. To which I used to respond: "Yes, but it's not one of mine."

But an autistic person perceives the world differently. Where you see the forest, he sees a tree. And then another tree next to that. And another tree next to that. A hundred individual trees, each exerting its own pull upon his attention. So you're walking over some landscaping rocks and suddenly he pulls up short because he has spotted this one rock out of the thousands and it fascinates him. What can you do? Simple. You stop and admire the rock. You take a few more steps, then stop and admire another rock. And next time, you keep to the sidewalk.

The lesson is patience, but not only that. It's also surrender. It's learning to release something that was never really in your hands anyway—meaning control of your own destiny. And it's faith, too.

That line in the serenity prayer—the one about having the courage to change the things you can—resonates differently with me now than it did before he came. Because it turns out that one of those things I must be brave enough to change is me.

I think it will make me a better person. But the process is not easy. It's hard to accept that sometimes, you just have to surrender the wheel and see where it takes you. And that when God is laughing, you might as well start laughing, too.

MARCH 15, 2001

DAUGHTER'S FIRST CRUSH LEAVES ME OUT OF SYNC

Dear Justin Timberlake:

I've got a major beef with you, dude. I figure it's time we had a few words.

Now, I know what you're thinking. Who is this guy and why's he calling me out? I don't even know him.

Well, Slick, you don't have to know me. I know you. In fact, I've known you for years. I knew you when your name was Davy Jones and you sang with the Monkees, knew you when you were Jermaine Jackson of the Jackson 5. I remember when your name was Ralph Tresvant and you belonged to New Edition, remember when it was Jordan Knight of New Kids on the Block.

Heck, I can even go back to the time you went by Paul McCartney and sang with the Beatles.

Now, of course, you're calling yourself "Justin" and your group is 'N Sync.

Doesn't matter what name you use, I know who you are. You're the "cute" one in the boy band, the one whose dimpled smile makes all the little girls weak in the knees.

But that's not why we've got beef, you and me. No, my problem stems from the fact that you are the First Boy.

The First Boy of Girlhood, to be exact. It's sort of like the first robin of spring—a harbinger of change. Except that the bird's appearance heralds blooming flowers and warmer days. You are the bearer of less welcome tidings.

You still don't get it, do you? OK, let me break it down for you. I have a daughter, Onjel. She'll be 11 this year.

I went in to paint her room the other day only to discover she's had it wallpapered instead. With pictures of you. Everywhere I turn, there's your grinning mug.

That really grates my cheese, pal. I can remember when I was the only man in her world, when all I had to do to make her smile was come home. But that was before you came around, before the arrival of the First Boy. Now my stock has fallen like a dotcom.

And it's only going to get worse. I mean, you know what comes after the First Boy? That's right, the Second Boy. He'll show up at my door in a few years. His unfinished voice will sound like James Earl Jones as impersonated by Michael Jackson. He'll be wearing a body he hasn't finished growing into and his mom will be waiting in a minivan at the curb. Naturally, he'll be uncomfortable. So I'll invite him in, offer him a seat, fetch him a soda and do my best to make him more nervous.

I'm thinking I might pepper him with questions about his intentions, interrogate him like a murder suspect on *NYPD Blue*. Or, I might glare at him in silence. Maybe I'll just sit there, casually cleaning my fingernails with a hunting knife.

Not that it matters. The Second Boy will inevitably give way to the Third and the Fourth. Somewhere down the line, maybe the Fifteenth Boy turns out to be the Right Man. Next thing you know, I'm sitting alone in some hotel ballroom wearing a rented tux and watching the cleaning crew sweep up confetti, poorer by $10,000 and one daughter.

All because of you. Thanks a lot, pal.

You say it's not your fault? Maybe you're right. Still, you're a harbinger. And I'm not quite ready for the change you're harbinging. Unfortunately, like the kid who's "it" in hide-and-seek, change comes, ready or not.

I bought my daughter and myself tickets to your summer concert tour, by the way. Thrilled her to pieces and made my stock rise, which is what I had hoped it would do. Hey, I'm not proud.

I expect to find myself sitting alongside a bunch of other fathers whose stock has taken a beating lately. We'll smile tolerantly when you storm the stage and our daughters turn into wild women. We'll remember that no one ever loves anything quite as ferociously as an adolescent girl loves a boy band. And we will also make mental notes to stop at Wal-Mart on the way home.

They do carry hunting knives, don't they?

JULY 5, 2001

RENEWING VOWS WITH MY WIFE—MY ANCHOR

"When we get married, we'll have a big celebration."—The Intruders

Guess what I did on my summer vacation? I went and got married.

It was to the same woman I've been hitched to for the past 20 years, so maybe "married" is not the right term. Maybe I should call it a "remarriage" or a "recommitment."

Or an "ordeal."

Granted, that doesn't sound as romantic as the others, but it's a lot more accurate. You want to break an enemy spy? Forget chemicals and beatings. Just make him plan a wedding. He'll break in three days flat, I promise you. This particular wedding required more extensive strategizing than the D-Day invasion. Caused more sleepless nights than major surgery. It was difficult, it was time-consuming, it was complicated.

But at least it was hideously expensive.

Seriously, I could have bought a car with what I spent here. I'm talking the luxury options package: CD player, seat warmers, the works.

Eventually, I found that the only way to keep my sanity was to pretend I was spending Monopoly money. And I'm thinking to myself, what a difference a couple of decades makes. The first time Marilyn and I got married—young couple in L.A., poor in everything but love—we rented a chapel in Hollywood for a couple hundred bucks. Few hundred more for the dress, the tux, the cake. Held the reception at my mother's house. The whole shebang probably cost us a grand.

This time around, the photographer alone cost more.

And what did we get for our investment? We got to say our vows and then retire to a hotel ballroom where friends and family from all over the country stood and told gracious lies about our wonderfulness. We got to hear our 18-year-old testify publicly that we had been pretty good parents, notwithstanding dozens of previous claims to the contrary. We got to have kids blow soap bubbles toward us as we danced to "our" song, an obscure number you've never heard of whose opening line says, "You're the smile that I've searched for on a thousand different faces."

In a word, we got to get married. Again.

I don't mean to sound too smug about a mere 20th anniversary. Mainly because, every time I've ever been tempted toward self-satisfaction about a marital milestone, some older person has cheerfully assured me that it wasn't diddly squat. Wait till you've been together as long as we have, young feller, they say. Then you can talk.

To hear some of those folks tell it, they've been married so long, their wedding pictures were by Rembrandt. So OK, already, I get it. Twenty years isn't everything.

But you know what? In a world where nobody gets married anymore, it still feels like ... something. Some triumph of covenant, maybe. Some rejection of impermanence. And maybe that seems like a big deal to me specifically because I'm a member of the generation that once declared marriage moribund and commitment passé. It's a lie we sold so effectively that, decades later, it sometimes seems there are no more wives and husbands. Just "the mother of my children" and "my baby daddy."

There was a time when family was bedrock. Now it often feels as fleeting, as evanescent, as ... well, soap bubbles. We are less anchored than we once were. Less centered. And it happened largely—though not solely—because my generation discarded ritual and held ceremony to be empty.

But we were wrong. I understood that all over again as the music swelled, the bubbles fell, and my wife and I danced with children and friends and family all around. It occurred to me that this moment wasn't empty. Indeed, it was almost painfully full.

Summer vacations are seldom cheap, I suppose. One year, I spent a fortune to stand in long lines at the Mouse House in Orlando. Another year, I broke the piggy bank to watch water fall over the cliff in Niagara. This year, I stayed home to reaffirm the promise I once made to a smile I'd searched for on a thousand different faces. Know what I got for my investment?

Everything.

NOVEMBER 1, 2001

SON PICKS UP FASHION TIP: MATCH SHOE, POCKETBOOK

Let me tell you about the day I didn't strangle my youngest son. Thought about it, mind you, but didn't do it.

There are several reasons. In the first place, I'm rather fond of the kid. In the second place, strangling people is against the law. And in the third place, I don't think my hands would fit around his neck. At 16, he's two inches taller than I am and outweighs me by a good 20 pounds.

I know what you're thinking: "Why, Mr. Pitts, of course you didn't strangle your own child. You'd never do such a thing."

Well, no. But you'd sure think about it if you ever went shopping with him.

My son worships at the church of cool. Worse, he has bought into the Madison Avenue con job that claims cool is something you can buy. That one becomes beloved by women and envied by men if only one wears the right gear.

I've tried to disabuse him of that notion, but naturally, he finds my cognitive ability suspect, given that I'm his father and all.

Anyway, our philosophical differences all came to a head the last time I took him shopping for shoes. And when I say "last," I don't mean "most recent." Rather, I mean last as in "final," "finished," "wouldn't do it again for a million dollars and Halle Berry's home phone number."

He's in front of the display in Foot Locker, right? Just pacing there, tortured like Hamlet. Communing with the shoe gods or something. I keep checking my watch. Finally I start checking my calendar, because, you know, there's a good *ER* coming on Thursday night and I don't want to miss it.

Finally, he chooses a shoe. At least, that's what I think it is. It's this basketball player's signature footwear, a plastic and metal contraption with lights and buttons and digital readouts. I think it even has a modem. And the price tag? Enough to retire the foreign debt of a small Third World country.

No way, I tell him. I consider this a definitive rejection. Unfortunately for me, he considers it an invitation to negotiate. So he wheedles and whines. I say no. He sulks and glares. I say no. He assures me I can afford it. I say no. He warns me that sending him to school in any other shoes will make him a pariah, thereby crushing his confidence and condemning him to a life of destitution and want.

I ask if it's the "n" or the "o" he's having trouble with.

We do this routine in five stores—eight, if you count the ones on the Internet. Finally, he starts to sense that Dad's a little resistant. With extreme reluctance, he allows me to buy him a pair of shoes that cost only as much as the weekly grocery bill for a family of five. Shuffles off to school muttering about child abuse. I begin to worry that I'm not going to come off so good in his memoirs.

But here's the upshot: The kid gets his first job. Brings home a fairly respectable paycheck. Rushes off to Foot Locker. Comes back wearing this homelier-than-heck pair of sneaks that look like something from the unenlightened days when we thought shoes were just something to cover your feet. No lights, no plastic, not even a digital readout. Price: $30.

I ask what happened to the other shoes, the ones he needed more than air. He shrugs. "Too expensive," he says.

This is the point at which I did not strangle my son.

So maybe you're saying to yourself, What's all this talk of strangulation? Sure, the kid was a pain, but at least he learned an important lesson about the value of money.

You silly person.

Took the boy shopping for a coat the other day. Went down aisle after aisle of them, most priced at less than $150. He stood there communing with the outerwear gods. Finally, pulled out this monstrous coat with pockets inside of pockets, zippers on top of zippers and some rapper's name stitched into the fabric. Price tag: 250 bucks. He gave me this hopeful smile. I felt my hands rising without conscious command.

So now we don't go shopping for coats, either.

NOVEMBER 4, 2002

SON'S ESSAY A REVELATION

So it's parents' night at school, and I'm there on behalf of my youngest son. I look at him sometimes and see a toddler with a gap in his grin and a penchant for gnawing his toes.

But that's just a memory lie. The toddler is a teenager two inches taller than I am, a youngster on the cusp of manhood.

It hasn't been a fun passage. Last year, we went through a phase where he seemed to feel compelled to challenge everything I said, down to and including, "Hello." These days, he doesn't so much challenge me as endure me. My son has perfected the thousand-yard stare, eyes fixed on something beyond your line of sight while you're yammering on about a good work ethic, the importance of education or some other bit of useless arcana from the book of responsible adulthood.

There is nothing quite as effective as a teenager for making one feel like a moron.

So anyway, I'm at parents' night. It's just me—my wife is with one of the other kids, my son couldn't be bothered. I'm in his social studies class, and I ask to see some of his work. The teacher finds his folder, I page through his papers, and I come across a short essay: "The Person I Most Admire."

Turns out it's two people. Some rap entrepreneur ... and me. Most of the essay, in fact, is about the overall wonderfulness of me—about the lessons I've taught my son and the ways I've shaped his life.

To say I was shocked is to understate by half. I guess you never know, do you? You flat-out never know.

This episode came to mind a few days ago as I absorbed the results of a new parenting study, *A Lot Easier Said Than Done*, by Public Agenda, a nonprofit, nonpartisan group in New York City. The study—you'll find it on the group's website, www.publicagenda.org—produced a number of fascinating statistics on parents and parenting.

One set of questions from the survey particularly intrigued me. It sought to ascertain how good a job parents feel they've done in transmitting basic values to their children.

The short answer: not very good.

For instance, while 83 percent of parents say it's essential to teach children self-discipline and self-control, only 34 percent feel they've successfully done it. Ninety-one percent say it's important to teach children to be honest and truthful, but just 55 percent think they've managed to do so. And so on.

I thought it was just me who felt overmatched. Turns out it's most of us.

You're anxious about what sort of job you're doing, what kind of adult you're creating. You struggle against the amorality of media, the cockiness of youth, the influence of peers and, most of all, the inadequacy of self, trying to ensure that the people your children become are, at heart, decent, responsible and good. But in the end, you wonder, you worry and you doubt. Because some days—most days—you'd swear they never hear a word you say.

I had to wonder if my son left that essay for me to find, but it seems unlikely. The students' work folders weren't put out for parental inspection, and he had no way of knowing I would request to see his.

Maybe I should have asked him about what he had written, but I didn't know what to say and didn't want to embarrass him. So he'll never know I saw it—unless, I suppose, he happens across this column someday.

If so, I hope it's after he has had some children of his own and experienced what it's like to want for them, to desire desperately and without regard to self, the very best for them. And to receive, in response, the thousand-yard stare and heavy sigh of someone who is being forced to endure an idiot's blather.

When he knows what that feels like, maybe he'll know why I made a copy of his essay. And why I put it in a trunk of things I mean to keep, always.

DECEMBER 17, 2004

A TOUGH LESSON: DEATH TOUCHES THE YOUNG, TOO

Torrie was buried on a Friday.

The day was cold and clear and there must have been a couple hundred people packed into the church. Most of the mourners were unbearably young—in their teens and 20s, I would guess.

One was a woman who had to wait out her tears while delivering a eulogy. Another was a pallbearer who dissolved into a shuddering heap. And then there was a man who came hesitantly down the aisle, stopping short of the casket and turning away. A moment later he was back, willing himself forward. He leaned over the body and cried out the dead man's name.

Torrie was 20. And let me tell you: Burying a 20-year-old is a special kind of awful.

Not just because it seems an obscene inversion of the natural order—parents burying a child. Not just because it reeks of untapped potential, an end too close to a beginning. But also because of what it does to the young people left behind, the brutal, unsentimental way it strips away their illusions of invincibility and immortality.

It is one of the defining conceits of youth, this conviction that time doesn't touch you, that 16 is endless and 20, forever. Yes, the conceit always ends, but you hate to see it end so abruptly.

I should mention that Torrie did not die as too many young people do. There was no gang fight, no random shooting, no beef in a crowded nightclub. He had an asthma attack. It led to heart failure.

In a way, that makes his death harder to grasp. We have grown sadly used to seeing young people die through senseless acts. To have one snatched away by sudden illness feels like a betrayal, the universe behaving with unfathomable meanness. It feels as if God is cheating.

Torrie practically grew up in my house, just as my youngest sons practically grew up in his. If you've ever had teenagers, you know what I'm talking about: that migrating flock of kids that seems to live nowhere in particular, stopping at each other's houses for days at a time to empty the fridge and commandeer the television before moving on.

So it was not at all uncommon for me to come downstairs on a summer morning and find Torrie sacked out on the floor in the den, maybe with my boys snoring in the chairs where they had fallen asleep playing video games or watching movies deep into the night. Sometimes, my wife had to order Torrie and his cousin to go home if only to shower and change clothes.

It had been two years since I saw him and I almost didn't recognize him in the casket. He was a young man with a beard and a head full of braids, no longer the kid I remembered—pudgy, fresh-faced and with a big, cheesy grin.

My sons had a hard time at the funeral. Everybody did, I guess, but it was my boys and their peers who broke my heart.

Young people—African-American men in particular—often meet the world with faces that give nothing away. Armored faces, I call them. They guard their feelings jealously, project an air of studied indifference as if to make us believe they are beyond the ability to be hurt. It's all a fraud, of course, a form of self-defense, a way of projecting an invulnerability one does not always feel.

You know this if you are an adult. And if the knowing sometimes leaves you exasperated over the conceits of kids, there is also a wistfulness that comes from realizing something they often do not: no one is beyond hurt, and nothing is forever.

Usually it's an incremental lesson, a wisdom you pick up with the years. But sometimes, life is a merciless teacher. That was certainly the case on the Friday Torrie was buried. So it hurt to sit in that church as armored faces broke and tears came streaming out.

My sons came away with a renewed understanding that every day is a gift. It's an important lesson.

But man, what a hell of a way to learn.

FEBRUARY 24, 2006

A PHONE RINGS, AND OUR LIVES ARE ON HOLD

I hate telephones.

Yes, they're indispensable tools of communication, but I hate them for the tension of that moment between the ring and the answer, that instant of apprehension before you know what the call will bring. It is a fraction of time when all nightmares seem possible.

I trace the feeling to an awful night 13 years ago when the telephone yanked us up out of sleep to the news that my wife's brother had been murdered 3,000 miles away. Ever since then, I've been this way. Intellectually, I know that a telephone brings tragedy only once in a thousand rings. But those seconds when you just don't know, when it could be anything, still call the hairs on my neck to attention.

So Tuesday afternoon, the phone rings. I pick it up and hear my daughter's voice. Her tone seems normal, and I breathe easy. I figure she's going to hit me up for money, tell me we're out of milk. Then I hear her say, "Eric got hit by a car."

And suddenly, I am hurtling. Out of the office. To the parking lot. Down the highway. Eric is my grandson. He is 10.

I hate Eric.

This occurs to me as I am driving. I hate Eric and all my children and my wife and everyone else I love for how much I love them and for how love inevitably brings pain.

They get hurt, they get sick, but it might as well be me for all the fear that stabs my heart. To love somebody is to make yourself hostage to the fortunes of others. It is to give a hundred people veto power over your happiness. Sometimes I think the smartest way to live is without affiliation—no family, no friends, no children, no spouse, no pet, no nobody who can hurt you.

You might say it's a pathetic man who goes through life neither loving nor loved. Most days I would agree. But there are days it doesn't sound like a bad deal. Days like this.

So here's what happened: Eric was trying to cross the street. Going to a friend's house to play video games. He looked both ways—

twice, just like we taught him. When he was halfway across, he saw a car, an SUV, coming around the bend. Instead of continuing safely across, he tried to make it back to the curb.

The car hit him. He smacked the hood hard enough to leave a dent. A shoe flew one way, a video game another. My wife saw it happen. She ran to him. He was writhing in the street, crying. He kept saying, "I'm sorry. I'm sorry."

I am sitting beside his gurney in the emergency room as these words are written. The doctor has been in. His diagnosis: two lumps on the head and two skinned knees.

Let's repeat that to make sure you got it. The boy gets hit. By an SUV. He bounces off the hood. And he winds up with lumps and skinned knees. I am reminded of the refrain from a gospel song I've always loved. It says, "There must be a God somewhere."

There must be. And obviously, He was in a forgiving mood this day.

Eric is more voluble than usual. He says Spider-Man would have dodged the car. He says that like Wolverine, his "healing factor" kept him from serious injury. He says he is glad to be alive.

I keep thinking how all the uncertainty of life can be summed up in the ringing of a telephone. But it comes with the territory, doesn't it? Uncertainty, I mean. You just never know. Life is a dance on the high wire above mortality. It unfolds in the shadow of tragedies past and tragedies yet to come.

There's nothing you can do about it except use the time in between to laugh, sing, hug, read comic books with your grandkid as often as you can.

And try to forget that you are a wisp in a wind. I hate that, too, but what are you going to do?

Eric is still chattering away, all nervous energy. He complains that I forgot to pay his allowance. He wants to go to Ruby Tuesday for dinner. And he says, he keeps saying, that he is glad to be alive.

I know just how he feels.

APRIL 17, 2006

SURPRISE! DREAM ROLLS UP IN FRONT OF HER

The car glides to a stop in front of the hotel. Light splashes off gleaming black metal as the valet gets out. He hands the keys to my wife.

Marilyn says, "These aren't my keys."

The valet says, "Yes, they are."

Marilyn says, a little more forcefully, "These aren't my keys. That's not my car."

The valet says, "That's your car."

Marilyn's brow knits in confusion. She looks at the key fob like she's never seen a key fob before. Then she steps through the crowd of us gathered there on the sidewalk, going to inspect the car this man insists is hers.

It is her 50th birthday, and no, she won't mind my telling you that, because she's always been one of those rare women who believes aging is a thing to be embraced, not feared. This evening, we've had a party for the ages. We've eaten fine food, we've laughed, we've danced to Elvis and Luther, the Tempts and the Gap Band. Now it's late and we're out on the sidewalk and the valet has apparently delivered my wife the wrong car.

Got to be the wrong car, she's thinking. It's sure nicer than any car she's ever had. In fact, it's her dream car, the one she always told me she wanted to own "someday."

She said this back when our car was a red piece of junk that required you to keep a foot on the gas when you were sitting at the light, else the engine would stall.

She said it back when our car was a wine-colored heap with a powder-blue door and a tendency to struggle going uphill.

She said it back when we didn't even have a car, when she was pregnant and sick and we had to bum a ride or catch the bus everywhere we went.

Someday, she said. Someday.

At the time—20 years ago, maybe 25—someday always felt like a synonym for never, a consolation prize you give yourself when reality smashes your day into little pieces.

As I watch her step dazedly through that crowd of family and friends toward the car, someday feels different. Feels ... real. Feels now.

In the movies, this is where they'd fade to black and let the credits roll. But real life is not a screenwriter's artifice. Tomorrow, we'll get up and go to work like always.

Still, there is a sense of summation, a sense that here is a moment in which to pause and appreciate what you came through and what you came to. The gospel song puts it best: "My soul looks back and wonders how I got over." It's a song appropriate to moments like these, moments redolent of things you hoped and pain you suffered and the realization that the clichés are true: If you hang in there, just keep struggling and stringing breaths together, anything can happen. Anything at all.

My wife starts screaming. "This is for me? This is *my* car?" Like she can't make herself believe.

The crowd yells, "Surprise!"

She starts running around the vehicle, hands to face, laughing, crying. I yell out, "Hey, Marilyn, remember how you said you wanted one of these someday? Well, it's someday."

Beaming, she climbs into the driver's seat. They yell at her to start the car. She can't. It's got a fancy ignition system she needs a minute to figure out. Even the valet laughs.

It's just a car, of course. Just metal and rubber and a lot of gadgets and doodads no car really needs. Just another material bauble that cannot follow you into the ground. But sitting there shining under the lights on the evening of my wife's 50th birthday, it feels like vindication and validation and I love you and thank you for persevering with me. Thank you for never giving up on us.

Everybody's talking at once. Some are climbing into the car with her.

I hang back, watching, smiling to myself, capturing the memory. It's enough.

Someday has come.

OCTOBER 7, 2007

A REFLECTION ON FIVE DECADES OF LIVING

On Thursday, it will be 50 years since I fooled around and got myself born. It's a personal milestone that raises a critical question I've been grappling with for weeks:

Can I get a column out of this?

I figured I could—obviously—but that raised yet another question. What approach do you take? Do you go for solemn reflection ("Two score and ten years ago, my foremother brought forth upon this continent a new baby, conceived in...")? Do you go for laughs ("...and I told the kid, 'Look, I've got underwear older than you!'")? I even thought about sharing some of the life wisdom I've picked up over the years, except it turns out an alarming amount of my life wisdom actually comes from old pop songs ("You've got to know when to hold 'em...").

It was as I was going back and forth with this that I learned a gentleman of my acquaintance was celebrating his own birthday milestone a few days before me. But Joe Engel of Charleston, S.C., isn't turning a piddling 50. He's turning a monumental 80. Between the time of my writing this and the time of your reading it, his family is throwing him a party. If I know Joe, wine will be drunk, pretty women will be flirted with, dancing will be done.

Joe is a survivor of the Holocaust, one of the one-in-three European Jews who escaped the Nazis alive. He survived the Warsaw Ghetto. He survived Auschwitz. When Allied troops closed in on the death camp, the Nazis loaded their captives on a train and ran. Joe jumped from the train, hid beneath eight feet of snow. He made his way to a barn, concealed himself under a mound of hay. German soldiers, searching for runaways, stabbed the hay with bayonets. Later, the barn wound up in a crossfire between the Germans and the Russians, gunfire punching through the walls. Joe survived all this, too.

Sometimes, I know, he wonders why. Others were bigger, others were stronger, others had more faith. Sometimes he wonders why he was one of the few who lived. I think maybe he lived so that he might someday lift a glass or bask in the beauty of a woman. Or dance. Not just to do these things, but to be *seen* doing them. That's an affirmation, isn't it? Testimony to the rest of us of the stubborn resilience of life.

Your humble correspondent has survived no death camp. To the contrary, I've seen Niagara Falls and Hawaiian sunsets. I've been in African shanties and French restaurants. I've seen Stevie Wonder dance on a piano, heard Aaron Neville sing "Amazing Grace." I've suffered loss, yes, but I've also seen birth.

It's been—so help me, Jimmy Stewart—a wonderful life. But there have been those hard days when faith was shaken, and I moped in the self-pitying conviction that life was a conspiracy against me. When I was a kid—and I suppose this is true of all kids—I always figured that one day I would Understand It All. At the end of five decades, I'm still waiting for that day. At the end of eight, Joe is, too.

That's reassuring, I guess. I've come to believe wisdom begins with the realization of how little of It All you truly do understand. And how little you likely ever will.

So I want to be like Joe when I grow up. I remember seeing him at dinner in Poland one night after a somber day spent touring death camps. The table talk had been of genocide and human cruelty. Then the band struck up "Hava Nagila" and Joe found a pretty woman and started dancing. In my notes, I wrote that he danced as if his bones were made of joy.

Which strikes me as the only way to dance. So, do you want to know what I've learned at 50? That there is no finish line, nor finished state. There is only now.

And now is always a great time to do a little dance. Maybe make a little love. And get down tonight.

Like I said, pop songs.

JUNE 1, 2008

TALKIN' ABOUT MY GIRL

Dear Daughter:

I have loved you from the moment I met you. You were still wet from the birth canal, hair matted to your scalp, eyes squeezed shut.

They dried you off, cut the cord, placed you in a bassinet under a warming light. I went over to you. My hand covered your torso.

And I loved you.

That was 17 years ago, 17 years that have moved as cheetahs move. The infant is a toddler, the toddler is a little girl, the little girl is an adolescent, the adolescent is you, a girl on the verge of womanhood, graduating high school—with honors!—this spring, going to college in the fall.

You are facing the future. I am facing the past, sitting here looking at old pictures of you and listening to songs whose lyrics make me sad.

There you are with a plastic pig snout from some restaurant strapped over your nose, looking up with crossed eyes. And the Temptations are singing about sunshine on a cloudy day. "My Girl."

There you are walking with your arms folded and your lips poked out, pouting because that bad old ground had the nerve to skin your knee. And Paul Simon is singing "there could never be a father who loved his daughter more than I love you."

There you are in your senior picture, your hair glossy and long, wearing a white cap and gown, facing the camera, smiling your confidence. Stevie Wonder is singing, "Isn't she lovely?" And she is.

There's this other song that really gets me, though. It's called "I Wish I Could."

A meditative keyboard and guitar frame the melody, and Peabo Bryson sings of watching his little girl playing in the leaves, of kneeling by her side to say bedtime prayers, of snapping pictures, trying to "hold on to the memory before the whole things slips away."

He sings:

I wish I could save these moments and put 'em in a jar/
I wish I could stop the world from turning, keep things just the way they are/
I wish I could shelter you from everything not pure and sweet and good/
I know I can't. I know I can't. But I wish I could/

Honey, you know your dad. Your dad doesn't cry unless there's a death in the family or a loss in the playoffs. But I swear, that song brings me too close for comfort every time. Every doggone time.

You know why? Well, in the last 17 years, I have used a Nerf gun to chase off the monsters under your bed, given you my shoulders as a throne from which to look down on the world, waited outside with other parents while you sat in the arena cheering some pop star who had stolen your heart away from me. I have endured your rolling eyes, your heavy sighs and your indifference (hated your indifference most of all).

But what comes now is harder than all that. Because what comes now is the beginning of goodbye.

Yes, I know. You're not going anywhere. You still live in that land-fill down the hall you call a bedroom.

But see, I am losing my little girl. She is waving her last fare-wells to me here and now. And some woman is about to take her place. Giggly, excitable and gawky on high heels, but a woman, all the same.

There is much I want for this woman. I want success for her. I want adventure and travel, dancing and laughter, discovery and joy. I want challenges, but I want contentment, too, that peace that comes from knowing you are exactly where you are meant to be in life, do-ing exactly what you are meant to do. I want her to be happy.

You see, I haven't met her yet, but already, I love this woman.

And yet, I'd give anything to make her go away, to cast her back beyond the horizon. I would trade her without a second thought for just one more chance to take out a Nerf gun and slay any monsters that dare trouble my little girl.

Oh, I know I can't. But I wish I could.

PART TWO:

WHITE MEN CAN'T JUMP (AND OTHER STUPID MYTHS)

OCTOBER 24, 1994

WHITE MEN CAN'T JUMP, AND OTHER STUPID MYTHS

The other day, my son Marlon, who's 12, picked up *Newsweek* and began reading the cover story. It was a report on *The Bell Curve*, a controversial new book that postulates a genetic basis for intellectual disparities between blacks and whites. Perhaps you've seen the articles that have also appeared in *Time, New York, The New Republic, The Wall Street Journal* ... the book is creating quite a stir.

It argues that lower average IQ scores for blacks have a genetic basis and that differences in the genetic pool of the two races doom us to continue as a society in which whites win the lion's share of Nobel Prizes for science, while blacks gallop up and down the hardwood of the basketball court.

I'm not real big on censoring what my children read, but I was sorely tempted to snatch that magazine from Marlon. A child's psyche is such a delicate thing, after all. What would it do to my son to have his impressionable young mind filled with odious stereotypes? I was worried.

I mean, I didn't want Marlon to feel that white children were inferior.

It is, after all, only a short hop of logic from white intellectual superiority to white athletic inferiority. On the other hand, perhaps it's good to bring that ugly old myth out of the closet. Perhaps by dealing with it openly, we can once and for all consign it to the dung heap of history where it belongs.

Certainly this isn't the first time that canard has been heard. White children have had to endure it for decades, had to learn to close their ears to all the mean-spirited taunts: You can't run! You can't jump! You can't play D!

The only difference is that now these stereotypes have been given a new patina of science, earlier research by Dr. Jimmy the Greek notwithstanding.

One wonders what those poor white kids must think, how their self-esteem must suffer.

Popular culture sure doesn't give them much support. Everywhere they look, they see black athletic achievement—sports pages and sportscasts dominated by the exploits of larger-than-life black multimillionaires and esteemed commercial spokesmen like Shaquille O'Neal, Charles Barkley, Bo Jackson, Deion Sanders, Barry Bonds, Walter Payton, Ken Griffey Jr., Karl Malone, Sugar Ray Leonard, Michael Jordan ... sure, a white athlete occasionally shines through. One thinks of John Stockton, Larry Bird, Fred Biletnikoff, Cal Ripken— guys who, through an extraordinary combination of tenaciousness and good fortune, somehow manage to become stars despite belonging to an oppressed minority. But they're always viewed as exceptions, aren't they?

It's a masterpiece of condescension and Catch-22 logic. Society tells white kids they can't compete athletically with blacks and then, whenever one breaks through and gives the lie to that thinking, he's called a special case. An exception. Some African-American bigot can even be counted upon to claim the guy must have black blood in him.

Is the disparity in athletic performances between the races a matter of genetics or environment? Nature or nurture?

I would suggest that we will never know the answer for certain. In a nation—and world—so consumed with race, you can never devise an infallible test of athletic ability that will completely rule out racism as a factor. Give a white newborn to a black family at birth, let them raise him in a completely black environment, then turn him loose on a basketball court. Even if he slams headfirst into the goal post, you haven't proven that genetics predestined his failure.

Why? Because unless they exiled him to an hermetically-sealed bubble, his black family would not be able to shield him from the fact that he was white in a society that's not particularly friendly to people like him. More, a society that did not expect a whole lot from him in terms of athletic prowess.

Indeed, his black family might unwittingly contribute to the problem.

You know, the other kids might get footballs for their birthdays but he'd get slide rules.

Then too, most of what he saw in the media would steer him away from athletics. Time and again, he'd see people who looked like him depicted as doctors, priests ... U.S. senators. But hardly ever as sports heroes.

Even his teachers would discourage him from going out for the team. "The best you can hope for is maybe to be a lawyer," they'd say.

How long do you think it would be before the child internalized that message, before the prophecy fulfilled itself and he accepted the image of himself as an athletic bumbler? It would happen early, believe me.

Which is why, when Marlon put down the *Newsweek* article, I watched him with concern. "So," I asked warily, "what do you think?"

He said—and this is a quote—"I think the guy who wrote that book is a butt-head."

Pretty intelligent kid, don't you think?

DECEMBER 19, 1994

WHO TOOK GOD AWAY FROM THOSE IN NEED?

No one knows how it came to pass that God got kidnapped. No one knows how He could have been taken unawares, then dragged away to some secret haven known only to the Most Righteous. No one knows how His kidnappers managed to recreate Him in their own images, convert Him to their politics, or make Him a standard-bearer for their causes. And their fears. No one knows how it happened, but that it happened seems beyond question.

What else could possibly explain the story that came out of Philadelphia last week, about the church where the HIV-positive and those with AIDS are forbidden to worship? These policies are outlined in a placard on the wall of the Old Ship of Zion Church, next to the sign that reads, "All Are Welcome."

Bishop Nathan Giddings, leader of the 38-member congregation, says his policies are based on his knowledge of God. The HIV-positive and people with AIDS, he says, are unwelcome "because they suffer from a plague." Gays too, are banned because they "have abandoned the way of the Lord." Giddings means his teachings to be a mixture of Christian and Jewish beliefs.

I was curious about that, so I spoke to a Christian, Richard Cromie, senior pastor of First Presbyterian Church of Fort Lauderdale. Giddings' teachings are "antithetical" to Christian beliefs, he said.

Then I spoke to a Jew. "We don't subscribe to anything like that," said Rabbi Simcha Freedman of Beth Torah Adath Yeshurun in North Miami Beach. "On the contrary, our tradition teaches us to open our hearts to those who are afflicted in any way."

And I spoke, too, to some of the front-line soldiers—and sufferers—in the AIDS fight. God's house, they told me, should be a refuge for the afflicted—not a fortress against them. "A condemning, judgmental God is alien to me," said John Weatherhead, executive director of CenterOne, a Fort Lauderdale AIDS support agency.

"I have a loving God," said Robert, a barber with AIDS from Coral Gables who doesn't want his last name used. "I don't have a God that hates me and wants to see me dead."

Nicholas Udall, an HIV-positive landscaper from Fort Lauderdale, said simply, "Church should welcome everybody. It doesn't matter if you're blue, green, sick, well, have a virus, don't have one. It should be for everybody."

Or, as a wise friend of mine liked to say, the whole of the Bible can be boiled down to a single, essential truth: God is love.

"All else," he said, "is editorial."

But who knows? Maybe that changed when God was kidnapped. Maybe things are different now that He belongs to the Most Righteous.

I poke fun at them, but I'd be lying if I said I don't also have a certain perverse envy of them. After all, I whisper to Him often, confessing questions and confusions on dark nights when the world lies fallow and too still for comfort. As I do, I wonder what it must be like to be like them—to have no questions or confusions. To know the mind of the Almighty.

God, says Nathan Giddings, wants him to bar the door to sanctuary. You look at the man in all his Most Righteous glory, and if your first response is anger, your second is to shake your head in disbelief at the way he is evidently able to say such things with clear eyes and untroubled conscience.

Then you look at the people on whom the bishop has closed the door, those who have come suddenly face to face with their own mortality and those already traveling the valley of the shadow of death. You look at them and remember Bible stories of Christ, loving and fearless among the lepers.

Get away from me, says Bishop Nathan Giddings to the lepers of the 20th Century.

It sounds nothing like what Jesus said, once upon a Bible verse: "Come unto me ... and I will give you rest." But then, that was before God was taken hostage.

And if God sometimes seems the exclusive property of the Most Righteous, whose fault is that? Theirs? Or those of us who let Him go and sat silent while they laid claim to Him? Either way, the failure—of courage, sensitivity and faith—lies not in Heaven but on Earth. Lies in the pulpit of Old Ship of Zion and the heart of Nathan Giddings, and all the other shadowed places too distant and mean for light to reach.

"The Lord created AIDS and the Lord can cure AIDS," said Bishop Giddings last week. Thankfully, the same holds true for ignorance and fear.

APRIL 1, 1995

A DAD FINDS PHRASE IN FRANK DIARY TROUBLING

With butchers stealing gold from the jaw teeth of corpses and peeling off human skin for use as lamp shades.

With flakes of ash that once were women and men spewing from the smokestacks of mass crematoriums, and infants being tossed live from third-story windows.

With hunger, privation and fear gnawing the joy from her soul, and with all the world at war, she wrote: " ... in spite of everything, I still believe that people are really good at heart."

Sometimes, I think it's the most troubling thing anyone has ever said. Sometimes, the distance between what we are and what that statement presumes us to be seems so vast as to be uncrossable.

I just re-read *Diary of a Young Girl* for the first time in years. In it, Anne Frank—50 years dead—is flightier than I remember, all petulant self-absorption and quicksilver moods.

And yet, also, a child of aching sensitivity and serious thought.

" ... in spite of everything I still believe that people are really good at heart."

That statement—written during the two years the teenager and her family hid from the Nazi regime bent on destroying them—has become an emblem of faith and resilience. As if, in the hope and courage of one child, we might find our own.

Yet the statement still troubles me, and I find the reason difficult to put into words.

If you're a parent, perhaps you've had the experience of being watched by adoring young eyes that think the world of you. Eyes that think you larger than life, smarter than Einstein, stronger than Hercules. Eyes that flatter, humble and ennoble you.

There is nothing you wouldn't do to be worthy of those eyes, to keep them from seeing how ordinary you really are.

That's more or less how I feel about what Anne Frank said. I fear she thinks us greater than we are. I fear we are not worthy of the adoration of her eyes.

And I fear that she is wrong about how good we are.

I fear it because I have seen corpses tumble over a cliff in Rwanda and dam a muddy creek below.

Fear it because of an "ethnic cleansing" in Bosnia-Herzegovina.

Fear it because of Anne herself. Because I look into her face—the deep-set eyes, the shy smile—and realize that they never became old. I cannot even imagine them old.

I fear because sometimes we are so woefully incapable of learning.

I fear.

She feared. And yet ...

" ... in spite of everything I still believe people are really good at heart."

Foolish child. Too naive and faith-filled to surrender her spirit to the bestial cruelty of nations and men. And so, in the end, her faith is more than a simple inspiration to those of us who survive her. It's a burden on our pessimism, a stubborn challenge to our world-weary angst.

It reposits more confidence in you than you want or need or even know how to handle.

But you have no choice in the matter—one seldom does with children. So you do what you have to do.

Teach the lessons and pray the prayers. Tell the truths and shame the devils. Push back the long shadows cast by ignorance and fear.

Remember the child whose faith braced her even as the inferno of war scoured the world.

And dream a day when it would be unthinkable to gaze into the eyes of a child and see flames reflected there.

JUNE 3, 1995

BLACK YOUTH: IT'S TIME TO PUT ASIDE THE BLOODIED N-WORD

This is an open letter to young black America.

People are asking me about you again. They're writing and calling, challenging me to explain why you sometimes call each other "nigger," then profess anger and hurt when a white person uses the same word.

They think you're hypocritical. They think you're hypersensitive. They think you should be more like the Italian guy who'll let a friend get away with the word "wop" or the Irish person who, in the spirit of good fun, now and then tolerates being called a "mick."

They think you should emulate those people in other ways, too: Stop whining about the names you are called and the mistreatment you have received. Life here has been no picnic for them, either. They worked, they educated themselves, they moved ahead and assimilated. Why can't you?

But you aren't Irish or Italian, are you? You're African. Skin the color of creamless coffee. Or pecan shell. Or sandy shore. Skin that makes you stand out in a crowd of Europeans like "a fly in the buttermilk," as the old folks used to say.

That's why your forebears and mine were chosen to bear the burden of slavery—the fact that it was beyond their ability to run off and blend in. And there you have the defining difference, the thing that makes our experience unique. With the possible exception of the original tenants of this land, no group of Americans—not Irish, Italian, Chinese, woman nor gay—ever suffered on these shores as we did.

Ten million to 20 million kidnapped from the bosom of home. Half again that many left dead by the horrors of the Middle Passage. Centuries of enslavement, rape, torture, disenfranchisement, theft, poverty, ignorance, murder and hate. And then someone asks in well-meaning innocence why we can't be more like the Irish.

Makes we want to holler.

That's why you call yourself "nigger" sometimes, I know.

Oppression long ago taught us how to build a mansion from a stack of debris, weave a symphony from a moan of pain. Look at the record. Given hog entrails, we made chit'lins. Given agony, we invented the blues. Given the bruising hardness of city streets, we created cool.

And given "nigger," a word white men meant as an emblem of our stupidity, meanness and filth, we made a multipurpose word useful in the expression of everything from anger and humor to sarcasm and fraternity. We made it our word. And the whole weight of history bars white people from using it the way we do—or even understanding it the way we do.

But here's my problem: unlike chit'lins, unlike cool and unlike the blues, this gift of oppression always took from us more than it gave. Meaning that if there's a certain sense of in-group smugness in greeting your brother as a "nigger," there is also, unspoken between the consonants, an admission that the white man was right when he said we were lower and lesser.

That word is drenched with four centuries of blood and tears. It hates us, even when it issues from our own lips.

And it is time we got beyond self-loathing.

I know what *Action News* says about you. I know how police act like you're a crime waiting to happen. I know the advice the crack man gives, know the terrible things family and friends sometimes say because they don't know better and they don't know you.

Love yourself anyway. Love yourself past the hateful words and the hurtful lies. Love yourself over the empty pockets of poverty and the bare walls of spirit. Love yourself through the narrowness of days and the meanness of nights.

Love yourself with a fierceness and an urgency, and I promise that it will lead you up to this truth: You are the flower of 400 years. You are the dream a slave once had.

And there is no such thing as a nigger.

There never was.

NOVEMBER 8, 1995

THE RISKS AND THE POWER OF PEACE

When the hatreds are ancient enough, when grudges are sufficiently nursed, they take on a life of their own. When that happens, when people hate so long they can't imagine themselves not hating, the most foolhardy thing a man can do is reach open hands over the ramparts and say the dangerous word:

Peace.

It is a cautionary truth worth remembering in an America that seems sadly determined to sunder itself along seams of gender, culture, race, religion and class. It is, perhaps, the one thing of value we can take from the assassination of Israeli Prime Minister Yitzhak Rabin.

I'm no student of the long history of blood and suffering in the Middle East. I grew up with it on the evening news, of course, but like the internecine warfare in Northern Ireland and Lebanon, it was something that was happening to someone else someplace far away. You sighed and shook your head when the rocks sailed and the bombs blew, but mostly you were just glad you didn't live there.

I took heed, however, that day in 1993 on the lawn of the White House when the Arab-Israeli peace accords were signed. Took notice of how the old soldier Rabin reached hesitantly past President Clinton, past ancient agony and the enmity of years, to grasp the hand of his mortal enemy, Yasser Arafat.

It was a profoundly courageous gesture.

How courageous we can only know now as Israel mourns and the world reels and men and women of good will agonize over what tomorrow will bring. Rabin apparently was killed by one of his countrymen—an Israeli right-winger outraged by the move toward peace. Seeing Rabin's fate, will anyone be in a hurry to be that brave again?

The words of songwriters float in fragments in my mind. Gil Scott-Heron saying "work for peace." John Lennon saying "give peace a chance."

But that's just the knee-jerk reaction of a pampered American child struggling to understand. We justifiably lament the violence of our society, but in truth, not one of us goes into the day worrying about the car bomber or mortar attack that are facts of life for someone else in that someplace far away.

For us, peace is something the songwriter sang, an expression the hippies popularized. It's a word rappers use, slamming it down at conversation's end like the winning bone in dominoes. "Peace!" they bark.

But elsewhere they are better acquainted with war, and so they long for peace, need it enough to risk everything for it.

And some fear it, too. After being defined so long by war, perhaps they wonder who they would be in war's absence.

We Americans will, if we are smart, use the shocked silence of this moment to assess those cautionary truths. To remember the power of ancient enmity to become its own engine and reason for being. To ask each other, what was it we were fighting about again? To get a grip.

Because when you look at America, when you see one nation under God fracturing into tiny fiefdoms ruled by fear, is it so difficult to imagine that the someone else living someplace far away may one day be us, here?

Already, the air in this nation is hot and mean, stifling with accusation and acrimony. Already, dialogue is being choked off like water gurgling to a halt in some rusty old faucet. Already, some of us are waiting, armed.

Would that more of us could be half as brave as the old soldier and his enemy were when they reached across and promised to study war no more. Surely they knew that old animosity was a perpetual-motion machine that might react in just this way—exacting blood to ensure its own survival. But they reached across anyway.

Would that we could do the same.

Maybe then even a pampered American child might learn to say the word and mean it. Not as the lyric in a song, or a greeting of the truly hip, but as a sacred trust, an urgent need, and the highest dream human hearts can muster.

Shalom.

Salaam.

Peace.

FEBRUARY 8, 1996

FEAR RULES IN CUSTODY VERDICT

You can tell a lot about a person by what he fears. Fear is like a picture in negative, an image inferred. Thus one can discern vanity by its fear of homeliness, modesty by its fear of exposure, stupidity by its fear of intelligence.

Knowing that, consider the child custody battle last August between John and Mary Ward. Dad is a convicted killer, an accused child molester, a fount of racist rhetoric and a deadbeat $1,400 behind in his child support payments.

Mom is a lesbian.

Guess which one a judge in Pensacola feared? Yup. Mom. Which is why Dad wound up with custody of their 11-year-old daughter.

This, even though Mom raised the little girl for 11 years. Even though she was by all accounts an attentive, involved and caring parent. It didn't matter. In Judge Joseph Q. Tarbuck's court, her homosexuality was the sole salient fact.

"I'm opposed to it and that's my beliefs," said John Ward righteously. I am reminded that if ignorance is the wellspring of fear, righteousness is its favored refuge.

Reading the story last week, I couldn't escape the sinking sensation that I had somehow awakened in the '50s, the scaredy-cat years when we feared all the wrong things for all the wrong reasons. And I was reminded again that you can know a person by his fears.

Does he fear with real reason? Or does he fear without rationale—fear based on half truth and superstition, as cave dwellers once feared flame?

Does he fear, in other words, like Ward and Tarbuck?

Consider the options the judge faced. Because Ward has threatened to disown his daughter if she ever comes home with a black guy, he might have feared the little girl would end up looking at life from beneath a pointy white hood. Because seven years ago a teenage girl accused Ward of molestation (charges were never filed and he denies the allegation), Tarbuck might have feared that the daughter would receive unwelcome midnight visits to her room. Because Ward spent eight years in prison for the second-degree murder of his first wife, Tarbuck might have feared that the child would learn to express her anger in violence. Or worse, become the target of such expression.

Instead, Tarbuck feared the mother. Feared that if left unprotected, the little girl would grow up to like women.

Truly, the mind boggles. Faced with a ruling this arrogant, retrogressive, wrong-headed, atavistic and brain dead, one hardly knows where to begin tearing it apart.

In the first place, Your Honor, homosexuality is not catching. In the second place, even if it were, given the chance that a girl might be influenced to grow up a killer on the one hand or a lesbian on the other, I have difficulty seeing "killer" as the preferable option. And in the third place, as far as I know, lesbians have not blown up any buildings, shut down the federal government or made media heroes of any radio talk-show crackpots. As far as I know, those crimes were all committed by heterosexual men.

One wonders where these boys get the gall. Ward opines piously that his wife's sexual orientation is wrong and you say to yourself, "Yeah, right. As opposed to the brilliant life choices you've made, eh, sport?"

Sorry. There goes the mind, boggling again.

But it's troubling to me what all this says about these men and others like them. That their minds are closet-small and fortress-closed. That you cannot reach them with logic, facts or truth. There is no light in the closet. There is no key to the fortress.

"I'm opposed to it and that's my beliefs," he says.

Fine. Here's mine. Two men in Pensacola fear a good mother who wants for her child only that she "grow up to be the very best that she can be, whatever's right for her ... I want her to be able to develop her own ideas."

They fear her. And you can tell a lot about a person by what he fears.

MARCH 30, 1996

IN THE END, JUST ONE SAD TRUTH: GAIL'S GONE

Call her Gail.

Maybe I should start by telling you that she was good people— that she got down in the floor and played Legos with my little girl, surprised my son with Power Rangers cookies because he's their biggest fan and used her own money to buy clothes for homeless people.

Or I could start by telling you that she was, as my wife puts it, "always looking for permission." She didn't think you would like her for who she was, so she looked for you to say, 'It's OK.' "

Maybe I should tell you that Gail was gay, since that seemed the most important thing about her to some who knew her—and thus, should have known better.

I could start a lot of places, but I suppose I should start with the fact that Gail is dead. She put a gun in her mouth in February and pulled the trigger.

Her suicide came eight years after a hysterectomy that plunged her into an abyss of depression. Six or seven years after she began using painkillers to ease the burden of feeling. And, says her companion of 15 years, three months after her brothers turned her away from their family reunion.

We will call her companion Pam. She and Gail lived together in South Florida. When I asked her why Gail's brothers shut her out of the family reunion, Pam said it was because one of them considered her an "embarrassment." She said the other one, who considers himself Christian, told Gail she would burn in hell for loving a woman. Gail used to complain that they said this stuff to her all the time.

I called her brothers, who live in another state, to ask how they feel about those things now that she's dead. Neither returned my call.

So Pam did all the talking. Her voice was filled with shadows and long silences where I groped reflexively for words before realizing that there were none. But she spoke through it with determination, and she told me things I didn't know.

That Gail's mother was abusive—an alcoholic—and her father chronically ill and that their home was filled with rancor. That Gail was sexually molested by a family acquaintance as a child. That she had a baby at 16 or 17, but put it up for adoption and regretted it ever after.

And Pam told me what happened when Gail decided to move back home a few years ago to be close to her sickly father. Her brothers said, "There's no way that you're moving anywhere in this vicinity. We're not going to have any lesbians living here."

And so she stayed in Florida.

"Her main thing was, she wanted to be accepted," said Pam. But that was the one gift her brothers never gave, Pam added.

My wife remembers Gail stopping her once and saying, "There's something about me that you should know." But Gail hemmed and hawed so long that Marilyn finally said, "What are you trying to tell me? That you're gay?"

Gail was astonished that Marilyn already knew, and that it didn't matter to her. What if more people had felt that way? Would those moments that haunt Pam to this day have happened still?

"She came in and asked me, 'Do you want me to fix you something to eat?' I said 'No thank you'. She walked from one bedroom into the next. All of a sudden, the gun went off. I ran. She was sitting in the chair, smoke in the room ... I could smell it like someone lighting a match. Blood was just pouring out of her mouth like a faucet. I gave her mouth to mouth and the more I tried to do it, the more my mouth kept filling with blood."

Gail left a suicide note. It said: "Well, you're rid of me for good now."

"I took it personally," said Pam. "(But Gail's therapist) said, it didn't necessarily have to be for (me), it could have meant to everybody. Everybody's rid of her. She was just in so much pain.

"I keep thinking, if I fix things up and paint the room and patch the bullet hole and put new carpet in and try to get things ready for her to come back..." Her voice trails into a silence.

As this story might have begun in many places, it could end in many, too. We could leave it with Pam, numbed beyond pain. We could leave it by pondering how it must feel to need your family's approval so badly—and be denied. We could leave it with a lament for ignorance and fear.

But I am sick at heart and grand conclusions are beyond me just now, so I would rather leave it, period.

Gail was 43. My baby girl says she'll miss her. She'll always remember how they played Legos on the floor.

MAY 16, 1996

BUT, DADDY, I'M TAN, NOT BLACK

My daughter didn't understand black. She insisted that she was tan. Patiently and with a child's faultless logic, she repeated it, even holding up her arm so I could see for myself.

Hampered by the imperfect logic of adults, I fumbled to correct her. No, I explained, you're black.

It was a conversation that could only happen in America, but I knew it had to be done. She had to be prepared for the day one of her friends, in a fit of pique, said some awful word picked up from the grown-ups at the dinner table. As prepared as possible, anyway.

But even so, some small part of me rebelled at the task of explaining race to a child. Was saddened by the reminder that we haven't yet managed to make it irrelevant.

One hundred years ago this week, the Supreme Court codified that failing into a law that, for the next 58 years, gave backbone to Jim Crow. At the center of the case was a man named Homer Plessy who wound up in jail while trying to get to Covington, a small town in Louisiana.

The facts of the case were simple. On June 7, 1892, Plessy bought a first-class ticket on the East Louisiana Railway and took a seat in a whites-only coach. In the language of the day, Plessy was an octoroon—one-eighth black.

That was one-eighth too much. He was arrested and charged with violating a Louisiana statute requiring separate accommodations for blacks and whites.

In its ruling, the high court upheld the concept of "equal but separate" facilities. Justices said it was a "fallacy" to think this meant government was calling blacks inferior.

Of course, that's precisely what it meant.

The Plessy case was historic, but it really only sanctioned what was already ingrained in American life. Blacks and whites had never lived side by side in the years before the ruling. For that matter, they haven't been neighbors in the 42 years since the decision was overturned, in the *Brown v. Board of Education* case.

Yes, the Civil Rights Movement shattered the legal foundation for segregation. And yes, a rainbow coalition of dreamers has since sought to build a new foundation based on the revolutionary idea that we can live together.

But that idea has been under fire since the moment of its making, savaged by separatists in white school districts, Black Muslim mosques and many places in between. Now the effort seems almost dead. Worse, it seems almost quaint—a relic of the tie-dyed years when some people thought you could have peace simply by saying it.

In its April 29th issue, *Time* magazine declared flatly that America has "given up" on school integration, largely because whites won't stand still long enough to be integrated with. Instead they've fled from the cities to the suburbs to avoid it.

Nor is the surrender a one-way street. A few days ago my wife and I were invited to my sister-in-law's college graduation—a separate ceremony for students of color, held under the banner of Afrocentricity. We received a similar invite a few years ago when my cousin came out of law school.

Some people don't see the problem. Some wonder what is gained when black and white live together. Better to discuss the things that are lost: ignorance and fear.

We trade that weight for wings. We gain a sense of nation that doesn't depend on war or crisis for lifeblood. We draw strength from the fact that we all sing America with different accents and dance it with different rhythms.

In theory, at least. We are not yet there in practice. Not even now, a century after the Supreme Court rebuked Homer Plessy, a generation after the Court said we must find a way to live together.

Which is why I felt a little sad at having to wear my little girl down with adult illogic to protect her from the cruelties that are yet to come.

I watch her sometimes as she plays, running across the lawn in a giggling flock of brown and blond children. And I know that while nothing has changed for her, everything, irrevocably, has. That Plessy's lesson is rushing at her, that it will take her innocence, pull her out of the moment of idyll.

And that it will make her forget what it was like to rush laughing across the lawn in the days when she was tan.

JUNE 29, 1996

THE TEEN WHO CHOSE HUMANITY OVER A MOB

He was a white man in a Confederate flag T-shirt come to a rally of the Ku Klux Klan. She was a face in the crowd, a black teenager who wanted to "verbally harass him."

But the crowd became a mob. They descended upon him, pummeled him to the ground, started stomping him with their feet and hitting him with sign posts. And Keshia Thomas faced a decision: to join the mob or to be a human being.

This was Keshia's choice: She fell atop the prostrate man, used her body to shield him from the blows. Ask why she did it and she says, "I was just doing what my parents taught me: Do what's right. You can't change a man's view by killing him."

It happened a week ago in Ann Arbor, Mich., the compelling sideshow to a human carnival. Fifteen Ku Klux Klansmen had come to rally for the cause of hatred. But an estimated 1,000 anti-Klan demonstrators, a multiethnic tidal wave of outraged humanity, went after them. They broke windows, threw rocks and eventually had to be driven back by police using tear gas. Eleven people were arrested, at least two were reported injured.

It's a story with multiple morals: that we must defend free speech, especially for those views we abhor; that it is too frighteningly easy for a rational group to become a blood-lusting mob; that supporting a noble cause doesn't give you license to beat a man's head in with a signpost.

But the most compelling lesson is embodied by Keshia's choice.

She is, in some ways, a standard-issue teenager. Eighteen years old, laughs easily, dreams of becoming a forest ranger, wants to go to college but worries that she can't afford it. She says when she rushed at the man in the Confederate flag shirt, "I wanted to say, 'What did I ever do to you? There's no reason to fear me.' "

About that man, we know next to nothing at this writing. Not his name, not his hometown, not his Klan affiliation, if any. We do know that that shirt, worn in that place, was provocative. And that the provocation gives the lie to lost-cause apologists who claim Dixie's battle flag is a benign banner of Southern heritage and nothing more. It certainly wasn't understood that way by whites and blacks on the streets of Ann Arbor. One suspects it wasn't even understood that way by the man who wore it.

Don't you wonder what went through his mind as that black woman saved his body and maybe even his life? Don't you wonder what he says to the face he meets every morning in the mirror?

Maybe we'll never know. But then, it doesn't matter. What does matter is Keshia's choice.

It's a choice that's remarkable because she's black, because she's young and yes, because it flies against the choices we as a nation have made in recent years: Black and white demagogues blustering, Reginald Denny and Rodney King bludgeoned, Jews burned out in Harlem, blacks shot down in North Carolina and sanctuaries of God, burning, blackening, in the heat of arson fires. Each representing a decision by some one of us to endorse rage, to permit partitioning, to seek comfort with racism.

And to harden—many of us calcifying our souls against the notion that it is possible, or even desirable, for Americans to cross the divide and embrace as families do.

But the most effective champion for human equality our nation has ever known believed that embrace inevitable and redeemed the hateful without once raising a hand in anger. The would-be disciples of tolerance who rampaged last week in Michigan should seek Martin Luther King's example and understand that he would have deplored their violence and applauded Keshia's choice.

That a scattered few do not, that some in Ann Arbor have been heard grumbling that she should have left the man to his fate, only speaks of how far they have drifted from their own humanity. And of the crying need to get back.

Keshia's choice was to affirm what they have lost.

Keshia's choice was human.

Keshia's choice was hope.

JULY 18, 1996

GOP'S IMAGE TARNISHED BY INDIFFERENCE

I keep trying to take at face value the GOP's oft-stated desire to attract black voters. But they keep making it more difficult.

As in Bob Dole's decision to pass up an invitation to speak at the NAACP convention in Charlotte last week. First, he claimed a scheduling conflict. Then, he accused NAACP chief Kweisi Mfume of trying to "set me up," and confessed a preference for audiences he can "relate to."

Ahem.

One wonders what Dole was expecting from an NAACP audience—a fusillade of rotting tomatoes? Sure, they might have been cool, even skeptical. But they would have listened, given him a chance to make the case that the big, Republican tent is the place for blacks to be.

Instead, he spurned them, and that forces a question: Do you really want us under your tent, Bob?

I mean, c'mon. This is courtship? If I'd gone courting like the GOP, I'd still be a bachelor.

Frankly, if the GOP wanted black voters, I think it could have some. The Democratic Party, after all, has been criticized—I'd say justly—for taking the black vote for granted. Meantime, polls show a strong, though not dominant, streak of conservatism in the black psyche.

So why hasn't the elephant made inroads? Simple. The GOP doesn't know how to talk to blacks. Talk in code about them? Yes. Use them? Certainly. Talk to them? Nope. Ronald Reagan and George Bush used to grimace like men in acute gastrointestinal distress when hobnobbing with blacks. Contrast that with Bill Clinton, sitting easy in the pews of some black church.

The hell of it is that some blacks may actually be receptive to the GOP's message. One often hears African Americans citing the need to do for self, spurning the notion of waiting on government rescue. Their rhetoric could come from a GOP playbook.

But come November, most will still vote Democrat.

Blame Dole. Blame Gingrich and Buchanan. And blame Jeb Bush. During his unsuccessful 1994 campaign for governor of Florida, Bush was asked, if elected, what would he do for black people? His stunning reply: "Probably nothing."

He went on to say that he backs "equality of opportunity," but it was "probably nothing" that made the headlines. It was curt and contemptuous, a back of hand slight unimaginable against any other constituency.

But it probably played well in Klan klaverns, where Dole's comments were doubtless another hit.

Which tells me that when the chips are down, to hell with reaching out. These boys will fall back on time-tested methods: Pandering in code to the extremists who fear, loathe and scapegoat black people.

So maybe the GOP silence is a guilty one, the muteness of a gagged and bound conscience. Hey, no one's expecting them to propose new government machinery to benefit blacks. That's antithetical to what they are. But shouldn't they at least be able to answer simple inquiries about how their existing proposals would benefit black people? Shouldn't they come to black neighborhoods, black churches, black places, and make their pitch?

That's outreach. Instead, the GOP offers blackface, trotting out their few black stars, hoping the sight of them will make blacks do a double take and grow warm and fuzzy toward the Grand Old Party. Last year, they unveiled their "Minority Outreach Strategy," which, as far as I could tell, boiled down to making sure black Rep. J.C. Watts of Oklahoma sat front and center at GOP events. Even Jeb Bush broke down and hired an "African-American outreach coordinator" for his campaign. All of which assumes a certain stupidity on the part of African-American voters.

It's sad that the GOP feels it must go through such extravagant machinations to simply talk to black people. Yet, until the party learns that skill, until it becomes more comfortable playing to an NAACP convention than to a Klan klavern, you know what will come of GOP efforts to attract the African-American vote?

Probably nothing.

DECEMBER 7, 1996

TRUE FRIENDS SPEAK OUT WHEN ISSUES DEMAND IT

Wait awhile. Hold off. This is a bad time.

In 1963, that was the prevailing sentiment of white liberal allies—"friends of the Negro," as they were known then—as the civil rights movement prepared for its defining moment in Birmingham, Ala. From Attorney General Robert Kennedy on down, they wrung their hands and pleaded for delay. Change was coming, they said, the Negro would get his justice, but he was pushing too fast.

Martin Luther King called those people a greater stumbling block than all the cross-burners and segregationists. These "friends," said King, valued order more than justice and paternalistically presumed to set the timetable for the freedom of others. "Shallow understanding from people of good will," wrote King, "is more frustrating than absolute misunderstanding from people of ill will."

I find those words instructive in light of the recent ruling from a Hawaiian court affirming the right of gay people in that state to marry. It occurs to me that perhaps I have been a "friend of the homosexual." That is, less the true friend I ought to be than a go-slow, be-cautious, I'm-on-your-side-but voice of prudence. A human speed bump on the road to progress.

Meaning that for the better part of a year, I've struggled to cobble together a coherent opinion on the issue of same-sex marriages. Frankly, the idea made me uncomfortable.

Gays in the military? Yes. Gays as parents? Certainly. But marriage? As in ... marriage? For some reason, that one gave me pause.

Problem was, I couldn't think of a single solid argument against it.

So I was left instead with a nagging unease, the inability to stand confidently in favor or say a definitive no. I felt dispassionate logic warring with unguarded emotion, and it made me wish gay people would just learn patience, slow down, realize that maybe now is not the time.

Funny thing about time, said King. People act as if it alone can bring transformation.

"Change will come in time," we are fond of saying. But time, he argued, is neutral. It is human beings who must make the change.

I know some people resent comparisons between the civil and gay rights movements. Or for that matter, comparisons between the civil rights movement and any other freedom campaign. And not without reason. The dynamics that drove African America's struggle were, after all, unique.

But I believe there is a useful parallel to be drawn here for gay people: Sometimes, your best friends can be your worst enemies. Sometimes, those who support you can undermine or even negate that support by their weakness of knees. Sometimes, moving ahead means leaving even your allies behind.

I don't mean to suggest that gay America shun straight supporters or that every disagreement about tactic, tone or objective is a sign of paternalism or tepidity. A wise person picks fights carefully.

But sometimes, the only reason not to fight is fear, unease, a vague sense that the time is not right or that change is coming too fast. We fail to understand that change always comes too fast, which is why it always scares us.

So I'm pleased by what happened in Hawaii. More, I admire the crusaders of gay America for the fact that it happened not just in the face of opposition from enemies, but also of ambivalence from friends. It speaks well of gay courage, pride and determination to be fully free.

All of which will be severely tested in the days ahead. The issue of same-sex marriage is likely to go to Hawaii's Supreme Court. I wouldn't be surprised to see it wind up in the federal court system after that. The cynically named Defense of Marriage Act that recently passed Congress gives other states the right not to recognize a same-sex marriage performed in Hawaii.

That would seem to be baldly unconstitutional, but the legal issues are tricky and no one knows how they will play themselves out. Gay people could be standing on the threshold of an historic victory—or a humiliating setback. Either way it goes, I have learned something valuable here about who I am and where I stand.

It's quite simple, really. I stand with my friends.

JANUARY 25, 1997

CAN WHITE APOLOGIZE? CAN BLACK FORGIVE?

On the day after the first episode of *Roots*, Joe Hudson was met at the water cooler by a white colleague named Norman. Norman said, If any of my ancestors inflicted harm on any of yours, I apologize.

Twenty years later, Hudson, who hosts a radio talk show in Detroit, is telling me this to explain his support for what I consider the most incendiary idea in race relations—about which, more in a moment.

"The only verdict that counts is when you look in the mirror," he says. "That mirror reflects who you are and what you are. If my white friend Norman needs a lung, I'm going to give Norman a lung, because I love Norman and because he said he was sorry."

The most incendiary idea in American race relations is this: that white can apologize, and that black can forgive. It is also the most electric.

There is, let me concede at the outset, no groundswell behind this. No sense of inevitability pushes it forward like the wind does the wave.

But it's out there nonetheless. I hear it from time to time, rising like steam from hearts sickened of acrimony. I saw it once in a letter from a white person who asked with urgency, "Why can't you just forgive us?" I read it in *My First White Friend*, by black author Patricia Raybon, who wrote of the heaviness her soul set free when she chose to forgive. Most recently, I heard it in Hudson's voice when he contacted me after reading a column I wrote on *Roots* and black anger.

Hudson's dream is that President Clinton, on behalf of the nation, will do for black America what Norman did for him. Apologize.

I was intrigued, so I pushed him on that. An apology, Joe? Against the weight of that awful history? Against whip scars and rope burns? Against torchlight justice and Whites Only signs? Against "nigger"?

"We have to start somewhere," replied Joe.

I pushed him some more. Could he take an apology in exchange for father's tears and mother's fears? For the tamping down of children's dreams and the emasculation of black men?

Joe sighed. "I'm tired of being angry," he said. "I'm tired of my eyes throwing flames at white folks every time I look at them."

Joe has no illusions that the Promised Land is upon us. He understands too well that racism still infects the body politic like a virus. And yet ...

"... Saying I'm sorry is certainly the first step in the healing process."

So simplistic. So naive. So ...

Electric.

Can white apologize? Can black forgive?

I find myself wary of asking too loudly; this is dynamite with question marks for fuses. Indeed, the same day Joe called, I heard from a white bigot who called me "nigger" and a black one who railed against honkies.

Who would dare speak apology and forgiveness to people like them? Who would say it to those pitiful whites who hate because they feel impotent, hate because they fear, hate because they are ignorant, hate because ...?

Who would offer it to those miserable blacks who cling to rage because losing it would be like losing their bones?

Can white apologize? Can black forgive?

Bigots black and white make me shudder and doubt.

But, ultimately, both are beside the point.

We ought to apologize, even to those who scorn the act. Forgive, even when brethren find it a cowardly response to horrific crimes.

We ought to do these things not as a kindness to the other, but as an act of mercy to ourselves.

Otherwise, these things hold us, and we, in turn, grip one another—unwilling to draw close, unable to let go—fastened together by the deeds of our fathers and the words left unsaid.

The deeds are immutable, but the words await only courage.

JUNE 5, 1997

GOD'S LAW IS SUBJECT TO DEBATE

This is for those who hated my recent column about Ellen DeGeneres and Jerry Falwell—the lesbian comic and the preacher who finds her disgusting. It's for the ones who pointed me to the Bible, specifically Leviticus 20:13, which calls homosexuality an "abomination" worthy of death.

Finally, it's for those who, in light of this, dared me to explain how I can scorn the preacher and defend the lesbian.

Let me begin by saying that I have no answer.

When it comes to reconciling the words in the ancient book with the conundrums of modern life, such is often the case.

This same chapter of Leviticus, for instance, also mandates death for cursing your parents (Leviticus 20:9) or committing adultery (Leviticus 20:10).

Why aren't those who quote Leviticus as literal law rushing to obey this injunction? Why aren't the streets running red with the blood of sluttish spouses and spoiled brats?

I have no answer.

It is emphatically not my intention to ridicule God's Book. However, I do mean to challenge those of His would-be soldiers who seem to take their faith as an excuse for spurning two of His greatest gifts.

Meaning a heart that knows compassion and a mind that entertains questions.

They claim there's nothing personal in their persecution of gays. They are, they say, just following God's law.

But we seldom hear of anyone getting this hot and bothered over faithless spouses or ill-mannered children, both worthy of capital punishment according to the Bible.

For that matter, you seldom hear rage over men with long hair (1 Corinthians 11:14) or women who speak out in church (1 Corinthians 14:34-35)—both also scorned by the Bible. And so, if these people are honest with themselves, they must admit that their antipathy toward gays has less to do with God's law than with human aversion—the visceral shudder of revulsion many still feel at the thought of all things homosexual.

Problem is, it's hard to say that, isn't it? Sounds mean and unreasoned. Feels better to parade your loathing and fear under the banner of God's law.

Some would have you believe that law is as immutable as stone and exact as tax code, but every application seems to prove otherwise.

I've known of churches where they thought God's law forbade the use of medical doctors, and churches where they thought it required them to wrap venomous snakes around their bare arms; churches where they thought it called them to sing His praises in reverent whispers, and churches where they thought it meant for them to rattle the rafters with soul shouts; churches where they believe God's law sanctions hatred, and churches where God's law seems to demand that you send a check to Rev. Bob. And yes, churches where it simply bids you to be a humble servant of that which is decent and good.

All that from the same book. So it would seem God's law is, at the very least, open to interpretation.

What's it say about us that so many are willing to interpret the Bible only to the limits of their own narrow-mindedness and bigotry? That so many are inclined to ignore the passages that say men ought not judge? Or that so many seem to disregard what happened when the scribes and Pharisees brought before Jesus a woman caught in the act of adultery and demanded that she be stoned in accordance with God's law. Instead, Jesus faced them and said the one who was without sin should cast the first stone.

Why is it so few ever take that literally?

I have no answer.

Is homosexuality an abomination?

No answer for that, either, except that if I was given heart and mind, the giver must have wanted me to use them. No answer except that my heart and mind find it difficult to justify loathing or impeding people who have done me no harm. No answer except to note that God is mercy. And, of course, He is love.

So it doesn't bother me to have no answers.

But I fear the man who has no questions.

JULY 10, 1997

A FUNNY THING HAPPENED ON THE WAY TO OUTRAGE: I FOUND MYSELF LAUGHING

I hated *Amos 'n' Andy* before I ever saw it. Hated it because I was supposed to, hated it because it was full of darky stereotypes, hated it because de characters talked lack dis a'year—all mush mouth and malapropism.

Didn't have to see it to hate it. I took the word of black people who loathed the radio rendition that began in 1928—two white comics doing dialect—and of the NAACP, which protested the black-cast television version that debuted in '51.

And I was ready and willing to loathe Amos 'n' Andy even more on the news of its return, 31 years after black protest drove it away. Was prepared to rip the home video distributor who's putting the sitcom back into circulation and Harry Belafonte, who's developing a movie about it.

But a funny thing happened on the way to outrage. I looked at what I loathed—and laughed. Last thing I expected, but it had the rhythm of my father's tall tales, the resonance of stories heard around home fires. With the exception of the shiftless Lightnin'—an empty caricature—these people were rich beyond stereotype.

Particularly Kingfish, the resident con man. When I heard his voice—a sound of thumbs in suspenders, chest poked out to here, misplaced importance and pontificating pretension—I recognized it as one I've imitated for years for the amusement of family and black friends.

And I wondered how I could mimic something I don't remember hearing.

Chalk it up to collective memory. To the fact that this was how we used to laugh. More, chalk it up to birthright, something passed to me on the way into this world by the generations that came before. Passed along with one admonition: Keep it among us, don't let white folks catch you doing it.

Because we laugh differently when whites are not around, when there's nothing to prove and no pressure to verify our humanity. The laughter is richer then, less restrained and more self-deprecating, as if we never saw anything so funny as ourselves.

Just don't let white folks catch you laughing that way.

As African-American writer Mel Watkins observes in *On the Real Side*, a 1994 book about black comic traditions, "One of the characteristics of black American humor—as is also the case with Jewish or Irish humor—is a tendency toward self-mockery. ... Having been so vehemently maligned and negatively stereotyped by mainstream society, blacks have been understandably wary of adding to the fire by revealing the often denigrating self-appraisals that emerge from their own humor. The furor over ... *Amos 'n' Andy* ... is an example of African America's thin-skinned reaction to public performances ... of their private humor."

That fissure he describes, that rip between public and private humor, is something every black clown has had to take into account. White people, after all, never laughed with us so much as at us. So Bert Williams, Moms Mabley, Redd Foxx, Bill Cosby, Chris Rock—even the great Pryor himself—they've all had to struggle with how to be while white folks are watching. The price of misstep could be high—censure by a black middle class that was rising, aspiring, and ill at ease with public displays of self-caricature.

Were they—we—thin-skinned? Hell, yes. Who wouldn't be? Ever seen a Mammy doll? A little black Sambo? Ever held a tube of

Darky Toothpaste, or seen the unedited *Fantasia* with all the little pickaninnies? Ever had someone tell you that a drawing of some long-limbed, red-lipped, coal-colored oaf was supposed to represent you?

If black people were thin-skinned, we had every right to be.

But one wonders at the price. One wonders if it did not cost us some unfettered part of ourselves.

Most of all, one wonders if we haven't healed enough, grown brash and bold enough, to take it back. To claim for ourselves the right a white person takes for granted.

I hated Amos 'n' Andy before I saw it. Now it just makes me wistful, makes me wonder.

How marvelous it must be to laugh without caring who hears it.

AUGUST 10, 1997

ELVIS' LASTING INFLUENCE: HE CUT ACROSS RACIAL DIVIDE

Twenty years ago this week, Elvis Presley died and I didn't care.

It wasn't antipathy I felt, but ambivalence. In those days I was associate editor of *SOUL* ("America's Most Soulful Newsmagazine"), a tabloid covering black entertainment. As far as I was concerned, Presley's death had nothing to do with me or my readers; he was irrelevant.

Nor was I alone in that estimation. Indeed I was, at 19, part of that post-Civil Rights school of black thought whose rejection of Elvis was pure reflex. We had a sense that Elvis Presley was an interloper who raided black culture and exploited it to a degree that blacks, being black, never could. It was like being made to live on the back porch of your own house and it raised a mighty resentment. Calling Presley the King of Rock 'n' Roll was, we felt, not unlike calling Jimmy Carter the President of Bolivia.

And then, there was this quote: "If I could find a white man who had the Negro sound and the Negro feel, I could make a billion dollars."

So said Sam Phillips, the man who would soon catapult Presley to glory in the mid-'50s. His words stung all the more for being true and for saying what they did about a black man's place in America. Stung so much that two, three, four decades later, we still felt the pain. What else explains the visceral hostility the black hip-hop community lavished on a man named Vanilla Ice, a white rap star of modest talents?

Presley's talents, on the other hand, were prodigious, which always made it tougher to dismiss him out of hand. Besides which, there's an inescapable irony in the fact that he has come to be called an icon of white cultural imperialism and racial division: In his years of greatest creative power, Elvis Presley brought black and white together, often at professional risk. Motown, disco and even rap, whose fan base is as much white as it is black, all grew out of that precedent he helped to set: the revolutionary idea that black and white could be brought together in—and by—the groove.

It's worth remembering that Presley arrived during the last—and in some ways, the fiercest—years of legally mandated separation of the races. It was a time when dance organizers might stretch a rope down the center aisle of an auditorium to keep black and white dancing apart. A time when police broke up white teen parties because it was thought the kids were swinging with too much abandon, swinging too much like Negroes. A time when sweaty white men with sledge-hammers smashed open juke boxes containing music by Negro artists, music variously described as "animalistic," "jungle-like" and "savage."

What might they have thought to learn that "juke" itself was an old African word meaning to jab or poke, in a sexual sense? It's probably best they didn't know: The poor men were already outraged enough, their sense of decency, their sense of place and self, all under assault by a new sound emanating from the shanties on the wrong side of the track. Because this was a time of fire.

And Elvis Presley came not to cool that fire, but to stoke it, to make it higher and hotter until it razed the old order and swept away the old men with the sledgehammers where they stood. He married black and white, made country more rhythmic and rhythm more country until what he had sounded like neither and sounded like both. He challenged what had never been challenged before, and the fact that he was a good-looking white boy born among the temples of the old Confederacy only made the act that much more seditious. And subversive. And daring.

Small wonder the establishment reacted to him with such unbri-dled revulsion. "Unspeakably untalented," said the *New York Herald*

Tribune. "Nightmare," said *Look Magazine.* Frank Sinatra called him "deplorable," Jackie Gleason promised that he wouldn't last, Billy Graham said, "I wouldn't let my daughter walk across the street" to see him. And then there's this sign, spotted on a used car lot in Cincinnati: "We guarantee to break 50 Elvis Presley records in your presence if you buy one of these cars today."

It wasn't simply the music that frightened them. It was what the music meant.

Elvis Presley brought separations together, resolved in one grand sweep the irresolution and interdependence of the black and white South. And he revealed segregation as a lie, unmasked white men doing what white men had done since the days of Thomas Jefferson and before: standing at the fence hole spying on black culture, taking notes. Unable to turn away, they stood there conjuring fantasies that blasted and offended their puritanical souls. The thing is, Elvis dared to live what he had conjured. With every throbbing quiver of his leg, every percolating note of rhythm guitar, with every whisper of loss, hymn of grace, thunder of righteousness from his outsized voice, he spoke what was then an officially unspeakable truth: that black and white are intertwined, entangled, woven together like braids.

Which is why James Brown's observation that Elvis "taught white America to get down" comes short of ultimate truth. What Elvis taught didn't stop with getting down, or even with white America.

Consider: According to *Billboard* magazine, Presley was the third most popular black music artist of the 1950s, after Fats Domino and Dinah Washington. Between 1956 and 1963, he posted 24 Top 10 hits on the R&B chart. "Hound Dog," Presley's version of Big Mama Thornton's 1953 hit, spent six weeks at No. 1 in 1956.

And black people, antennae preternaturally attuned to currents of culture and nuances of behavior, sensed something in him the charts could not quantify. Something sweet and genuine, something that respected and admired them. And they responded in kind. Upon spotting Presley one day, black girls on storied Beale Street in Memphis took off after him "like scalded cats," according to a black reporter. The black press noted with approval the way Elvis profusely and publicly thanked a Memphis friend, B.B. King, for "the early lessons."

In his book, *Last Train To Memphis*, Peter Guralnik recalls how *Jet* magazine once undertook to verify Presley's rumored disparagement of black people ("The only thing Negroes can do for me is buy my records and shine my shoes.") Presley denied making the statement and *Jet* found no end of black acquaintances willing to vouch for him.

They seem small gestures now. Even Presley's black chart success has been repeated (though less spectacularly) by such white performers as Teena Marie, the Doobie Brothers and Hall and Oates. But in its time, in the days of fire, this was revolution.

And on the anniversary of Presley's death, it seems that the least we can do is remember these things and honor him for them. Elvis Presley has, after all, become rather a foolish figure these last years—a tabloid mainstay kept alive by kitsch, an army of impersonators in rhinestone jumpsuits and the unwillingness of the easily gulled to believe him truly dead.

So it seems only fair to remind ourselves that whatever else he was, he was also this: one of the most dangerous men of a very dangerous time, a performer who dared integrate the two pieces of a disparate whole and tell the truth about what it means to be American. He forced raw-boned, hill-country white to look into kinky-haired, son-of-Africa black and see its own reflection. More, he forced us all to see a shared legacy of hardscrabble days and sweltering nights, of loving and longing and guitar twang, of train whistle and mule-drawn plow and front porch lemonade, of pea-picking and Moon Pie and the kind of yearning you can't speak, the kind that starts high in the throat as a keening sound and ends up low in the soul as a weary sigh.

This was music, yes. But it was also miracle.

Twenty years ago Elvis Presley died and I thought it didn't matter.

I was wrong.

SEPTEMBER 20, 1997

THE PILGRIMS DIDN'T INVADE ENGLAND FOR THIS

In 1492, when George Washington and a crew of hardy explorers stepped off the Mayflower and discovered the United States, who could have guessed that it would someday come to this?

I'm talking about a new poll indicating that many Americans know next to nothing about their own Constitution.

Out of a thousand citizens surveyed by the National Constitution Center in Washington, over half couldn't say how many U.S. senators there are. Over a third believe the Constitution names English as the official language of the United States. One in six thought the Constitution establishes the United States as a Christian nation.

It was only the most recent addition to the mountain of evidence indicating that when it comes to American history and government, Americans know, well, diddly squat. As Philadelphia Mayor Edward Rendell, the chairman of the center, pointed out, most native-born Americans would fail the citizenship test immigrants must pass to become naturalized citizens.

This situation is intolerable. Inexcusable. Really, really bad.

And it is time to make a change.

As President Coolidge said so memorably during the most hopeless days of the Civil War, "When in the course of human events we ask not what our country can do for us, but what we can do for our country, when we act with malice toward none and charity for all, that is one small step for a man, one giant leap for all mankind."

Gives me the chills just thinking about it.

The question, my fellow Americans, is can we surrender to a tide of ignorance? Is that why Martin Luther King freed the slaves? Why Thomas Jefferson chopped down the cherry tree? Is it why Ronald Reagan stood on the floor of Congress and uttered those imperishable words, "Give me liberty, or give me debt!"

No, I think not.

But you know, it's ironic that this study comes out right as the nation is suffering through yet another of its dreary cycles of anti-immigrant hysteria. It's a strange malady, given that the American colonies were founded by people who came from someplace else, brought disease with them, were a drain on resources, lacked salable skills and refused to learn the language. For some strange reason, the natives—at least initially—took them in anyway.

Yet we have, in our righteous xenophobia, come down hard on new arrivals in recent years. We've tightened rules, restricted rights, instituted English-only laws, done everything except sandblast the welcoming inscription off the Statue of Liberty. We have made ourselves as clear as language allows:

Go back to Mexico, María.

Go back to France, François.

Go back to China, Chang.

Go back.

It occurs to me, though, that maybe we ought to keep a few immigrants around. You never know when we'll need someone to explain our history or interpret our Constitution. Lord knows most of those born here have no time for that, what with Steven Seagal movies to see and a new TV season getting under way.

It's a shame, though, when you pause to consider all that we have lost. We won't be able to tell our children heroic stories of Franklin Roosevelt's Rough Riders charging up Bunker Hill or the Confederate soldiers standing their ground at Iwo Jima. Won't be able to explain how the president's Cabinet was made with wood from the three branches of the federal government. Won't even be able to talk about how the Second Amendment gives us the precious right to bare arms. And legs.

We should not accept this sad state of affairs.

I'm reminded of what Abraham Lincoln so eloquently said during one of his famous fireside chats at the height of Great Depression: "Them that's got shall get, them that's not shall lose. So keep hope alive because a mind is a terrible thing to waste."

Frankly, I think that says it all.

NOVEMBER 22, 1997

BARBIE'S MAKEOVER MAKES HER MORE REAL, LESS HATEFUL

Let's call this column "Barbie Does The Right Thing" and let's begin it with a declaration: I've always hated Barbie. Indeed, I've had it in for ol' Plastic Head for as long as I can remember.

When I was a boy, it was because she was one of my sister's favorite toys. Obviously, I had to hate her—she was covered with cooties.

As a man, though, the animus has more to do with Barbie's status as an icon of our expectations for women. Meaning a pinched waist, a painted face, an empty head and bazooms out to here.

Sure, they'd put her in a lab coat sometimes and call her "Dr. Barbie," but anyone with eyes knew how this doctor operated. Let's just say that her stacked-to-the-max proportions were probably more influential on the psyches of young girls (and boys) than her plastic stethoscope ever could be.

At some level, it's probably unfair to blame Barbie for retarding little girls' perceptions of themselves and their abilities. That's a dishonor shared by many of us. But Barbie has always been the embodiment of that retardation, symbol of all that is patronizing and paternalistic about our relationships with women. So it never bothered me to see her take her lumps.

Maybe it bothered Mattel, though. Maybe that's why the toy maker recently announced that beginning next year, it will be phasing in an updated Barbie. Less makeup, less prodigious chest, less pinched waistline. In short, a Barbie who looks less like a trollop with too much time on her hands and more like real women and girls.

Some have questioned the wisdom of tinkering with a billion-dollar-plus franchise. Some girls and women say they like their synthetic sister just the way she is.

Hey, hard plastic.

I think the change is good, if for no other reason than that I'll be able to watch my little girl play with Barbie without wanting to punt her (the doll, not the daughter) into the trees behind the house.

I've always thought there was something insidious about Barbie Doll. It wasn't simply that her beauty was, in the most literal sense, unattainable, but that she codified beauty as the single most important—indeed, the defining—attribute of a woman's worth. Barbie was nothing but beautiful. Had no other dimension.

I know that "lookism"—the tendency to judge people by appearance—goes both ways these days and that women stand readier than ever to evaluate men by raw physical attributes. But women, by and large, don't control the machinery of perception in this country. So they'll never be able to do to men what men have always done to them—meaning judge us solely and completely as a collection of body parts. For that, men ought to be thankful.

We couldn't handle it. Yet women do everyday, straining to meet criteria that are, for all but the most genetically blessed, impossible. And when failure comes, as inevitably it must, it too often leaves women devastated, doubting and, sometimes, dead of self-starvation.

So, yeah, I can get behind a more realistic Barbie. I can get behind anything that helps a girl see herself as more than a rack upon which breasts are hung.

But why stop here? Why not let Barbie carry her realism deeper into the shadows of despair where imperfect girls live? Let her reflect their reality.

Mattel could make Smart Barbie. Comes with Threatened Ken.

Or Abused Barbie. Comes with Abusive Ken with Special Kung Fu grip.

Or ... Teen Mom Barbie. No Ken available.

Yes, I know, Barbie is not supposed to be real; she's a fantasy. And I have no problem with fantasy; I love a pretty woman as much as the next guy. But I want girls to understand that pretty is only one of a million wonderful things they can be. That's why it cheers me to see Barbie do the right thing.

At least I'll no longer have to indulge fantasies of sending my daughter's dolls sailing over the roof. Already had my excuse ready, though.

"Ooh, look, honey. It's Astronaut Barbie."

DECEMBER 6, 1997

A QUESTION OF FAITH: BLIND DEFENSE OF RACE DOOMS SEARCH FOR TRUTH

I'm not here to change your mind about Tawana Brawley.

For 10 years this young black woman has told a tale of how, when she was 15, white men kidnapped and raped her and left her smeared with excrement and racial epithets. Her refusal to cooperate with investigators and the fact that a grand jury said the attack never happened have convinced many that this story, which outraged, galvanized and polarized New York City and the nation, was never anything but a hoax.

I'm willing to concede that reasonable people could consider the same body of evidence and come to different conclusions.

What bothers me is embodied in something one of her supporters told a reporter a few days ago: "If Tawana Brawley was to get up ... and say it was a hoax, I'd say she was lying. We know what happened to her."

In other words, this woman will not allow for even the possibility that Brawley's tale is untrue. She believes it without question.

I wish I were surprised.

Tawana Brawley returns to the news as her advisers, including the Rev. Al Sharpton, defend against a defamation suit brought by one Steven Pagones, whom, 10 years ago, they identified as one of her attackers. Brawley was the star attraction at a recent rally where she reasserted the truth of her tale before an audience of hundreds of people.

That many of them believed her doesn't trouble me. That some believed her without question does.

Black people, some of us, are victims of a perverse dynamic born of both paranoia and hard experience. A dynamic which says that the more a black person is reviled or simply doubted by the white mainstream, the more fervently we must rush to his or her defense. To diverge is unthinkable. To question, traitorous.

It's a reflex born of the too many times we've seen ourselves lynched by that mainstream, physically and otherwise. But ultimately, such unguarded faith makes sense only if one accepts that every black person is a saint and every black mouth a fount of gospel truth.

And that just ain't so.

The issue is not, should we support the brother or the sister. Rather, it's should we support without question. Support in the face of overwhelming evidence. Support although it expends moral capital on those who don't deserve it. Support even when it makes us look gullible and foolish. Support at all costs and by any means necessary.

No. We have a right to question. More than that, we have an obligation.

Which we need to exercise. Otherwise, we'll continue to see ludicrous scenarios like those that have played themselves out in recent

FORWARD FROM THIS MOMENT   **113**

years. Black folks rallying around O.J. Simpson like a brother even though he didn't remember he was black until the handcuffs went on. Black folks claiming Mike Tyson was unfairly maligned right up until he tried to bite off Evander Holyfield's ear. Black folks voting to support—with a standing ovation, yet!—National Baptist Convention chief Henry Lyons, and never mind that he's an accused swindler and his wife an alcohol-abusing arsonist.

We forgive too easily, forget too readily, rally too quickly behind any crook, creep or cretin with the right paint job. Now we are told that even if Brawley admits to telling a lie, at least one woman will continue to believe her tale. "We know what happened to her," she says.

Really? How exactly do "we" know this? Why do we invest ourselves so deeply in a story that is, by even the most charitable interpretation, questionable?

But that's just the point: Some of us find tales of black woe literally unquestionable. Some of us are so maimed by racism—both previous and anticipated—that we accept the word of kinsmen uncritically. That stifles honest discourse and feeds mob mentality. And it's inimical to the search for truth.

There can be no answers where there are not questions first.

JANUARY 15, 1998

ATHLETE PICKED THE WRONG BATTLE

"A man can't ride your back unless it is bent."—Martin Luther King Jr.

We begin by returning to the scene of the crime.

Last month, Latrell Sprewell, a black man and professional basketball player, choked his coach, who is white. The reason? Coach yelled at him in practice. In response, the team tore up Sprewell's $32 million contract and the NBA suspended him for a year.

I wrote a column about the incident, saying, in part, that for $32 million, Coach could yell at me till he popped an artery. Thirty-two mil buys a lot of earplugs.

Most of those who took the trouble to respond felt the same way, an opinion that cut a wide demographic swath across black, white, male and female. But a tiny minority saw it differently. While careful not to condone Sprewell's actions, they felt he should not have to stand there as a black man and be yelled at—"disrespected"—even for $32 million.

You can't trade "dignity for dollars" is how one of them phrased it.

The dissenters had two things in common. All were male and all were black.

In their insistence on respect at all costs, I heard an echo of gunfire—saw all the young black men gut-shot and brain-shot by other young black men over petty affronts and minor offenses these last years. It struck me that brothers are literally dying for respect.

Which is not hard to understand. They seek only what history and society have conspired to deny them: a way to be somebody. So some young black men on some unforgiving streets have come to practice a studied macho harder than concrete. For them, there are no minor slights. It is, they'll tell you, an issue of respect and they guard that respect to the point of extreme behavior and diminishing returns. Even, sometimes, to the point of violence.

When such a man perceives disrespect, when he has the barriers up and the warning lights flashing, a prudent person keeps his distance. Tellingly, the last civil thing Sprewell said to his coach was, "Don't come up on me."

Yet, even understanding all this, I can't quite agree with my dissenters. They don't get it. The cold fact is, the world does not operate according to the mores of hard streets. If one seeks to get ahead, one adapts to society, not the other way around. Latrell Sprewell failed in this, and to make excuses based on who he is and where he's from is to insult both. Somebody should've pulled his coat. Somebody should've schooled him better.

He got upset because Coach yelled at him?!? So what? Yelling is what coaches do. They get in your face and push you through your limits. It's not like the coach insulted Sprewell's mother or something. What he said, according to *Sports Illustrated*, was, "Put a little mustard on those passes!" Sprewell should have done just that and kept his hands to himself.

Is that "dignity for dollars?" To ask the question is to miss the point.

Sprewell satisfied a short-term impulse at the expense of his own long-term well-being. And how many times have we seen young men do that? Wreck their lives to gratify some petty need or retaliate for some imagined act of disrespect.

You want respect? Real respect? Bump the dumb stuff. Keep your eyes on the prize.

Latrell Sprewell should have done that, should have valued his career more than he ultimately did. And yes, he should have remembered the money. Do you think that's crass? Well, the money is important here not because of the flashy things it can buy, but the substantive ones. Thirty-two million dollars is higher education for everyone in the family, businesses and properties to be handed down to the next generation. It is advantages and options most people don't have, blessed security of which they can only dream. Freedom.

Sprewell could have protected that. Instead, he choked.

Anyone who thinks that by doing so he kept his dignity intact needs to think again. If that's dignity, give me dollars instead.

MARCH 26, 1998

BLACKS: OFFENDED BY USE OF N-WORD? THEN STOP SAYING IT

As Richard Pryor told it years ago, he was sitting in a hotel lobby on a trip to Africa when he heard a voice within. "What do you see?" it asked. "Look around."

"I looked around and I saw people of all colors and shapes. And the voice said, 'Do you see any niggers?' I said, 'No.' It said, 'Do you know why? There aren't any.'"

Pryor told an audience that he started crying then. The comedian, whose speech had always been peppered with that ugly word, abruptly realized that it had not passed his lips in the three weeks he'd spent among the blacks of Africa. Pryor subsequently renounced the word altogether: The most profane man in America decided that here was a term too profane even for him.

I mention this only because there is, in case you hadn't noticed, a renewed struggle under way over the use and abuse of the N-word.

And it's left me a little ticked off at the blatant hypocrisy. Of black people.

I'm sorry, but I just don't get it. Over recent months, black activists have battled the people who put out the *Merriam-Webster* dictionary, a black educator has challenged Mark Twain's *Huckleberry Finn*, and Spike Lee has lambasted Quentin Tarantino, all over the use and abuse of the N-word.

But I haven't seen anybody say a damn thing about black comics who fly it like a dirty flag. Haven't heard a peep about the tiny talents of raunch rap who spill it into the ether like sewage. Haven't heard anyone say the obvious: that if we as African-Americans truly abhor this word, then the protest ought to begin on our own doorstep.

Yeah, yeah, I know the rules. It's OK for us to say it, but not for whites. Except that some young blacks say it is OK for whites if those whites are honorary blacks, down with the brothers. Yet if those same whites mistakenly use the word outside their circle of black friends, they're likely to incite a riot.

I know the rules, but the rules are stupid. Contradictory. And confusing. If white people are baffled about what is and isn't allowed, I can't blame them. I blame us.

We've become entirely too casual, too gratuitous, with this instrument of disparagement. These days, one is less likely to hear the word from a white jerk with his bedsheet draped on his head than from a black one with his pants sagging off his butt. I once heard a young black colleague make a point of saying it in front of a white woman, who was properly flummoxed. The colleague explained with blithe self-satisfaction that she enjoyed dropping the word into conversation in order to observe white folks' stunned reaction.

All of which suggests to me that we as black people suffer from historical amnesia. A blindness to the suffering of ancestors. And a stubborn refusal to learn the lesson Pryor did—to grow up and leave this evil thing behind.

So the last word some beaten black man heard before gravity yanked him down and the rope bit into his neck becomes a shock tactic for a callow youth. The word that followed his torn corpse as it was dragged down dusty roads behind the bumper of a car now serves some oafish rapper who can't find anything else to rhyme with trigger.

That's grotesque. It is obscene.

And it renders just slightly hollow all these recent protests of mortal offense.

I'm supposed to be outraged that the word is used—with historical accuracy—in a classic novel that came out 114 years ago? No. Mark Twain doesn't bother me. Snoop Doggy Dogg does. Def Comedy does.

Because they suggest to me that behind the facade of arrogant cool, we still hate us.

That self-loathing is slavery's hardiest legacy, Jim Crow's bastard child. And I'm impatient to see it dead. Impatient for a day when we love ourselves enough to be offended by anyone who uses this word. Moreover, love our children enough to stop teaching it to them.

Here's a new and much simpler rule for the use of the N-word:

Don't.

JUNE 6, 1998

HATE CAN'T WEIGH YOU DOWN WHEN YOU'RE IN CHARGE

By popular request, today's column discusses the pressing problem of black racism in America—a topic second in importance only to the question of safety locks on squirt guns.

I shouldn't laugh, I suppose. There are people who take the "issue" of black racism quite seriously. I know, because many have called or written me in the last few weeks.

Seems they're exercised over a recent column of mine that dealt with a white driver who swerved toward my son while someone in the car yelled racial epithets. A sizable minority of white readers complained: Why the ongoing emphasis on white racism against blacks? What about all the black racism against whites?

I kept waiting for them to tell me about black banks that turn down their loans, black employers who pay them less, black courts that hand them harsher sentences. ... man, I was ready to read those African-American so-and-sos the riot act.

But turns out that what these readers were calling black "racism" really amounted to any unpleasant encounter with a black person.

Been mugged by a black guy? Racism.

Called a nasty name? Racism.

Beaten to a parking spot? Racism.

But the problem is that if you're mugged, it's crime, not racism. Insults prove rudeness, not racism. Losing a parking spot is tough luck. Not racism.

Although some white people don't get that, David Iverson probably would.

He's a 51-year-old Miami immigration attorney who sent me an e-mail describing his own experiences with "black racism." Of all the folks who made that claim, he's the only one I took seriously. Of course, it helps that Iverson's experiences took place not in the predominantly white United States, but in the predominantly black U.S. Virgin Islands, where he lived for 13 years. See, it's hard to be an effective racist in a land where you're not in control.

I laughed when he told his stories—not in amusement, but in recognition. He talked about being stopped on petty pretenses by black cops, about being hesitant to call authorities for help "because you never know ... if you're going to go from victim to defendant." Even about social gatherings where a speaker rails against the inferiority of your people, then catches himself and says, 'But not you. You're different.'"

Sometimes, he said, after a day of racial slights, he'd find himself facing a rude sales clerk. Up went the antennae, probing for racial subtext. Only when she proved equally insolent to the black customer behind him could he exhale.

It's an exhausting existence, one whites in America, by and large, know nothing about.

"I wish every white person ... could go through that kind of experience," Iverson told me. "I don't regard it as a traumatic, terrible thing, because it does put you in a similar situation to what black people go through in the United States."

The point isn't that black Americans are incapable of hating white ones; they do it all the time.

But there's a different resonance, isn't there? The hate carries a different weight depending on whether you belong to the dominant group or the one that's perceived as inferior. If the former, the hate stings but doesn't cut, because you live in a culture that reinforces your worth. If the latter, the hate draws blood and that same culture salts the wound with words your grandfather would recognize: You have no worth.

Understand: Bigotry is never right. And yet hating white people in America is not unlike hating Icelanders in Iceland. Not a good thing, but not terribly threatening, either.

I'm amazed that some otherwise clearheaded people don't get that, so fixated are they on the idiotic "issue" of black persecution of whites. It's as if, in a nation where victimhood is all the rage, they feel left out.

So, fine, they're victims. And I feel sorry for them. As sorry as I do for all those kids maimed each year in squirt-gun tragedies.

JUNE 20, 1998

RACISM INFLICTS PAIN IN DISSIMILAR DEGREES

"Your blues ain't like mine."—Bebe Moore Campbell

Spousal abuse. That's probably what I should've written about.

If I'd said that husband beating, while a serious problem, pales in significance next to wife beating, people would probably have thought it an unremarkable statement.

Problem is, I didn't write about spousal abuse in a recent column, but race. Made essentially the same argument, though—ridiculed the notion that black prejudice against whites is a pressing national issue.

Naturally, all hell broke loose, caller after caller taking vitriolic exception, citing for support a rogue's gallery of coarse, criminal and bigoted blacks they'd had the misfortune to encounter. Then there's the woman from Michigan who told me in a disappointed voice that she thought the column unnecessarily "snide." Too much poison in the pen.

Maybe she's right. This subject does that to me. I get impatient with this offense against common sense.

The Housing Department is requesting more money to deal with housing bias against blacks and other minorities; the Agriculture Department confessed last year to a long pattern of discrimination against black farmers; the Justice Department says that in 1996, blacks suffered more hate crimes than all other racial groups combined; the Labor Department reports that black unemployment stands at 9.0, better than twice that of whites; the Sheriff's Department in Jasper, Texas, reports that James Byrd Jr. remains dead at this hour, his body torn to pieces because it was dragged behind a truck by three alleged white supremacists ... and I'm supposed to stand here and say with a straight face how pressing is the issue of discrimination against whites?!?

Not to be snide again, but get real.

Do not misunderstand me. I wouldn't minimize the frustration and pain felt by anyone—white, black, brown or magenta—singled out for mistreatment or violence on account of color. Or, for that matter, religion or sexual orientation. Nor did I ever say or imply, as some people insist I did, that African Americans are saints incapable of bigotry. Ask Reginald Denny about that. Question the corpses left by the Long Island massacre.

What I did say—and reiterate—is that blacks lack any meaningful or widespread power in this society, and so have precious little ability to use their biases to impose wholesale, life-altering discrimination against whites. Yes, there are isolated exceptions to that, but there are isolated exceptions to everything. The point stands. Indeed, it should be self-evident. That it isn't troubles me.

I first wandered into this quagmire by recounting an ugly incident involving my middle son.

Several months ago, he was walking away from the school bus when a carload of white kids buzzed past, swerving toward him while someone inside yelled a racial epithet. My wife went to one of the kids' parents hoping to resolve the issue. She never got the chance. Marilyn was met by about a dozen kids on the porch, loudly jeering while the mother of one stepped forward as if to fight. "I'm sick of you people," she said. "Everything is always about race with you."

I was 3,000 miles away when my wife told me about this episode. Helpless to help my family.

When I put down the phone, I was fatigued, discouraged and in despair. The kind of despair that comes to true believers when the world kicks them hard in their optimism. The kind of despair that says, "Play by the rules, do the right things ... and what does it matter? Nothing changes."

I wanted so badly in that moment to get away, to escape, to stand outside this thing that obsesses America. To find another place, another country, where it would not dog my days, where I could slow down, stop, breathe ... be.

The words are inadequate, I know. I wish I could explain how I felt but I can't, and maybe that's the point of all this. Most black people don't need the explanation, most whites could never understand it.

Believe me, they should be grateful for that.

AUGUST 29, 1998

STRAIGHTENING OUT THE ISSUE OF 'CHOICE'

This is for a mother in North Carolina.

She wrote in response to a recent column of mine that criticized conservative Christian groups for newspaper ads attacking gays. She wants me to accept that God exists and "does not make mistakes. He does not make a person gay."

"People like you," she writes, "make it easier for my son to convince himself even more [that] he is gay. My son is 25 years of age, good looking, personable, friendly, popular, witty, college-educated, and a very confused young man who has allowed Satan to rule his life right now. You cannot convince me deep down in your soul [that you don't] know this is abnormal."

She closes by saying that she'd love to hear from me. Well, here's my answer.

Dear North Carolina Mother:

Thank you for writing. I appreciate your concern, but don't worry. God and I talk all the time.

But then, it doesn't matter much what you think of me; I'm just a guy in the newspaper. It does matter what you think of your son.

It sounds like you did a great job raising him. I imagine that you kissed a lot of skinned knees and tended more than one fever. And I imagine, too, that some nights before you went to bed, you looked in on him as he slept, small and unaware, and maybe touched his hair, breathed his scent, and loved him helplessly.

Now there's this. And you're frightened.

But you know what? Your son probably is, too.

I don't know about "confused," though. Indeed, this might be the first time in his life that he isn't confused. The first time he's ever been honest with himself and those around him about who and what he is. And if everything that came before was a lie and this is finally the truth, then, will you deny it, and pretend it doesn't exist? Will you reject him as a "mistake?" Or will you still love him helplessly?

God makes no one gay, you say. In other words, homosexuality is something one chooses.

Here's my question, then: Why? If being gay means carrying a secret that sits on your heart like stones, if it means being reviled by preachers, rejected by family and ridiculed by strangers, if it means living with the fear that someone might take from you your career, your child, your very life, why would a person freely choose it?

Oh, I know that being gay has become chic in recent years. But gay people were with us long before that.

And I'll grant that science has reached no conclusive verdict on the origins of homosexuality. On the other hand, I don't recall "choosing" to be heterosexual. Do you?

As you see it, your son is a victim of satanic wiles. Yet the same Bible that is interpreted as forbidding homosexuality also forbids adultery, the disrespect of parents and working on the Sabbath. Maybe I'm wrong, but I don't think you'd be as upset if your son's sin was that he mowed his lawn on Sunday afternoons.

But is God truly that selective? Does He somehow prefer Sabbath-breakers to gays?

Or isn't it true that none of us is perfect and that all fall short of grace in some way or another?

So many people claim to know the mind of God, but the funny thing is, everyone who invokes His name seems to be thinking of something different, something that speaks only to his or her individual feelings or fears. For one guy, God is the bringer of wrath, for another, He is a booster for the home team and for still another, He is the force that makes the bus wait when you're running desperately to catch it. For me, He is a silence heard above the cacophony of the world, a blessed quietness that spills inside, a stillness that slips over you with the stealth of twilight shadows.

We choose the God we need, Mother.

If I were you, I'd choose the one that allowed me to meet my child where he is and love him helplessly, still.

OCTOBER 16, 1998

ABOMINATIONS FROM AMERICA'S PAST HAUNT US, READY FOR AMBUSH

Maybe in the watchful darkness of a moon-bathed night when all the world lies too still for sleeping.

Maybe when unwelcome thoughts rattle like skeleton's bones in the dark places of your mind.

Maybe when old fears and distant failures, loved ones and raw aches from long ago come sit together at the side of your bed to watch you watching them.

Maybe then, with rationality cowed to silence, the question might better be faced:

Do you believe in ghosts? And it occurs to you: Maybe you should.

Toni Morrison does. Oprah Winfrey, too. At least, if we are to judge from the celebrated book Morrison wrote and the film Winfrey adapted from it. *Beloved* is, after all, a ghost story. Yes, it's about those spirits of the dead who bring torment to the living. But it is also, in the larger sense, about the unwillingness of a hard past to stay buried, about the way we are tormented by the awful things we saw, suffered and did in the dreadful long ago.

In *Beloved*, Winfrey is Sethe, a former slave haunted by the spiteful spirit of her own dead child and, more, by the ghastly, unthinkable thing she did on the day slave catchers came to get her years ago. (This thing, by the way, is real; it actually happened.) Sethe drags her pain behind her daily, like weights. She lives only by force of habit.

It cannot have been easy to shape Morrison's sometimes-dense, often-demanding prose into a film narrative, and *Beloved* cannot be said to be a perfect movie. It lapses sometimes, fails to make emotional connections. But those shortcomings are balanced by moments of serene power, unbearable pain and tender mercies too beautiful to behold.

Even though the titan Winfrey stars in it and co-produced it, you still find yourself wondering how *Beloved* ever got made. Same thing you wondered about *Amistad, Malcolm X, Get On The Bus, Rosewood* and *Once Upon A Time ... When We Were Colored*. It occurs to you that we are living a moment without precedent here, a moment when black American passages, the same stories once dubbed too painful for mass consumption, are suddenly crowding into the multiplexes in growing numbers.

What makes it all the more amazing is that so much of the nation remains as discomfited as ever by black history. Just a few weeks ago, a school system in Prince William County, Va., rejected a black history poster because, along with images of people like Duke Ellington, Frederick Douglass and Jesse Jackson, it also includes a famous photo of a 1930 lynching. Black history without racial violence—rather like U.S. history without the Revolution.

And one doesn't have to look very far to find a white man who will wonder why any of this offends, why black people are always harping on history. Get over it, he will say. You're stuck in the past, he will say. That stuff is dead and gone. He will say.

Then, that same man will sit and weep copious tears at the latest documentary on the Holocaust. It isn't difficult to guess why this happens. Talk about the awful things that happened to the Jews during the Nazi regime, and your villains are distant figures way over in Europe. Talk about slavery and Jim Crow, its 100-year sequel, and your villain might be found in the family Bible or even, God help you, in the mirror.

It becomes a thing too near. So you seek to push it down, bury it deep. But as a character in *Beloved* points out, that which dies badly never sleeps peacefully. That which dies badly will return to bedevil the living.

In that sense, America is a haunted house. We've tried to kill what happened to black people in this country. Sought to rid ourselves of it by ignoring it, hiding it, sanitizing it, pushing it deep or simply by growing impatient with it and crying, Enough! As if a ghost cares that we are vexed.

Instead, each time we think it's buried, the ghost just slips from the soil and steps out to wander among us. Look in the eyes of weeping mothers, gaze upon the fists of angry men, hear the lament of lost children, see the sundering of hopeless families and ask yourself: Is this really a new pain? Or is it, rather, a pain that has been gathering itself for generations, a deep and powerful ache that stretches from a man in slave shackles to a boy in handcuffs?

The past shapes the present. And the future, if it has any sense, trembles.

Because you cannot bury what won't stay down, can't wish away what will not go. You can only face it, touch it, incorporate it, nurse it, make peace with it. And then climb to a higher place from there.

In *Beloved*, Sethe is nearly destroyed by that process—at the end, she is scarred and drained, eyes too sad for dreaming. Yet for all that, something in her seems steadier and more certain than it was before, as if her suffering has cleansed her and left grace in its wake. When we leave her, we believe—or is it just a prayer?—that she'll be all right.

Get over it, says a white man who believes with an earnestness that he's telling you right, telling you for your own good. The past is dead and gone, he says. And it makes you marvel all the more at Sethe's strength, wonder all the more at the depth of her soul because, somehow, she has stood in the face of a cutting truth that man's fear won't let him know.

That which is dead ain't necessarily gone.

NOVEMBER 5, 1998

IT'S NO SURPRISE THAT JEFFERSON WAS A HYPOCRITE

Not Thomas Jefferson. Oh, no, not him.

For generations, that's been the response of biographers and historians to rumors that our third president fathered children by one of his slaves, Sally Hemings. Not Jefferson, they said; he couldn't have done it.

After all, he was a strong believer in the inherent inferiority of black people and an ardent foe of so-called miscegenation—sexual contact between black and white. Moreover, he was a great and moral man. For him to be guilty of something he so loudly abhorred impugns that morality and bespeaks a hypocrisy too galling, too gargantuan, to be credited.

Not Thomas Jefferson. Oh, no, not him.

That bang you just heard was the sound of jaws hitting the floor. Turns out T.J. had a thing for brown sugar after all.

At least, that's the conclusion reached by researchers whose work is reported in the Nov. 5 issue of the science journal *Nature*. They took DNA samples from a present-day descendant of Sally Hemings and compared them to samples from members of Jefferson's family. The results were a match, indicating to a near certainty that Jefferson fathered at least one of Hemings' children.

So how are we to respond to this turn?

Some will seek to construe this as a love story and, granted, there may have been affection between master and slave. So what? It seems obvious to me that intercourse between property and owner constitutes nonconsensual sex—de facto rape. To consent to sex implies that one has a choice in the matter, the ability to freely decline. If you are owned by the person asking for sex, that ability does not exist. You don't say, "Not tonight, dear, I have a headache," to a man who can have you whipped or your children sold.

Others will suggest that the real story here is Bill Clinton. They'll say the fact that the great Jefferson fooled around with a woman young enough to be his daughter and dissembled—if not outright lied about it—casts Clinton's carnal sins in a different light.

It's a thought. But for me, at least, it's a thought for another time.

Because here in the first blush of revelation, it's the hypocrisy that gets me. More precisely, it's the fact that some people find that hypocrisy such a surprise. Jefferson scholars and descendants are reportedly flabbergasted by these findings. One report describes the news as a "bombshell."

Not Thomas Jefferson. Oh, no, not him.

And I can't help but wonder, why the hell not? Why should anyone be surprised that Jefferson was a hypocrite on the issue of race? Wasn't that established beyond doubting on the day this slaveholder wrote that "all men are created equal"?

More to the point, when has hypocrisy ever been absent from America's dealings with its racial, ethnic and religious minorities? From the natives whose "Great White Father" lied to and brutalized them, to the Jews who, in their hour of greatest need, found open doors closed and welcoming arms folded, hypocrisy has ever defined us. Ever soiled us.

Not Thomas Jefferson? Oh, no, not him?

Please.

From his day to ours, hateful hypocrisy has been woven through us as inextricably as the threads in the flag, its filth touching everything from our highest institutions to our most innocent idylls, from the White House—where leaders demonized select citizens in the name of political expediency—to the schoolyard, where children recited a couplet that went, "Eenie, meenie, minie moe, catch a n----- by the toe." From top to bottom, there's nowhere we are not touched by bigotry and its attendant duplicities, whether as beneficiary of unearned advantages or heir to undeserved handicaps.

We have always been smaller than our largest ideals. That's a given. What defines a person is where she goes from there, what truth she tells in the face of lies, how she struggles toward grace.

To hold a great man above that struggle on account of his greatness is to impede the effort and miss the point. This filth touches all. You, him, her, me.

And yes, Thomas Jefferson. Oh, yes, even him.

JANUARY 14, 1999

WHAT'S IN A NAME? A SIGN OF NEW TIMES

I imagine the news fell like a thunderclap upon certain ears. A small item it was, appearing early this week. But in those corners where they fly "English only" banners and speak with angry fervor of the need to "take back America," I expect that it hit like a hammer from the sky, producing spasms of apoplexy glorious to behold.

It seems that in California and Texas, the most popular baby boy's name is no longer John or James, Michael or David.

It's Jose.

California and Texas are, respectively, two of the most populous states in the country. California in particular is regarded as the bell-wether, harbinger of trends for the rest of the nation. And according to the Social Security Administration, folks in those states are naming their newborns Jose.

Ain't that a kick in la cabeza?

I know I'm enjoying this more than I should. Can't help it. It seems such an apropos rejoinder to these last years of Hispanic-bashing, a fit reply to the man who complained in a 1995 poll, co-sponsored by the *Herald*, that Cuba was sending "trash" to these shores ... to Patrick Buchanan, who wants to build a fence along the U.S. border with Mexico ... to all those people who feel personally insulted when Spanish is spoken in their presence. It seems an appropriate answer to those who've spent so much time fighting—and fearing—the future.

The future comes regardless, doesn't it? Ask the Census Bureau, which has been saying for years that Hispanics are on track to replace African Americans as the nation's largest minority group. Or, ask all those little boys named Jose.

Either way, you see the same thing—a nation that's changing dramatically and profoundly. Which is quite frightening to some people—conjures up troubling visions of a torn, polyglot America taken from "us" by "them" through sheer weight of numbers. Why do "they" insist on sticking out? Why don't "they" become more, you know ... American?

A tricky thing, assimilation. The Holy Grail of immigrants ever since Eastern Europeans started rushing to these shores late in the last century. You gave up your "funny-sounding" name, you hid your religion, you lost your accent, and you thereby "became American"— which almost always meant some close approximation of the, white, Anglo-Saxon, Protestant ideal.

But many have come to a different understanding of what it means to be American. They've come to feel that it doesn't require them to give up identity and heritage, doesn't demand that they become Smiths and Joneses.

Rather, it requires them only to believe in American ideals: equality, democracy, justice, freedom. Including the freedom to be who and what you are.

Granted, that's not the way it used to be. But it is the way it is and the way it likely will be from now on. The demographic shifts we face now are seismic and profound. My high school was almost 100 percent black—25 years later, the overwhelming majority of students are Hispanic. I'd be lying if I said that a visit there a few years ago didn't take me by surprise for reasons that had nothing to do with the passage of time.

Change strikes away comfort zones. It is unsettling. But still, we ought to be able to face it with something better than the xenophobic paranoia some of us have embraced. Something that honors and advances our national ideals. After all, everything that lives must change. And grow. Our country, to its credit, is doing both.

It's worth noting that nothing stops Hispanic parents in Texas and California from naming their sons John or James, David or Michael. If they wanted to, they could send their kids down the same path generations of immigrants have already trod, the one which says you change who you are to join the mainstream. Instead, they've chosen a different path.

More to the point, they've chosen this name, which speaks explicitly of Spanish heritage and implicitly of American faith—a trust in the ability of the rest of us to understand the obvious:

Jose is an American name.

FEBRUARY 4, 1999

IT WOULD SERVE US WELL TO BE MORE NIGGARDLY WITH OUTRAGE

English-major humor ...

One day back when I was in college, I approached a friend who was standing in a small group of people and asked him, "So, is it true you like to masticate in public?"

The world stops. The poor guy teeters there, mouth open, mortified. Then a grin unfolds itself slowly as he gets the joke. For those of you who don't, "masticate" means chew, but it sounds an awful lot like that other word which means to pleasure oneself sexually.

I laughed my fool head off at my pal's discomfort.

As you may know, something very similar happened in Washington recently, only nobody's laughing. It started with a guy named David Howard, who's white and a top aide to Mayor Anthony Williams. In a meeting with subordinates, Howard lamented how little money was available in the constituent services budget. "I will have to be niggardly with this fund," he said.

Oops.

Now you and I, because we're so erudite, understand that "niggardly" means penurious, parsimonious ... stingy. Howard's staff members, unfortunately, did not know this and were offended at what they thought he had said—even after he apologized and defined the word. The rumor soon circulated that Howard had used the infamous racial slur that sounds like niggardly but, in fact, has no connection to it.

Before long, Howard was besieged by phone calls from angry black constituents. Feeling compromised in his ability to do his job, he submitted a letter of resignation. Instead of round-filing the letter and requisitioning dictionaries for the offended staffers, the mayor let Howard go.

Now Williams is being criticized by everybody from editorial writers to gay leaders (Howard is gay) to the NAACP. And me, I'm just sitting here thinking of how I've always liked "niggardly." Maybe it's just more English major humor, but sometimes I enjoy using that word to describe white bigots. It amuses me to imagine them scratching their pointy heads and saying, "Whud that boy call me?"

I'll grant that Howard probably should have chosen another word—some terms that work perfectly well in written communication leave too much room for misunderstanding or offense when used in informal speech. But that's not quite the same as putting the onus for this mess on him. No, that weight is properly borne by the aides who blew a minor misunderstanding out of proportion, the members of the black community who jumped on Howard for no good reason, and the mayor who lacked either the gumption or the judgment to do the right thing.

If some people say this all represents political correctness at its most extreme, I can't argue. If some feel it illustrates how hypersensitive we've become on issues of racial insult, I have to agree with that, too.

But for my money, this misadventure speaks to another failing I find even more distressing—a recent tendency among black people to waste their credibility, to lavish it upon dubious causes. Consider the recent record. We spent our credibility on O.J. Simpson's innocence and Tawana Brawley's honesty, spent it chasing a white teacher out of her school because she read students a book celebrating nappy hair, spent it decrying a silly Internet rumor that black voting rights were about to be revoked. Now we've spent it to chastise David Howard for something he didn't say.

I'm sorry, but as causes go, this ain't exactly Selma in '65.

The bad thing is, there's no shortage of real concerns we should be expending that energy on—housing discrimination, banking-industry racism, educational inequities, institutionalized poverty, police malfeasance, hate crimes ... the list is endless. And instead, some of us are going after David Howard?

Ridiculous.

It saddens me to see black people do things like this. We only compromise our voice, only make the nation less likely to credit it when we do declaim on issues of substance. Only become that much more like the boy who cried wolf.

His example ought to give African-American people pause next time they're tempted to expend moral capital on a cause this foolish, this empty, this ... inutile.

And if that word is unfamiliar, gentle reader, please do what they should've done in Washington. Look it up.

FEBRUARY 13, 1999

FRED? BARNEY? YOGI? YOU JUST NEVER KNOW

This is an open letter to the Rev. Jerry Falwell.

Dear Rev. Falwell:

Just wanted to drop you a note of support in your recent campaign against *Teletubbies*, the children's TV program imported from Britain. I daresay most people would have looked at these characters—four little elves with televisions where their tummies should be—and found them rather harmless. It took you to warn us that one of them, Tinky Winky, is gay.

Thanks to the "Parent Alert" in the latest issue of your *National Liberty Journal*, we can now see what should have been obvious all along. Tinky Winky is purple—the gay pride color! He's got a triangle atop his head—the gay pride symbol!

What more proof do we need? Tinky Winky is obviously an agent of Satan, sent to lead our preschoolers into an unhealthy fascination with show tunes!

Rev. Falwell, you're going to take a lot of grief for your courageous stand. But you can take comfort in knowing that millions of right-thinking Americans are with you.

Because you know, the homosexual agenda—which they hammer out every year at a secret meeting above a beauty parlor in Duluth—doesn't stop with *Teletubbies*. Oh, heck no! To the contrary, gays have been slipping coded messages into children's entertainment for years.

Think of Kermit the Frog, for example. Forever running away from Miss Piggy, a beautiful female swine who adores him. But he always has time for Fozzie Bear, doesn't he?

How about Fred Flintstone and Barney Rubble? Their friendship seems awfully ... close, wouldn't you say? And remember the last line of their theme song: "We'll have a gay, old time!"

Don't even get me started on *Bananas in Pajamas*. Two bananas— hey, we know what bananas symbolize, don't we?—who walk around dressed for bed!

Let's be frank here, Rev. Falwell. We both know what people are going to say about you. That you've lost your mind. That you've been wearing your halo too tight. That you're an obsessed, self-righteous, paranoid homophobe who sees gay people popping out from behind every stone wall.

And some people will even argue that it's strange, Rev. Falwell, that a man who professes to know the path to glory has a worldview so filled with fear.

Don't pay them any attention. That's just reason and common sense. People will use that sometimes to confuse a guy like you. But zealotry is its own defense, and that should be more than enough to keep you on the path of the straight. And narrow.

That's good, because there are so many other dangers people need you to warn them about.

Like Yogi Bear and ... Boo-boo. Kind of a smutty name, don't you think? And what exactly did they mean when they said Yogi was "smarter" than the average bear? Maybe it was a hint that his desires don't stop with picnic baskets, hmmm?

What about Barney? Hey, he's purple.

Donald Duck? Never wore any pants.

Popeye? Always crying, "I yam what I yam."

And we can't forget Batman and Robin. How obvious can it be? Two single guys, living together, carrying on a double life. Worse, they tooled around in the Batmobile, a powerful machine they kept driving into the dark, mysterious recesses of the Batcave.

Granted, some people won't find gay subtext in any of this. And they'll wonder: What's it say about you, Rev. Falwell, that you're able to see the homosexual agenda where others see only a harmless diversion for preschoolers? What's it tell us about your character, common sense and grip on reality that you find it necessary to warn us about Tinky Winky?

I think you know how I'd answer that question.

If not, just know that I consider you an American of the kind we haven't seen in a long time. Not since the late Paleolithic Era, at least.

I want you to know, too, that I stand behind you. Way behind you. And upwind.

No need to thank me for this. Watching you do battle with a Teletubby is all the thanks I need.

NOVEMBER 13, 1999

GANGSTA RAP'S INSIDIOUS LIE: LIFE'S USELESS

On Tuesday night, right before they executed him for murdering police officer Kenny Wallace in 1994, Virginia officials asked Thomas Lee Royal Jr. if he had anything to say. He did. Royal, a 32-year-old black man, asked them: "... How you're going to kill a man when a man is willing to die?"

I came across that story as I was preparing to write this column commemorating the 20th anniversary of the hip-hop revolution. It struck me because it seemed to crystallize the ways in which rap music has proven poisonous to the spirit and aspirations of African-American men.

This is not, I realize, an entirely fair thing to say. In the first place, I haven't a clue whether Royal was a fan of rap. In the second, I must concede that, since a song called "Rapper's Delight" first brought it to national attention in November 1979, rap has concerned itself with a variety of subjects. It has been a music of Christian faith, defiant feminism, adolescent rebellion, black nationalism, party fun and cheating hearts.

My problem is that rap is also largely—perhaps even primarily—a music of thug values, also a laconic beat and hard rhymes celebrating that which deserves no celebration: drug dealing, dream stealing, woman pimping, man killing. I refer, of course, to so-called gangsta rap, a death-affirming music of scabrous explicitness and coarse joys, its icons young men in gaudy diamonds and gangster derbies who scowl at the camera as if it were a mortal enemy. Violence is an ever-present threat.

Nor is the violence simply implied or merely pretend. It has become common for rappers and their hangers-on to die by gunfire. Arenas are reluctant to book rap concerts because of security concerns and high insurance premiums. The CEO of one of the major gangsta rap labels is a hoodlum doing time for a parole violation.

It's worth noting that the biggest sin in the world of these men is to be "soft"—to be caught feeling something. So Thomas Royal's doomed bravado resonates. "How you're going to kill a man when a man is willing to die?" It could be a rap record refrain.

It's no coincidence that the gangsta genre was born in the '80s, just at the moment when everything was going to hell in urban America, the moment when something ugly crept into the heart of the city, when Mama became a crack addict and Daddy the invisible man, when nobody knew, nobody saw and nobody cared. When children began to plan their own funerals.

The point is not that gangsta rap caused this. But it did—and does—represent the attempt to romanticize it, to turn life in hell into a badge of awful honor. It did—and does—represent the triumph of a cynical, values-free vision exploited and mass-marketed so effectively that it becomes possible for a sheltered suburban kid who couldn't find the inner city with a road map to adopt its hopelessness as his own. It did—and does—reek to high heaven.

"How you're going to kill a man when a man is willing to die?"

And you wonder what he wished us to conclude from that statement. That the man who holds to life with both hands is weak, but the one who has nothing to lose is strong?

Better to recognize the statement for the lie it is: a man's desperate attempt to assert control over the barrenness of his own existence. It's an attempt that finds echo in the self-destructiveness of too many black males, in the wanton way they fling themselves from the high cliff of oblivion. Dead from gunshot, dead from drugs, dead from lethal injection, dead.

And you struggle to make them hear you over the beat of a song that romanticizes the death, that rewards it with that badge of awful honor. Struggle to make them know that when they leap from oblivion's cliff, they take us with them. Struggle to make them reject a limiting vision of who they are and what they might be.

We already know they're not afraid to die. We must challenge young black men to prove a more difficult thing.

That they're not afraid to live.

JANUARY 20, 2000

FLAG OF LIES STILL FLIES IN FACE OF TRUTH

Masochist that I am, I think I'll talk about the Confederate battle flag again.

Last time I did so, I argued that the state of South Carolina needs to remove that dirty symbol of slavery and racism from its spot above the capitol building. Which, naturally, produced howls of outrage, loads of racial invective and not a few lamentations for my ignorance of history. As one writer put it, "If you are intelligent, and I think you probably are, then you know the Civil War wasn't about slavery."

Ahem.

If you know me, then you know I can't let that one pass unchallenged. Especially since it is repeated ad nauseum by apologists for the old Confederacy.

The war wasn't about slavery, they say, because only a fraction of the Confederate soldiers owned slaves. It's a nonsequitur masquerading as logic. Put another way, I'd be willing to wager that the average American soldier had never even heard of Kuwait before George Bush ordered him or her to defend that desert kingdom. Because, you see, it's not the soldiers who determine whether or why a war is fought—it's the leaders. In the case of the Confederacy, the leaders could hardly have been more explicit.

In an early message to his Congress, Confederate President Jefferson Davis flatly cited the "labor of African slaves" as the reason for secession.

His vice president, Alexander Stephens, called slavery "the immediate cause ... of the present revolution." And he added this: "Our new government is founded upon ... the great truth that the Negro is not equal to the white man, that slavery, subordination to the superior race, is his natural and moral condition."

Not about slavery? Oh, please.

Yet, the attempt to separate the Civil War from its dominant cause proceeds apace, without the barest hint of shame. Defenders of the Confederacy huddle behind euphemisms—"state's rights," "economic issues"—but always, it devolves to the same thing, the bondage of African people. A century and a third later, much of the South still finds it impossible to face that truth squarely.

Instead, there's this taxing insistence that if Grandfather fought bravely and truly believed in his cause, then surely this must transfigure the cause, must leave his deeds somehow ... ennobled. But that's just another nonsequitur, another blind alley of logic. I mean, surely there were Nazi and Japanese soldiers who, during the Second World War, fought bravely and truly believed in their cause. But who among us would call their cause anything but reprehensible? Who among us finds honor in what they did?

Indeed, some years back, when Japan issued school books that distorted or ignored that nation's wartime aggression and atrocities, American observers promptly condemned it as an attempt to whitewash the past.

Small wonder. The Japanese can never be allowed to forget how awful that past was—else they might be tempted to relive it.

What would we say to the Germans if they chose to fly the swastika above their capitol? How would we reply if they told us they were simply honoring the heritage of forebears who fought for what they believed? Would we call it a "controversy," suggesting there were competing opinions of roughly equal validity? Would we, in the manner of certain rubber-spined presidential candidates, declare it a local issue of no concern to "outsiders?"

Or would we be alarmed? Would we say that here was a people too deluded to learn the hard lessons of history?

And if that's the case, then how can we say less about the South? How can we say less about the region where, five years ago, a governor proposed educational standards that would have required teachers to refer to slaves as "settlers?" Where in 1998, a school district rejected a black history poster because it included an image of a lynching? Where a banner symbolizing slavery and white supremacy flies above a house of the people?

Every day that sunrise finds it there, South Carolina shames itself, shames its ancestors, shames the nation, shames the very truth—and profanes the ideal of liberty and justice for all.

Yet there it hangs anyway, a cloth lie flapping in the Dixie breeze. Look away, look away.

JANUARY 22, 2000

WHY LOSE YOURSELF IN GROUP'S CAUSE?

Our question for today: How much of you belongs to you?

I'm moved to ask this by one of the students in my writing class. The assignment was to compose and read aloud an essay describing themselves and their lives. The piece this student wrote was about how confusing and painful it is to have people pigeonhole you just because you're black. It's difficult, wrote this 14-year-old, to have others always expect you to operate, be confined by, or bend your behavior to, their expectations.

What was intriguing is that the people the child was complaining about were not white, but black.

It seems my student gets a lot of grief for speaking standard English, singing the songs of a white pop group, and cultivating a rainbow coalition of friends. Some black folks in the kid's immediate circle have responded with the harshest epithet they can muster. They call the child ... "white."

If this were a movie, this is the spot where you'd hear scary music and a shriek of unadulterated horror.

If you're a member of a minority—racial, sexual, cultural, religious—there's a good chance you already understand what's going on here. If not, I can only refer you back to that opening question: How much of you belongs to you? You may think the answer is self-evident. Truth is, it's anything but.

The life of the American minority group is governed by a deceptively simple equation—oppression from without creates cohesion from within. People who find themselves besieged because of their sexual orientation, skin color, culture, or way of approaching God tend to draw together with similar others. They circle the wagons, raise the drawbridge, close the gates, and make of themselves a community—a people.

It can be a soul-saving thing, belonging to a people. You love them unreservedly for providing you an emotional home, for instilling in you a sense of worth, for giving voice to your aspirations. Most of all, you love them for standing up on your behalf when the world comes calling with reproach and accusation.

A soul-saving thing, yes. But you find, not infrequently, that you are expected to pay for this wonderful gift at the cost of bits and pieces of your own individuality. When you belong to a people, when you are born into this association that exists on a basis of mutual defense, of watching the world from a bunker and waiting for the next attack, it's easy to lose your very self to them. So easy to become the group.

Small wonder. The group enforces its cohesion strictly. Its members are discouraged from doing, saying or thinking that which does not reflect the consensus of the whole. Sometimes, one is discouraged from even associating with members of the "enemy" camp. And there's a heavy penalty for transgression: One is cast out, ostracized.

As in a colleague I once had who told me his people constantly criticized his work. Their complaint? He was "not Cuban enough."

It's a charge that finds its echo across the American demographic. Not lesbian enough. Not Jewish enough. Not black enough. The unstated irony is that all these peoples who plead for tolerance of difference sometimes have so little tolerance for the differences within their own ranks.

So sometimes, yes, a person wonders: How much of you belongs to you? Where's the point beyond which fealty to the group becomes a compromise of self?

I wish I'd had an easy answer for my student but of course, I did not. I did tell the kid this: What you are should never be the sole determinant of who you are. You have the right to your own taste in music, your own choice of friends, your own self. These are your prerogatives, no one else's. Otherwise, what's the point?

Someday, I hope my student will learn. That you have to honor what you belong to, yes. But you must also protect the things that belong to you.

JANUARY 29, 2000

HARD FACTS SHOW BIAS IS HARDLY 'THEORY'

So it seems this newspaper in Jacksonville ran an editorial that's got a lot of people steamed up. Funny thing is, most of those people work for the paper.

It goes like this: Earlier this month, the *Florida Times-Union* published a piece condemning affirmative action. This, in itself, was not the problem. Affirmative action is a difficult topic on which people of good will can certainly disagree.

What has *Times-Union* folks riled is not so much what was said as the way it was said, the way an editorial writer managed, in a few paragraphs of condescension and arrogance, to trivialize arguably the most profound tragedy in American history. Meaning slavery, which was dismissed in the editorial as something that "existed briefly in America but ended more than a century ago."

That's bad enough, but the *Times-Union* was just getting started. While conceding it's "unfortunate" that Africans once were slaves, the paper wants us to know the experience was not unique, since "virtually every American" can trace himself or herself to slavery. We are reminded that Jews were once subjugated in Egypt and that the Japanese once enslaved other Asians.

None of those people gets affirmative action based on ancestral suffering. So what is black folks' problem?

"The theory," says the *Times-Union* editorial, "is that some undefined thing 'lingers' today that results in prejudice and discrimination against African Americans ..."

In the wake of those words, a coalition of *Times-Union* journalists, the majority of them white—hello?—has lodged strenuous objection against the newspaper. And the local chapter of the National Association of Black Journalists has rejected a $1,000 donation the paper offered to help sponsor an upcoming conference.

Allow me to get my two cents in. The first thing I have to do is point out that the period of African subjugation lasted 246 years. That's "brief" in precisely the same sense that Shaquille O'Neal is "dainty." Especially considering that there followed another century of de facto slavery in which bondage was enforced not by iron shackles but by systemic ones—government condoning and enforcing the denial of jobs, voting rights, justice, education and sometimes, life. This ended in the late '60s. So black people have been free, in any meaningful sense, only for a little over 30 years.

And while it's certainly true that other Americans' ancestors were slaves, the crucial difference is that they were slaves somewhere else.

African Americans are the only Americans who have tried to make a life in the land of their enslavement among the heirs of those who enslaved them.

If you think that's easy, talk to the three or four Holocaust survivors who still live in Germany. They'll tell you otherwise.

But over and above misrepresentations of history and failures of logic, the thing that troubles me most is the simple fact that in 2000, the paper of record in a major American city is found mocking the existence of "some undefined thing" that harms African Americans. I find myself wondering if the people at this newspaper read newspapers.

Haven't they seen the stories documenting with hard numbers the racial discrimination that goes on right now, this very minute, in housing, employment, medical care, criminal justice and, ahem, journalism?

All that is "theory?" It's "some undefined thing?"

Silly soul that I am, I'd have thought the thing quite well defined. Would have figured that somewhere between the broomstick sodomy of Abner Louima and the dragging murder of James Byrd, between the Agriculture Department mistreating black farmers and Denny's harassing black diners, somewhere between all those news stories, statistics and tears, the thing had been quite effectively concretized.

How edifying to discover that it remains instead ... "undefined."

It occurs to me that the very ability to call it that, to airily dismiss reams of proof like some UFO hoax, speaks poignantly to the reason black folk sometimes feel frustrated enough to scream.

I won't subject you to that. I'll only say this: The "undefined thing" is real. And the good news for the editorialists at the *Times-Union* is that if they ever want to see what it looks like, they only need a mirror to do so.

MARCH 18, 2000

HE FAILS TO SEE MY 'DARK' SIDE WHEN I'M LIGHT

His name is Larry, and the other day, he read a column of mine that made him laugh. This seems to strike him as a minor miracle.

"Before reading your column," he writes, "it is standard procedure for me to ... brace myself in case the angry black man side of you is aroused...

"I am a white, middle-class, Southerner, baby boomer. Because most of the black man's problems appear to be blamed on me and my contemporaries or my ancestors, I tend to read many of your columns with a defensive posture."

Then came the column that made Larry laugh—a disbelieving tirade about $80 fashion jeans manufactured to look scruffy and old. After reading it, he found himself wondering if your humble correspondent might be, after all, just a "regular guy."

"I had fun with you today," writes Larry, "and enjoyed our camaraderie. I will miss you when you retreat to your facade of anger."

A thoughtful letter. Here's my reply.

Dear Larry:

Thank you for writing. You raise interesting points. I hope I can do them justice.

First off, I have to admit to being intrigued by one term you used. Are you sure "facade of anger"—with its connotation of artificiality—is what you meant to say? If so, I can assure you the anger you sense when I write about racial or cultural inequity is quite authentic.

I think what confuses the issue is that guys like you sometimes assume the anger of guys like me to be something it's not. Meaning hatred.

Larry, anger is just anger, just impatience with the unfairness of status quo. When a group of Americans, your countrymen and mine, must live lesser lives simply because of the amount of melanin in their skin, it seems to me that decent people—all decent people—should be angry.

For all that, though, the issue of anger isn't what makes me respond to your letter. No, what got me was the part suggesting that yours truly might be, at the end of the day, just a "regular guy."

Larry, I get letters like yours fairly often. They generally arrive following columns that focus not on race or other prickly social issues, but rather on small things—a disbelieving rumination on the price of fashion jeans, a meditation on life as a chocolate addict, a treatise on surviving teenagers. In other words, the everyday minutiae of life as an American, a parent, a "regular guy" trying to make it to Friday intact.

The letters are invariably suffused, as yours was, Larry, with wonder. Wow, they say, you and I could be twins. Same experiences, same needs and fears, same basic outlook on life. We are so much alike.

So how is it, they ask, that my judgment fails so completely when the subject is race?

Not one of these good men has ever made what seems to me the more obvious inference. That if we are indeed so fundamentally similar, so alike in all those other things, perhaps we are alike in this, too. Perhaps I only say the things and feel the things that they might say and feel if they wore my skin.

Has it ever occurred to you, Larry, that I might be you?

I don't want to activate your defense reflex, but, candidly, I don't think it has. You sound surprised that I could turn out to be a "regular guy." Me, I never thought I was anything but.

It's just that I'm a regular guy who has spent 42 years dealing with all the stuff regular guys deal with and then, in addition, with the other crap—it's an indelicate word, but the right one—that comes of being an American dreamer with a brown face.

What I'm trying to get you to see, Larry, is that all of it—the things you can relate to and that one you can't—is of a single piece. They are who I am. They are who you, but for accident of birth, might have been.

So it troubles me when you say you miss me on the days I'm angry. How can this be, when I've never gone away?

OCTOBER 26, 2000

GANGSTA RAP'S MASK A RIP-OFF

"We wear the mask that grins and lies."—Paul Laurence Dunbar

The great black vaudevillian Bert Williams is supposed to have been a very funny guy. "The funniest man I ever saw," W.C. Fields once said.

Offstage, Williams was reputed to be exceedingly intelligent and reserved to the point of snobbishness. He was a great reader, too, favoring the likes of Twain, Goethe, Kant and Voltaire.

Onstage was another matter. Every night before he went on, Williams put on his mask. That is, he applied to his face gleaming black cork and whitewall tire lips. Then he shuffled out there, a shiftless ne'er-do-well, slow of foot, slower of mouth and slowest of mind. He and his partner, George Walker, billed themselves as "Two Real Coons" by way of assuring white audiences that they were getting something they were not: authentic black comedy.

This was obligatory behavior for black performers a century ago.

I was reminded of Bert Williams' life as I watched Spike Lee's movie. *Bamboozled* is easily the most controversial release of the season; a satire about the rise and fall of *Mantan's New Millennium Minstrel Show*, a TV variety show built on the coarsest racial stereotypes you can imagine. Two shiftless clowns, grinning from blackface and red lips, perform in a watermelon patch. Featured players include Aunt Jemima, Sambo and assorted pickaninnies. Mantan is the brainchild of a disgruntled black television executive who only wants to get fired. Instead, he gets acclaimed. Mantan becomes a sensation.

It's not a great movie—the final act is a mess, and the characters are sometimes unrecognizable as human beings. And yet *Bamboozled* is, at times, strangely compelling.

One scene in particular. You watch the characters played by Tommy Davidson and Savion Glover burn the cork black, mix it with water, then apply that paste to their faces. Watch them draw lips with lipstick the color of fire trucks. Watch them disappear behind the mask. Then they take the stage for the first time, these human caricatures straight out of a segregationist's fever dream. There's a moment of stunned, airless silence. White members of the studio audience turn hesitantly to black ones, looking for a cue, wordlessly asking if they should find this funny.

And, softly at first, the black people laugh. That laugh stays with me. There's something in it both troubling and true.

Because the better part of a century later, the "coon" act has changed and yet remains disturbingly the same. Consider that some of us now sell a crude, violent, values-free music that's supposed to be as definitively black as Bert Williams' shuffling jive.

Consider, too, that we still wear masks: A few years ago, there was a church-going ballet student who, seeking success as a rapper, remade herself as a foul-mouthed, malt liquor-swilling homegirl called Boss. Then there's the guy who began his career wearing lipstick and rouge until that went out of fashion and he transformed himself into a crude street punk called Dr. Dre.

Some of us still wear the mask that grins and lies. Only now they do it not because they have to, but because that's where the money is. Because black kids—white ones, too—will pay good money for fake lessons in authentic blackness.

"Keepin' it real," they say. And it's hard not to hear a ghostly echo of Williams and Walker: "Two real coons."

I'm not mad at Bert Williams. Not mad at Mantan Moreland, Butterfly McQueen, Nick Stewart, Stepin Fetchit or any other black performer who had to shuffle his feet, bug his eyes, slur his words, or wear blackface because the white men who did the hiring would not accept them otherwise.

But I am mad at gangsta rap. And at those of us who passively accept the insult. Have we, African Americans, become so numb, dumb, despairing or disconnected that we've forgotten who we are? Forgotten how to give a damn?

Or have we just worn the mask so long we've forgotten the face that lies beneath? Forgotten everything except the rictus grin of the clown. And betrayed ancestors' sacrifice in the process.

Because there's only one difference between Bert Williams and Dr. Dre.

Bert Williams had no choice.

APRIL 21, 2001

CLOTHES ENCOUNTERS OF THE THUG KIND

The subject was gangsta chic—that distinctive style of urban fashion that says, I am here to rob and injure you. I was speaking at a forum in West Virginia a few days ago when it came up.

I said what I usually say: It's troubling to me that young men, particularly many young African-American men, would dress in a style that's universally perceived as the uniform of the career criminal.

Whereupon a black woman rose from the audience, eyes flashing danger signs, mouth full of rebuke. Her own sons, she said, dress like this and she thinks they look darn good. Why should they change? So white folks will like them? White folks are going to think what they want about young black men, regardless. Besides, you can't judge a book by its cover.

I'm here to tell you the same thing I told her: Sometimes, you can.

Indeed, as she spoke, I was reminded of something that happened to me maybe four years ago. I'm standing on a subway platform waiting for the train. A group of teenage boys is standing nearby and I'm watching them with a wary eye. You know the type. Loud and profane city kids dressed like street thugs. Hats to the back, shirts hanging open, pants sagging low so you can see their drawers. When the train pulls in, I wait to see which car they board. Then I board another.

You will have a hard time convincing me I did not do the right thing. Don't take that as an argument in favor of stereotyping. It's illogical to make sweeping judgments about a person based on some accident of birth or circumstance. None of us can choose the color of our skin, the nation of our origin, the orientation of our sexuality, the ability or disability of our limbs, the religion of our forebears. How stupid, then, is the person who attempts to draw conclusions about us by observing these things over which we had no control.

No, the argument I'm here to make has to do with the things we do control. One of which is dress.

I'm sorry, but if I see a woman tricked out as the rapper Lil' Kim was at the *MTV Video Awards*—breast exposed, nipple covered by a pasty—I feel justified in assuming she's not on her way to morning Mass. Similarly, the man with the Confederate flag T-shirt is probably not en route to an NAACP meeting. And the guy who walks around wearing white greasepaint on his face, a big red nose and floppy shoes ought to expect that once in awhile, people are going to throw cream pies at him.

The point being that all of us make judgments all the time based upon how people present themselves. This is only natural.

•

Certainly, we make special dispensation for the fact that young people always dress so as to annoy the old folks. This, too, is natural. From the flappers of the '20s to the poodle skirts of the '50s, from the tie-dyed hippies of the '60s to the polyester fashion victims of the disco years, kids have always outfitted themselves according to ever-shifting ideas of what constitutes cool.

But gangsta chic is about more than cool. The universal perception and frequent reality is that it's also about sending an implicit threat. It's no accident that the style rose just as rap went West, finding its inspiration—and performers—among black street gangs in South-Central Los Angeles. Indeed, observers say the whole sagging-pants style came out of jails where prisoners are denied belts as a matter of security.

What does it tell us about their mindset, their perception of self, that young African-American men from hellish neighborhoods would adopt that style as a badge of honor? And how grotesque is it that kids from the middle class adopt the same style as a statement of fashion?

I often hear such kids insist that dress is neutral and how dare you stereotype them based on what they wear. Fine. It's the argument you would expect them to make. But it's an abrogation of responsibility for adults to encourage them in that delusion. Better to explain to them that what you show to the world, how you allow yourself to be perceived, will have profound implications for the way people treat you. This is a fact of life that has little to do with stereotyping, racial or otherwise.

I mean, I perceived a threat by those boys on the subway platform and acted accordingly. Anyone who thinks that constitutes racial stereotyping needs to understand something.

They were white.

JULY 12, 2001

NO EXCUSES!
'BABY BOYS' SIMPLY NEED TO GROW UP

The first thing we see is a black man curled up in a womb. The first thing we hear is a voice-over explaining a psychologist's theory that black men are babies. That because of racism, the African-American man remains an unformed person—infantilized, immature and incapable of exploiting his own fullest potential.

Thus begins the new movie, *Baby Boy*. In it, we are introduced to Jody, a jobless, aimless 20-year-old from South Central L.A. Though he has fathered two children by two women, he flees commitment, whether that means marriage or just cohabitation. Instead, Jody lives with his mother, who's in her middle 30s. Apparently, he would be content to do that forever, except that Mom has begun keeping company with a hulking ex-con whose very presence makes plain that it's time for Jody to grow up and get out.

That he seems unable to do this, we are asked to believe, is ultimately because of the white man. Which brings me to the following conclusion:

Everybody should have a white man. Even white men should have a white man.

Because when you have a white man, nothing is ever your fault. You're never required to account for your own failings or take the reins of your own destiny. The boss says, "Why haven't you finished those reports, Bob?" and you say, "Because of the white man, sir."

I'm not here to sell you some naive nonsense that racism no longer exists. One has only to look around with open eyes to see that it continues to diminish the fiscal, physical and emotional health of African-American people. All of us are obligated to raise our voices in protest of this awful reality.

But black folks are also obligated to live the fullest lives possible in the face of that reality. To live without excuses.

Instead, director John Singleton begins with an excuse. He will demur that *Baby Boy* is a movie, not a message and that he intended nothing higher than a summer diversion. And he will be full of crap.

The theory he cites—and explores uncritically—is by Dr. Frances Cress Welsing, a black psychiatrist who has espoused black supremacy. According to one published account, she believes black men are inadvertently emasculated by their mothers, often single women, who coddle them in fear of what their fate will be in a hostile world.

Yet the world is full of white men, too, who refuse to grow up, white men for whom the avoidance of commitment is their prime directive. And surely there are also profound psychological reasons those men remain boys.

At some point, though, a problem ought to be defined less by our ability to explain why it happens than by our willingness to demand that it happen no more. Meaning, I don't care why some white men are infantile. They should grow up, regardless. And similarly, it only makes me impatient to be told that racism has supposedly left some black men in the same boat, as if that means they themselves bear no responsibility.

Frankly, I know too many hard-working black men to believe the "baby boy" phenomenon is as widespread as Singleton seems to suggest. To the degree it exists at all, there's something offensive about his attempt to pin it upon racial animus. There's never been a time that animus didn't exist and no such moment is on the near horizon.

Meantime, black women, children and communities are dying, spiritually and literally, for the lack of fully formed, grown-up black men. So I have limited tolerance for the idea of Jody as helpless victim. Racism doesn't excuse weakness—it demands strength.

And forgive me for being simplistic, but maybe if we were less eager to rationalize personal failure like Jody's, we would see less of it. Maybe if we required men to be men, more of them would.

It's telling that in the movie, Jody never encounters a white man. I might sympathize if I had seen him turned away from school or turned down for a job because of his skin color. Truth is, getting an education and doing honest work never seem to occur to him.

Maybe you think that means the white man is keeping him down. Me, I think it means he's has saved the white man the trouble.

FEBRUARY 7, 2002

DON'T BLAME RACISM; POWER IS REAL CULPRIT

"Look how white I am," he writes. "Am I lame or what?"

That's Rick Reilly's "Life of Reilly" column from the Sept. 4 edition of *Sports Illustrated*. Several readers have passed it along, inviting comment from your humble correspondent, who is happy to oblige.

For those who missed it, Reilly's piece delineates what he sees as a double standard that allows black athletes to insult white people with impunity. How, he wants to know, could Shaquille O'Neal get away with writing in his book how embarrassing it is to be dunked on by a white guy? Didn't John Rocker get pilloried for saying things like that?

And what about Mike Tyson grabbing his crotch at a recent disastrous press conference and making a vulgar and racist remark to a white reporter? Former Denver Nuggets coach Dan Issel just torpedoed his career by doing less. Why is there no firestorm of reproach and censure when the offender is black?

I think Reilly makes a valid point. I'd quibble with him over some of the examples he chooses, but in the main, the guy is right on target in challenging blacks in sports—and, by extension, blacks at large—to give the same respect they demand.

He should know that there is, however, more going on here than a simple double standard.

After all, when he notes the absence of any response to racially inflammatory remarks by black athletes, Reilly is in effect indicting not just black observers, but white ones as well. Indeed, white ones perhaps primarily. Where is their outrage?

Reilly believes their silence grows from a kind of racial inferiority complex, a sense that, where sports is concerned, denigration is deserved.

He may be on to something. But that surely doesn't tell the whole story. I mean, race and sport are not the only arenas where one party is allowed to say things the other is not.

Consider gender. And if you're a guy, you probably already know where I'm headed.

According to a generation of female comics, the fact of malehood means several things. That you worship beer, bosoms and the internal combustion engine. That you communicate emotion by grunts and shoulder punches. That you choose each day's wardrobe by determining which shirt stinks least. That your cooking qualifies as a crime against humanity. That your love-making is worse than your cooking. That you are proud without cause, clueless without apology—a channel-surfing, football-obsessed talking ape who would be helpless but for the civilizing influence of women. Who are, of course, superior.

A woman can say pretty much what she wishes about a man. The man who tries to do the same becomes Andrew Dice Clay.

I'm not here to suggest you feel sorry for that Neanderthal. No, my point is simply that most men don't spend a lot of time fretting about the disparity—nor should they, nor can they, without sounding whiny and small. The disparity is, after all, part and parcel of belonging to the gender that, for the most part, still controls the levers of power.

As much as we like to pretend equality has arrived, the truth is that access to those levers is still largely a matter of gender and race. It is, when all is said and done, power that's the true dividing line here. Most of us instinctively observe different rules, give broader latitude, depending upon whether one is part of the group that wields power or the group power is wielded upon. That's why the secretary who yells at her boss is considered audacious, but the boss who yells at the secretary is overbearing.

We make an automatic perceptual adjustment depending upon who's doing what to whom. So there's usually no outcry, even among whites, when some black public figure says some stupid thing. Reilly is right in suggesting that black athletes ought to be called to account when their rhetoric is racist. Such behavior braces up stereotypes injurious to blacks. It is also offensive.

But if he truly expects to see a day when the sins of a Shaq O'Neal call down the same fury as those of a John Rocker, he needs to understand that it's not coming.

You can have pity or power, but you can't have both.

FEBRUARY 9, 2002

WHICH CAME FIRST?
CHICKEN OR EGG ON HIS FACE

To the manager of the Giant Food supermarket in Union Deposit, Pa.:

So, I see where you hacked off some of your customers with a recent promotion. You put fried chicken on sale "in honor of Black History Month." Which begs the question:

What, no watermelon?

Seriously, I'm trying to imagine the thought process that went into this. Wasn't there a point at which klaxons began honking in your brain and a voice like the robot's from *Lost in Space* started chanting "Danger, Will Robinson! Danger!" Apparently not. From what I hear, even after a customer complained, you couldn't understand why it bothered him.

So now your corporate office has been obliged to issue an apology. That will surely do wonders for your career. Plus, the head of the local NAACP is weighing in.

I'm going to make an assumption here. I'm going to go out on a limb and speculate that you didn't wake up that morning thinking to yourself, "What can I do today to insult black people?" And assuming that assumption is correct, what's it say to you that you somehow managed to do so anyway?

I'll tell you what it says to me: That our level of intercultural dialogue in this country is abysmal. That all we different kinds of Americans live at an intolerable remove, one from the other. That a significant portion of the insult and hurt feelings that pass between races, genders, sexual orientations, religions, probably grows not out of intent, but ignorance.

Not that I find that comforting. The person who slurs me because he doesn't know any better is, in some ways, more vexing than the one who does so out of pure hate. I mean, at least I can write off the latter as a defective human being. The former I must find a way to deal with.

And that, take my word for it, is not easy.

The problem is that we live cookie-cutter lives, go through our days hemmed in by comfort zones, cloistered by our perspectives, surrounded by people who look and sound just like us. We don't know the exotic-looking people who live just across the street, just down the block, just around the corner. All we know is that they are, in some highly visible way, Not Like Us.

Maybe we're curious about them, maybe we're dying to know why they wear what they wear or speak as they speak or believe what they believe, but for some reason, we never ask. We have, almost literally speaking, no way to ask. So instead, we assume.

And you know what happens when folks assume.

I'd like to recommend a website to you: www.yforum.com. A journalist friend of mine set it up a few years ago. It's designed for people to post questions, ask that nagging thing they've never understood about blacks or whites or gays or Jews, and have people from those communities respond.

My friend, Phillip Milano, tells me he's "continually amazed" by the things people don't know about one another. "The level to which people are still disconnected is sometimes shocking."

Speaking of which, let me do my part to close that disconnect. Let me explain about fried chicken. It's not that black folks don't love it as much as anybody. But for longer than you or I have been alive, the eye-rolling, slow-talking, chicken bone-sucking black has been a staple figure of white racist propaganda, immortalized in movies, music and song. So African Americans are, understandably, I think, sensitive about anything suggesting a greater-than-average love for the bird.

Silly, isn't it, when you think about it? Here's something sillier.

As a child on a school field trip, I once refused to eat my boxed lunch—chicken—because there were white kids around. A lonely little stand against stereotype that would have been a lot easier, let me tell you, had white racist propaganda accused us of an unnatural desire for some other food. Like liver, maybe.

But I digress. My point is that you have to know that you don't know before you can learn. So find some way to invite into your comfort zone somebody who's not like you.

You may save yourself some grief.

In the meantime, just in case you weren't aware: a sale on bacon in honor of Yom Kippur?

Bad idea.

AUGUST 9, 2002

COLOR DOES MATTER, BUT IT'S NOT ALL

"I have a dream that my four children will one day live in a nation where they will not be judged by the color of their skin but by the content of their character."—Martin Luther King Jr., 1963

"The truth is that so-called colorblindness is neither possible nor even desirable."—Me, 2002

Recently, some nice people asked me, in effect, to reconcile what I said in a column a few weeks ago with what Martin Luther King Jr. said 39 years ago on the steps of the Lincoln Memorial. This is for them.

Let me begin by telling you about myself.

I am a linear descendant of Mississippi slaves. My ancestry—and I suppose this is true of all ancestries—is a fundamental part of who I am, a wellspring of challenge and pride, my spiritual and emotional home. I am black.

That's not, however, all that I am. I'm also a man. I am a native of Southern California. I am a husband and a father. I am a comic-book geek. I am a Christian. I am in my 40s. I am a hope-to-die Lakers fan. I am, in other words, many things, each relevant to different circumstances and occasions. The same is true of anyone.

Of course, not one of the many things I am puts people on edge quite like blackness. Which is why some well-meaning people think it would be best if we could somehow factor race—race alone, of all the things I am—out of the picture. Their mantra: Let us be colorblind. If all they meant by that was "equality," I'd have no disagreement with them.

But for them, the term seems to mean something considerably more radical. For them, colorblind means making oneself literally blind to color.

I didn't notice that you were black, they will say. Or, I don't see you as black. Journalists writing about the popularity of Michael Jordan or Oprah Winfrey frequently note how they have "transcended" race.

Here's what bothers me: No one has ever felt the need to not notice I'm from California. No one has ever made a point of not seeing me as Christian. And I have yet to encounter a journalist who felt compelled to note how Jordan "transcended" his sex or Oprah her Mississippi roots.

Given that each of us is a combination of many characteristics, why is it necessary to make such an ostentatious show of not seeing one: race? The unavoidable answer is race isn't perceived like other characteristics.

Rather, it's one that makes some people nervous. For them, it's That Which Must Be Overcome. Where I see ancestry, challenge and pride, they see something onerous and burdensome. Where I see one of the things that makes me whole, they see something that polite people should ignore and I should work to transcend.

I can appreciate the frustration of white Americans whose only desire where race is concerned is to know what's OK, what's allowed, what behavior will allow them to finally consider themselves enlightened. Frankly, black folks don't always make that easy. Some of us are never too far from outrage. Some of us could find a racial conspiracy in a phone booth.

So maybe if you're white, just ignoring blackness altogether comes to seem like a good idea. But that's naive and faintly insulting. How do you foster equality by making an essential piece of who I am vanish?

Decent people should seek balance instead—to make race neither smaller than it is nor larger. Because race is neither a defining facet, nor a demeaning facet, of individual identity. It's a facet, period. Unfortunately, much of what passes for racial dialogue in this country is the chatter of two extremes: the Afrocentric-to-the-point-of-paranoia one that says race matters always, and the "colorblind" one that says it matters never.

That's a false dichotomy. Race matters when it matters, and it doesn't when it doesn't.

So there's no need to reconcile what I said about color with what King said, because there is no dissonance. He didn't say avoid color, ignore color, pretend it doesn't exist. The key to what he said lies in four words:

"Not be judged by."

NOVEMBER 15, 2002

'8 MILE' EXPOSES HOW RACE DIVIDES

Jimmy is just a poor white boy trying to make it in a black man's world.

To which the black men, some of them anyway, react with unbridled hostility. As depicted in the compelling new movie *8 Mile*, they brand him with names one can't repeat in a daily newspaper.

But for all that, perhaps the harshest thing they say about him isn't a curse word at all. They call him Elvis.

Black folks have always had this thing about Elvis.

On the one hand, we loved him—the fact that *Billboard* magazine counts him one of the most successful black music artists of the '50s seems ample evidence of that. But in some ways we hated him, too. Every time they called him the king of rock 'n' roll, it felt like a bone wedged sideways in the throat.

Because we knew that rock 'n' roll was simply the name white folks gave our music when it crossed to their side of the tracks. And that even though the sound was ours, a shantytown plaint born of our rhythm and nursed on our blues, they would never acknowledge any black man—not Fats Domino, not Little Richard, not the mighty Chuck Berry himself—as its king.

So when some of the black guys tag a white rapper with that name, it's not a compliment, but an accusation. They are charging him with trespass, calling him a cultural imperialist out to colonize, exploit, and ultimately, take what they have made. They are telling him that rap will have no white king.

8 Mile, for those who don't know, stars the famously vile Eminem as the rapper wannabe, Jimmy "Rabbit" Smith.

No Eminem fan am I, so it surprised my wife and kids when I went to see his movie the other day. A bigger shock: I liked it a lot.

Not just because of the profane poetry of its script or the fact that it manages to encapsulate its place, time, generation and culture as vividly as *Saturday Night Fever* did 25 years ago. No, what intrigued me most was the movie's take on the politics of race and culture.

Rabbit lives with his alcoholic mother and her good-for-nothing boyfriend in one of those trailer parks where hope goes to die. He pilots a rusted old sedan through grimy streets on the edge of nowhere. Watching him is a visceral reminder of how often we use race as proxy for ain't got and can't get. We say black when we mean crime, black when we mean squalor, black when we mean poor.

But Rabbit is poor as dirt and white as snow. *8 Mile* forces us to either say what we mean or discard our outmoded paradigms altogether.

In the movie—as in life, for that matter—the rappers meet for weekly "battles," freestyle competitions where success hinges upon your ability to conjure rhyming, rhythmic insults off the top of your head. And some of the black rappers don't want the white rapper joining those battles because he is, after all, a white rapper.

You begin to wonder what that means, come to marvel at its power to define and divide, when you realize that all of them come from the same place and all want the same thing: to wake up one morning in lives they do not hate.

The movie suggests that if we were wiser, race would not be the difference that trumps those similarities. If we were wiser, we would understand that poor people, of whatever color, have shared grievance and common cause.

It's not a new thought. Martin Luther King was exploring it when he died. But it is a thought with power to rattle the creaky battlements of race, the tired old fortresses of us and them, privilege and want, acrimony and recrimination. A thought to make us wonder if there are not, or ought not occasionally be, concerns that surmount ethnicity and tribe.

Rabbit, not unlike a photonegative Jackie Robinson, simply longs to belong to something he loves. To be judged for who he is, and not what.

Ultimately, it's any individual's right to demand that. But watching a white man forced to demand it of black men is a reminder that the world has changed some in the last half-century.

Maybe Elvis really has left the building.

JANUARY 10, 2003

OPEN CASKET OPENED EYES

If you ever saw that picture of Emmett Till, you never forgot it.

Not the one that shows a handsome brown teenager, hat tipped up slightly off his forehead. Not, in other words, the "before" picture.

No, I'm talking about the picture that was taken after. After he went from Chicago to visit family in Mississippi in the late summer of 1955. After he accepted a schoolboy dare to flirt with a white woman working behind the counter of the general store. After he called her "baby" and allegedly gave a wolf whistle. After her husband and his half-brother came for him in the dead of night. After his body was fished from the Tallahatchie River.

The picture of him that was taken then, published in *Jet* magazine and flashed around the world, was stomach-turning. A lively and prankish boy had become a bloated grotesquerie—an ear missing, an eye gouged out, a bullet hole in his head. You looked at that picture and you felt that here was the reason coffins have lids.

But his mother refused onlookers that mercy, refused to give him a closed-casket funeral. She delayed the burial for four days, keeping her son's mutilated body on display as thousands came to pay their respects. "I wanted the world to see what I had seen," she later explained. "I wanted the world to see what had happened in Mississippi. I wanted the world to see what had happened in America."

The world saw and was electrified.

Mamie Till Mobley died in Chicago on Monday of an apparent heart attack. And if one were seeking to sum up her life, it might be enough to say that she spent 47 years keeping the casket open, speaking, writing and agitating in the name of her murdered son. Indeed, her book, *The Death of Innocence*, is due for release this year.

I met her once, maybe 30 years after her son's death, by which point she must have told his story a million times. And she still welled up as she spoke, her voice stammering and turning gray.

At the time, I was writing and producing a radio documentary tracing over 500 years of African and African-American history. I'll never forget my narrator's response when he reviewed a script that recounted Emmett's ordeal and the ordeals of other black men and women who were hanged, burned or hacked to pieces for the crime of being. He jokingly dubbed me "the Stephen King of black history" for my insistence on including the grisly details.

But I happen to believe Mamie Till Mobley was right to keep the casket open.

We're always so eager to hide the horror. Close the casket, turn your eyes, use euphemism to obscure truths too obscene.

Consider Trent Lott's first attempt at apology, when he blithely described segregation as "the discarded policies of the past." If you didn't know any better, you might have thought he was talking about farm subsidies or tax codes, so bloodless and opaque was the language.

But segregation wasn't opaque and it surely wasn't bloodless. It was a Mississippi courtroom where the sheriff sauntered in every day and greeted spectators in the colored section with a cheery, "Hello, niggers." It was two white men freely admitting that they had kidnapped a black Chicago boy. It was witnesses who placed the men at a barn inside which they heard a child being tortured.

And it was a jury of white men who heard this evidence, then deliberated for less than an hour before returning an acquittal. As one of them told a reporter, "If we hadn't stopped to drink pop, it wouldn't have took that long."

This is the fetid truth behind the flowery words, the stinking fact much of the nation would prefer not to know.

But by her very presence, a murdered boy's mother demanded that we be better than that, demanded that we be, at least and at last, brave enough to face the horrors we have made and that have, in turn, made us.

Mamie Till Mobley was 81 years old at the time of her death. Her only child was 14 at the time of his.

JUNE 16, 2003

EVANGELICALS COME LATE TO AIDS FIGHT

The story goes that one of the Pharisees decided to test Jesus with this question: Which commandment is the greatest?

Jesus replied: "'Love the Lord your God with all your heart and with all your soul and with all your mind.' This is the first and greatest commandment. And the second is like it: 'Love your neighbor as yourself.'"

I know what you're thinking and, no, you haven't wandered into a Sunday school lesson by mistake. Not even close. What you've wandered into is a knotty moral thicket at the intersection of money, faith and AIDS.

By way of illustration, let me tell you about Mr. Stearns, who went to Washington, D.C. last week. Actually, Richard Stearns, president of the Washington State-based Christian relief group World Vision, wasn't alone. Dozens of evangelical Christian leaders traveled to Capitol Hill to lobby Congress on President Bush's plan to allocate $15 billion to the fight against AIDS in Africa and the Caribbean.

Contrary to what you might expect, they're for it. No, that's not a typo. These conservative religious leaders really do want Congress to fully fund a program designed to fight a disease once known as the gay cancer.

Assuming you haven't fainted into your corn flakes, let us continue.

Because that's not the reason I'm telling you this. No, what gets me is something Stearns said. As reported in the *Washington Post*, these evangelical leaders acknowledge that they've come late to the fight against HIV/AIDS—an understatement, given that AIDS has been killing for nearly 25 years now.

Stearns explained the tardiness by saying that in the 1980s, evangelicals saw AIDS as an affliction of drug users and gays and "had less compassion for the victims." Deal with that one for a minute. Because they thought less of the sufferers, they cared less about the suffering.

Contrast that with Jesus' saying that loving your neighbor is Christianity's second greatest commandment and tell me you don't see a disconnect wider and deeper than canyons.

Unfortunately, we've seen that disconnect before. I'm thinking of the Christian Coalition's 1996 apology for generations of white evangelical support for segregation and opposition to civil rights.

Then as now, it was good to see conservative Christians move to where they should have been all along. Then, as now, their support was more than welcome.

But then, as now, you wondered: What took you so long? Why did you not understand what everybody else figured out long ago? Why are you the last to pitch in when, by rights, you should have been the first?

Christ, after all, had compassion for tax collectors, adulterers, prostitutes, lepers and others who were not welcome in most homes.

He famously walked with the disregarded, the dispossessed and the despised. But these days, many would-be Christians walk by them instead.

"Love the sinner, hate the sin," they chirp.

Even if you buy that dubious formulation, it's hard to see evidence of love in their decision to ignore a deadly pandemic.

Indeed, some evangelical Christians even employ God to justify their callousness, arguing that AIDS is a divine curse upon gay people. Somehow, they never get around to explaining how the "curse" managed to strike people like 13-year-old Ryan White, whose only sin was to be a hemophiliac in need of a blood transfusion.

Was God's aim that bad?

Or, as seems far more likely, is the problem simply that some of His people are distressingly small of spirit, disturbingly slow to respond to pain, disappointingly selective in their obedience to the second greatest commandment?

Makes you wonder what they'll do the next time some outcast is suffering and in need.

Maybe I'm being uncharitable. It is, after all, a good thing that the evangelical community has joined the fight against HIV/AIDS. Better late than never, as they say.

But late, nevertheless.

JUNE 27, 2003

AFFIRMATIVE ACTION NEEDS A DEADLINE

Race matters.

Boil it down, and that's what Monday's milestone Supreme Court rulings in the University of Michigan case reduce to, an acknowledgment of the obvious.

Not that the rulings were one-sided. As you surely know by now, justices struck down a formula that awarded a certain number of points toward undergraduate admission to applicants based upon race.

But at the same time, and to the relief of affirmative action advocates, the court affirmed that race can be taken into account in college admissions. There is, a majority of justices reasoned, a social benefit to be derived in fostering diversity in higher education, a benefit important enough to justify overriding the equal protection clause of the Constitution.

Predictably, Clarence Thomas was among the justices who disagreed. In a dissenting opinion, Thomas, an ardent opponent of affirmative action and the only African American on the court, repeated the oft-stated argument that racial preferences taint the achievements of racial minorities.

"When blacks take positions in the highest places of government, industry or academia," he wrote, "it is an open question today whether their skin color played a part in their advancement."

It's a myopic argument. The reasoning proceeds, after all, from the implicit assumption that skin color has played no role in the advancement of white males, that their predominance in "government, industry and academia" stems solely from their hard work, talent and skill. One has to be naive, if not downright ignorant, to believe that, to think that laws and customs designed to exclude blacks, Hispanics and women from the field of competition did not also play some small part in that success.

White males have benefited from a de facto affirmative action for the entire 227 years of the American experiment. And for many of us, the issue of whether their race or gender played a part in their advancement is not an "open question," but a settled certainty.

It is important to remember that, for all the talk of affirmative action as a tool of diversity, its original mission was to redress years of systemic racism and sexism, enabling blacks, Hispanics and women to enter arenas that had historically been closed to them.

Had we been wiser at the point of conception, this might not be such a contentious issue now. Affirmative action would have, should have, come with a built-in expiration date—say a generation or two, during which we would have worked to change the circumstances that made it necessary in the first place.

Unfortunately, we remain a society riven by "isms," racial and sexual. We are also a society in which some people use isms as an all-purpose excuse for failure. Not just failure to succeed, but also failure to try.

Take, for example, the low collective test scores of black students. You can argue that this academic incompetence is the byproduct of the negative, anti-intellectual self-image those kids are fed from birth and I wouldn't disagree.

But at the same time, we probably shouldn't be surprised to discover that the people who, statistically speaking, watch the most television, do the worst in school.

You don't need the Supreme Court to fix that. But you do need to take ownership of the problem. Preferably sooner, rather than later.

Because this will not, cannot, ought not, go on forever. Indeed, in writing in support of affirmative action, Justice Sandra Day O'Connor speculated upon a day, 25 years from now, when it might necessarily end.

That ought not be seen as an obstacle, but a challenge, a spur to finally confront all the hindrances to minority achievement. Affirmative action is not an end unto itself, only an imperfect means. Its goal should be its own obsolescence.

Meaning not a nation where affirmative action no longer exists, but one where it no longer needs to.

AUGUST 4, 2003

GAYS MAY BE HOPE FOR MARRIAGE

So what is it you have against gay marriage?

I'm not talking to the guy next to you. He doesn't have a problem with it. No, I'm talking to you, who is fervently opposed.

The number of folks who agree with you is up sharply since June, when the U.S. Supreme Court struck down anti-sodomy laws in Texas. As recently as May, 49 percent of us supported some form of gay marriage, according to The Gallup Organization. The figure has since dropped to just 40 percent. That's a precipitous decline.

So what's the problem? What is it that bothers you about gay people getting married?

Don't read me that part in Leviticus where homosexuality is condemned. I mean, that same book of the Gospel mandates the death penalty for sassy kids and fortune tellers, by which standard the Osbourne children and Miss Cleo should have been iced a long time ago.

I read The Book. I believe The Book. But I also know that it's impossible to take literally every passage in The Book, unless you want to wind up in prison or a mental ward.

So don't hide behind the Bible. Let's just be honest here, you and me. Why do you oppose gay marriage, really?

It just feels wrong to you, doesn't it? At some visceral level, it just seems to offend something fundamental.

Hey, I understand. It's one of the emotional sticking points for us heterosexual types, this primeval "ick" factor where homosexuality is concerned. I won't try to talk you out of it.

I will, though, point out that once upon a time, the same gut-level sense of wrong—and for that matter, the same Bible—was used to keep Jews from swimming in the community pool, women from voting and black people from riding at the front of the bus. All those things once felt as profoundly offensive to some people as gay marriage does to you right now.

The issue has been vaulted to the forefront in the last few days. Political conservatives have been galvanized by it. President Bush says he wants to "codify" marriage as a heterosexual union. And the Vatican has told Catholic legislators that they must oppose laws giving legal standing to gay unions, unions the church describes as "gravely immoral."

Which is funny, given the level of sexual morality the church has demonstrated lately.

Anyway, the reasoning seems to be that gay people will damage or cheapen the sanctity of marriage and that this can't be allowed because marriage is the foundation of our society.

I agree that marriage—and I mean legal, not common law—is an institution of vital importance. It stabilizes communities, socializes children, helps create wealth. It is, indeed, our civilization's bedrock.

But you know something? That bedrock has been crumbling for years, without homosexual help. We don't attach so much importance to marriage anymore, do we?

These days, we marry less, we marry later, we divorce more. And cohabitation, whether as a prelude to, or a substitute for, marriage, has gone from novelty to norm.

We say we shack up because we don't need a piece of paper to tell us we are in love. I've always suspected it was actually because we fear the loss of freedom. Or because we're scared to bet forever.

I'm not trying to beat up cohabitors. A long time ago, I was one.

But it strikes me as intriguing, instructive and poignant that gay couples so determinedly seek what so many of us scorn, are so ready to take the risk many of us refuse, find such value in an institution we have essentially declared valueless. There's something oddly inspiring in their struggle to achieve the social sanction whose importance many of us long ago dismissed.

So tell me again why it is you don't want them to have that.

I mean, yeah, some people say they are a threat to the sanctity of marriage. But I'm thinking they might just be its salvation.

OCTOBER 20, 2003

TO IRATE READERS: RACE HAS ALWAYS BENEFITED WHITES

I guess I touched a nerve.

That much seems apparent from the dozens of responses to my recent column about a hospital in Abington, Pa., where a white man asked that no black doctors or nurses be allowed to assist in the delivery of his child. The hospital agreed, a decision I lambasted.

Which has produced the aforementioned dozens of critical e-mails. The tone varies from spittle-spewing bigotry to sweet reason, but they all make the same point: that affirmative action entitles white people to question black people's competence.

As a reader who chose to remain nameless put it, many people wonder if a given black professional "is there because of his/her skills and abilities, or because of affirmative action. Unfortunately, affirmative action policies leave many unanswered questions about a black person's education and training, as well as skills and abilities. ... How do we answer these questions?"

I will try my best to answer them with a straight face. It's going to be difficult.

Because there's an elephant in this room, isn't there? It's huge and noisy and rather smelly, yet none of these good people sees it. The elephant is this simple fact:

White men are the biggest beneficiaries of affirmative action this country has ever seen.

That's not rhetoric or metaphor. It's only truth.

If affirmative action is defined as giving someone an extra boost based on race, it's hard to see how anyone can argue the point. Slots for academic admission, for employment and promotion, for bank loans and for public office have routinely been set aside for white men. This has always been the nation's custom. Until the 1960s, it was also the nation's law.

So if we want to talk about achievements being tainted by racial preference, it seems only logical to start there. After all, every worthwhile thing African Americans achieved prior to the mid-'60s—Berry Gordy's record label, John Johnson's publishing company, Alain Leroy Locke's Rhodes scholarship, Madame C.J. Walker's hair care empire, Dr. Daniel Hale Williams' pioneering heart surgery—was done, not just without racial preference, but against a backdrop of open racial hostility.

By contrast, nothing white men have ever achieved in this country was done without racial and gender preferences. Affirmative action.

I know that will be hard for some folks to hear. I know it will leave some white brothers indignant. And I expect many recitations of "up by my bootstraps" and "know what it's like to be poor." We all want to feel that we made it on our own merits, and it's not my intention to diminish the combination of pluck, luck, hard work and ability that typically distinguishes success, whether white, black or magenta.

On the other hand, there's a word for those who believe race is not a significant factor in white success: delusional.

It is not coincidence, happenstance or evidence of their intellectual, physical or moral superiority that white guys dominate virtually every field of endeavor worth dominating. It is, rather, a sign that the proverbial playing field is not level and never has been.

My correspondents feel they should not be asked to respect the skill or abilities of a black professional who may or may not have benefited from affirmative action. They think such a person should expect to be looked down upon. But black people have spent generations watching white men who were no more talented, and many times downright incompetent, vault to the head of the line based on racial preference.

So, here's my question:

Would African Americans be justified in looking down on white professionals? In wondering whether they are really smart enough to do the job? In questioning their competence before they had done a thing?

Yeah, you're right. That would take one hell of a nerve.

OCTOBER 27, 2003

'HARD-CORE RAP' IS CASHING IN ON STEREOTYPES

I guess I'm obligated to be offended by this new board game. After all, Al Sharpton says I should.

And not just Rev. Al, either. Many other people—including NAACP President Kweisi Mfume and radio host Tom Joyner—have pronounced themselves offended by the game.

Not that I blame them.

It's called "Ghettopoly," a take-off on Parker Bros. venerable "Monopoly." Except that this game isn't about moving a car or a top hat around the board, buying properties and landing on Boardwalk after somebody has put up a hotel.

In "Ghettopoly," your token might be a crack rock, a 40-ounce bottle of malt liquor or a basketball, and your goal is to build crack houses while pimping "hos" and getting carjacked. The game reportedly features an image of Martin Luther King scratching the front of his pants and proclaiming, "I have an itch."

So, no, you won't find "Ghettopoly" under my Christmas tree. Nor does it break my heart that retailers have been pressured into removing it from their shelves or that Hasbro, which owns Parker Bros., last week filed suit against the game's creator, David Chang of St. Marys, Pa.

For all that, though, I am not angry at Chang, who seems more misguided than malicious.

To the contrary, it's the campaign against him that gets my dander up—not because it's wrong, but because it's about 15 years late. I keep wondering where all this fury was when rappers like 50 Cent, Nelly, Ja Rule and Snoop Dogg first started pimping, drug-dealing and drive-by shooting all over the video channels.

Where were the boycotters when these people and others were creating the template that Chang drew from? Where was the moral indignation when African-American people were reducing African-American life to caricature?

Or is it just easier to raise rage against Chang because he is not black?

With a few isolated exceptions—activist C. Delores Tucker, the Rev. Calvin Butts—African Americans have been conspicuously silent as black music, once the joy and strength of black people, has detoured into an open sewer of so-called "hard-core rap."

The vast majority of that genre's practitioners are nothing more and nothing less than modern-day Uncle Toms, selling out African-American dreams by peddling a cartoon of African-American life unencumbered by values. It is a cynical, knowing act, promulgated by young men and women who get rich by selling lies of authenticity to young people, white and black, who are looking for lessons in blackness. They are as much minstrels and peddlers of stereotype as Stepin Fetchit, Bert Williams or any black performer who ever smeared black goop on his face or shuffled onstage beneath a battered top hat.

The only difference—the only one—is that Bert Williams and Stepin Fetchit had no other choice.

My personal theory is that black people of my generation—I'm 46—have resisted speaking forcefully against this because, like all baby boomers, we are deathly afraid of appearing less than hip. But as I recall, our parents never worried about that. They understood their role to be not hipness, but guidance.

I am of a generation that has largely failed that role, that turned "judgment" into a four-letter word. The fruit of that failure lies before us: an era of ahistorical young people who traffic in stereotypes that would not be out of place in a Ku Klux Klan meeting.

And I'm supposed to be angry at David Chang? I'm not. He's just a good capitalist, just regurgitating what he has been taught in hopes of turning a buck. My anger is not for the student, but for his teachers. And not just my anger, but my sorrow, too.

I'm not losing sleep worrying about what David Chang thinks of black people. I'm more concerned with what black people think of themselves.

DECEMBER 8, 2003

CINCINNATI CASE NOT A TOUGH CALL: MAN KILLED SELF

The coroner says he only called it homicide because he had no choice.

Under Ohio law, he explained, his only other options were to categorize the death as accidental, natural or suicide. None of those, he felt, adequately accounted for how Nathaniel Jones died—i.e., after being beaten with nightsticks wielded by Cincinnati police officers.

The officers say they were only seeking to subdue the 41-year-old black man after he began acting strangely—dancing and barking out numbers—and then became combative during an encounter outside a fast-food restaurant.

Video of the Nov. 30 beating, captured by a camera in a police cruiser, has been played on television nonstop, heightening racial tension in a city where tension doesn't need the help—a city which, two years ago, endured days of street violence after police shot and killed an unarmed black man. Last week's ruling by coroner Carl Parrott appears to have only splashed gasoline on this latest fire.

This, even though the doctor took pains to stress that the term "homicide" was not meant to suggest "hostile or malign intent." Jones, he pointed out, bore only superficial bruises on his lower body from the beating. Far more important in determining a cause of death were the facts that he weighed 350 pounds, had heart disease and high blood pressure, and was on cocaine and PCP. The coroner ruled that Jones died, in essence, because his heart couldn't take the exertion.

Those caveats aside, Cincinnati police are infuriated by the word "homicide."

Local activists, on the other hand, say it bolsters their contention that Jones was just the latest black man brutalized by police.

I understand their anger. My problem is that I also understand PCP, having lived in Los Angeles during the years that city became the epicenter of its illicit production and use.

PCP is phencyclidine hydrochloride, an animal tranquilizer we knew as angel dust. We also knew that people who were "dusted" might dance naked in the middle of busy intersections or hurl themselves from skyscrapers believing they could fly. PCP users sometimes seemed to possess a freakish strength, an impression created by the fact that the drug leaves some people in a violent, agitated state while simultaneously desensitizing them to pain.

That would be a dangerous combination in a man who only weighed 120 pounds. Consider it in a man Jones' size and it offers a certain context for the images captured on that video. Might even induce a fair observer to give police the benefit of the doubt.

Of course, where police and black people are concerned, many would say there can be no benefit because there is no doubt: the police are racist, the police are unjust, the police do not value black life as highly as white. End of story.

Except that it's not. For all the many valid reasons black people have to distrust the police, it's a mistake to automatically presume malfeasance on the part of every officer in every encounter. To do that is to put the good cop on the defensive and give the bad cop no incentive to change. Worse, it undercuts African-American moral authority, undermines the argument it purports to advance, makes anger seem not righteous, but reflexive.

The facts as they stand simply do not justify adding this case to the dishonor roll of police misconduct. Jones did not have his head broken like Rodney King. He was not sodomized with a stick like Abner Louima. He was not executed in a doorway like Amadou Diallo. He was, in the final analysis, a morbidly obese man with a diseased heart and high blood pressure who chose to use cocaine, chose to use PCP and then, under their influence, chose to slug it out with cops.

Which is why, from where I sit, there is no choice but to reach a very different conclusion than the coroner: Nathaniel Jones committed suicide.

DECEMBER 22, 2003

FOR THURMOND, POLITICS THICKER THAN BLOOD

"All the laws of Washington and all the bayonets of the Army cannot force the Negro into our homes, into our schools, our churches and our places of recreation and amusement."—Strom Thurmond

So I guess ol' Strom didn't mind a little integration after all.

Granted, he made opposition to it the cornerstone of a political career that took him to the South Carolina statehouse and the United States Senate. True, he ran for president in 1948 on a segregationist platform. Yes, he staged American history's longest filibuster in an effort to block a 1957 civil rights bill.

But back when he was in his 20s, Thurmond apparently had no qualms about integrating with his family's 16-year-old black maid.

The result of that union is Essie Mae Washington-Williams, a 78-year-old retired teacher from Los Angeles who spoke at a news conference in Columbia, S.C., on Wednesday. "My father's name was James Strom Thurmond," she said.

She had kept it secret all her life for fear of damaging his career. Thurmond, who died in June at 100, sent money over the years. She seems to have cared for him and believes he cared for her, too. Unfortunately, he didn't care enough to stop oppressing black people, which is what she considers herself. Blood may be thicker than water, but politics is thicker than both.

One senses the media's uncertainty with how this story should be framed. A radio anchor called it "surprising." *60 Minutes II* made it warm and fuzzy, the tale of a father's affection for a daughter he couldn't claim.

Given that a TV movie turned Thomas Jefferson's liaison with Sally Hemings into a "forbidden love" soap opera, I guess I should count my blessings. At least no one has tried to cast the senator and his maid as Carolina's answer to Romeo and Juliet.

Still, the media uncertainty is disappointing. What Thurmond did was hardly unique. From slavery through Jim Crow, it was common for young white men to test their sexual wings with black women their families owned or employed. Women who could not say no.

This, at a time when the black man who so much as cast a stray glance at a white woman risked torture, murder and mutilation from white men crying rape. Indeed, a black porter once let a white woman fall to the ground rather than steady her as she stumbled from his train and have his intentions fatally misconstrued.

If it all sounds absurd and hypocritical, well, those are two words that attach quite handily to Thurmond's racial legacy. And to the nation's.

We tend to think of race as an unbreachable wall—black over here, white over there. But America is full of Essie Mae Washington-Williamses, full of people who fall on both sides. After all, white men spent centuries sneaking across the color line they themselves had erected in order to bed black cooks and maids. African Ancestry, a company that uses DNA to trace African-American lineage, reports that fully 30 percent of its clients discover that their paternity lies not in Africa, but Europe.

It's a drama that has played out a million times. A million black women, a million babies, a million white men.

It is said that this particular white man changed in later years as the civil rights movement he had opposed gave the ballot to black voters. He was, bless his heart, one of the first senators to hire a black aide.

And yet there was still this daughter, forbidden to call him father. For all he may have done and felt for her, he still saw his oldest child as a shameful secret. Could not bring himself, even at the end, to publicly acknowledge her.

That's not a surprise or a warm and fuzzy tale.

It's just a fresh reminder of the hypocrisy of bigotry, the fluidity of identity. Just evidence that American lives are often American lies.

And that race is the biggest lie of them all.

JANUARY 30, 2004

BLACK MEN, STAY CLEAR OF RIGGED GAME OF JUSTICE

This is an open letter to African-American men.

I suppose I could as easily have addressed myself to the broader world, but I know how the response to that would go. Folks denying, rationalizing and arguing that facts are not truly facts.

That's how it always is when the subject is crime and you.

Earlier this week, the *Herald* ran a jaw-dropping series called "Justice Withheld." It detailed the abuse of a legal procedure called a withhold of adjudication. This is a tool Florida judges can use at their discretion that allows felony offenders to avoid a conviction.

Receiving a withhold allows you to legally say you've never been convicted of a crime, even though a court found you guilty. There are many benefits: You retain your right to vote and hold office and you don't have to put the crime on your application for a job or a student loan.

In theory, withholds are handed out sparingly to deserving people in extenuating circumstances. The *Herald* found that in practice, they are handed out like Halloween candy.

Four-time losers get withholds. Rapists and car thieves get withholds. Drug dealers and batterers get withholds.

If you commit fraud or forgery, you've got an even chance of getting one. Abuse or molest a child and your chances are actually better than even.

All those folks enjoying all that judicial mercy. Guess who gets left out?

Yup. You.

Even if you commit the same crime and have the same record, a white offender is almost 50 percent more likely to get a withhold than you are. Some folks say that's not a function of racism but of socioeconomics. Meaning that whites are more often able to afford private attorneys, less likely to have to rely on some overburdened public defender.

There are two answers to that. One: socioeconomics can't be disconnected from racism where black people are concerned; the disparity in black and white accumulated wealth is hardly an accident. And two: the *Herald* report shows that, even when you adjust for type of attorney, African-American defendants are still much less likely to receive withholds.

So I have a question for you:

Can we please stop being such good customers of the American injustice system? I am sick to my soul of watching shaggy-haired black boys and men in orange jumpsuits led into courtrooms to be judged for doing some stupid and heinous thing. I'm weary of the truth in that old Richard Pryor line about how he went to court looking for justice and that's what he found. Just us.

Contrary to what society has told us, to what so much of our music claims and to what too many of us have internalized, the reason isn't that we carry some kind of criminal gene. No, it's that we don't get second chances, don't have the same margin for error a white guy would. One strike, and you're out.

We need to recognize this. Need to make sure our sons and brothers recognize it.

The *Herald* report is not the first, the fifth, or even the 10th to come back with results like these, results that codify the painfully obvious: the injustice system sees no value in us, is comfortable throwing us away like so much used tissue. It doesn't give a damn about us.

But our children do. Our women and mothers and fathers do. So let us love them—and ourselves—enough to stay as far from that system as humanly possible. Because once you're in it, you're like a dinosaur in a tar pit. Dragged down.

No, it's not fair that we are held to a different standard. Say that loudly and clearly. Fight to make it right. But do not stop there.

You see, when you discover that a game is rigged against you, you have every right to complain that you're being cheated.

But a smart man does one thing more:

A smart man stops playing.

MARCH 12, 2004

BLACKS SHOULD BE SUPPORTIVE OF GAYS' STRUGGLE

Call it an object lesson in the quality of equality.

I refer to last week's Senate subcommittee hearing on the proposed constitutional amendment outlawing same-sex marriage. And specifically, to an exchange between two leaders of the African-American community.

The first, Hilary Shelton, director of the Washington bureau of the NAACP, argued that the amendment "would use the Constitution to discriminate." Which brought a sharp retort from the Rev. Richard Richardson, chairman of political affairs for the Black Ministerial Alliance of Greater Boston Inc. Defining marriage as the union of a woman and a man, he said, "is not discrimination. And I find it offensive to call it that."

If you polled black folk, Richardson's view would doubtless prove typical. Though it's not generally appreciated by the wider world, African Americans are among the most socially conservative Americans there are. Particularly on gay issues. Indeed, if you want to start a fight, suggest to a group of black folk that there are parallels between the civil rights movement and the gay community's struggle for equality.

Even African Americans who are sympathetic to the gay cause often bristle at the comparison. As the Rev. Jesse Jackson recently put it, "Gays were never called three-fifths human in the Constitution."

Those who are not sympathetic are even harsher. Gene Rivers, a Boston minister, accuses gays of "pimping" the civil rights movement.

Granted, the comparison between the black struggle and the gay one is inexact. But here's the thing: Every freedom movement from Poland's labor uprising to America's feminism to China's Tiananmen Square protests has been compared to the civil rights movement. When Czechoslovakians threw off communist rule in 1989, they sang "We Shall Overcome." Yet no one bothered to point out that the Czechs were never slighted in the U.S. Constitution, much less to accuse Poles of "pimping" the civil rights movement. What's that tell you?

It tells me this stinginess about the movement arises only when gays seek to embrace it. And that black people—some of us, at least—ought to be ashamed.

How can we of all people, we who know the weight of American oppression better than almost anyone, stand in the path of those who seek simple equality? How can we support writing anyone out of the Constitution when it took us so long to be written in?

And how can we stand with the very people—social conservatives—who not so long ago didn't want us in their churches, their schools, their parks or their restaurants? Yet more and more, we act and sound just like them.

We use our Bibles to justify our bigotry, just as they did.

We describe equality as unnatural, just as they did.

We invoke the sanctity of tradition, just as they did.

And we are wrong, just as they were.

Worse, we have wrapped our community in a conspiracy of silence, made being homosexual something one simply does not discuss. So that if you are black and gay or black and lesbian, there is often no sane thought of "coming out," no safe place to be who you are. The black community has no resources for you, no tolerance of you, no compassion for you. Yes, there are exceptions, but not enough. Not nearly.

Is it any surprise, then, that blacks lead the nation in new cases of HIV and AIDS?

Too many of us fail—or refuse—to see the great generality that overarches the specificity of our struggles. Meaning that it doesn't matter whether you are gay or black or woman or Jew or even Czech: people have a right to be free.

This is the principle gay people are fighting to vindicate. And no, it isn't *the* civil rights movement, but make no mistake: it's definitely a civil rights movement.

Except that this time, black people are on the other side.

JULY 9, 2004

COSBY'S REMARKS ON BLACKS' WOES ARE REFRESHING

Our question for today: Do white people matter?

It's Bill Cosby who inspires me to ask. In May, you'll recall, he made headlines for criticizing the "lower economic people" in African America for what he saw as their ungrammatical locution and dysfunctional behavior. On July 1, he was at it again, saying in an appearance at the annual Rainbow/PUSH Coalition Conference in Chicago that African-American youth are the "dirty laundry" many people would prefer he not criticize.

"Let me tell you something," he said. "Your dirty laundry gets out of school at 2:30 every day, it's cursing and calling each other [the n-word] as they're walking up and down the street. They think they're hip. They can't read. They can't write. They're laughing and giggling, and they're going nowhere."

Predictably, that set off another heated debate, even though Cosby is not saying anything black people have not said themselves, albeit privately. What makes Cosby's comments extraordinary is not what he is saying, but where. Meaning, forums to which white people are privy. Because the danger of black self-criticism is always that bigots will use it to bolster their bigotry.

Cosby addressed that concern in May during an interview with Eugene Kane, columnist for the *Milwaukee Journal Sentinel.* The comedian, who turns 67 on Monday, said he's simply at an age where he no longer cares what white people think of black people's dirty linen.

"I'm a tired man," he said.

Make no mistake: It's much easier for a black multimillionaire to dismiss white people's opinions than it is for a black man or woman living paycheck to paycheck. But, even granting that not-insignificant caveat, I must confess that I find Cosby's attitude refreshing, mainly because it points toward a freedom African Americans have never enjoyed before. Meaning the freedom to stop pretending perfection.

The calculus of the freedom struggle once required, demanded, that we constantly prove our worth. Conversely, some people—black and white—began to romanticize black folk, idealize us, as if the very fact of long suffering made us better, nobler. Such thinking was considered a sign of enlightenment. Actually, it was just a quieter bigotry that suggested we had to be better in order to be equal. It never allowed us to be simply human with all the frailties that implies.

African Americans have never gotten beyond that mind-set. Sometimes, we act as if conceding the slightest blemish would validate the whole canon of white racism. Never mind that nobody is perfect and every culture contains dysfunction.

We know that a white boy on crystal meth will be called troubled, while a black one on crack will be called proof that 37 million people are irredeemable.

Maybe, however, it's time we reconsidered the lengths we go to to change the minds of those who subscribe to that kind of "thinking." Maybe we ought to question whether we can ever win the approval of such people and frankly, whether we'd want it if we could. Do white people—bigoted ones, at least—matter?

Especially if the price of their approval is to stand silent while the future burns?

You have only to visit the schoolhouse or jailhouse to see the flames. And one need not be blind to racism's role in the equation to know that we bear some accountability, too, that elements of black pop culture are toxic, that some of us have undervalued fatherhood, disinvested in education, rationalized dysfunction.

It should make us all sick to our souls to watch our children die— spiritually, intellectually, physically—knowing that black people can do, and indeed have done, so much better than this.

So when Cosby calls himself a tired man, I read it less as a statement of fatigue than one of frustration. And who can blame him?

Hell, I'm a tired man, too.

SEPTEMBER 24, 2004

DON'T BE FOOLED:
RACISM PERSISTS, IT'S JUST HIDDEN

Sometimes, we act as if it just dissipated long ago, all the heat, all the hate, gone one milestone day. Like everybody got religion simultaneously, repented their sins and went forth to sin no more.

We consider ourselves enlightened now, beyond it now, so much so that some of us resent you even bringing it up. Indeed, the very word we use to describe it feels 20th century, like rotary dials and vinyl records.

Racism, the word is. Racism. So frequently misused and over-used, you are sometimes faintly embarrassed to use it at all. After all, it's no longer a word that makes anybody say, Oh, my God. It has become sonic wallpaper. Cliché.

Then you read a story from the *Clarion-Ledger* newspaper of Jackson, Miss. It says the State Fair is opening next month. And that, along with enjoying the fun house and the State Championship Mule Pull, fairgoers will have the chance to shake hands with, or get an autograph from, the chief suspect in the Ku Klux Klan's 1964 murders of Andrew Goodman, James Chaney and Michael Schwerner.

Shake hands. Or get an autograph.

For those who don't know: Goodman, Chaney and Schwerner went to Mississippi seeking to register black voters. In the South in 1964, that was a crime sometimes punishable by death.

Seven men were convicted of the murders, but their alleged ringleader, an alleged preacher named Edgar Ray Killen, went free after a jury deadlocked 11 to 1 in favor of conviction.

According to the *Clarion-Ledger*, the juror who held out said she could not bring herself to convict a preacher. The 79-year-old Killen reportedly remains under state investigation for the 40-year-old crime. He has never recanted his hateful views.

Killen was invited to man a booth at the fair by a lawyer named Richard Barrett, head of a white supremacist group. He intends to hand out cards bearing images of Goodman, Chaney and Schwerner with a circle around them and a line through them.

A legend on the card describes the martyrs as communists who "invaded" Mississippi. These are what fairgoers will be encouraged to have Killen sign.

Your immediate urge is to ignore it, to sequester it in that far place in the mind we reserve for the atavistic few who didn't get the memo that this fight is over, this hate repudiated so thoroughly that even our word for it has fallen into disrepair.

From where I sit, that urge gives us more credit than we deserve.

Forty years after the bodies of those three men were dug out of an earthen dam, racism has not left us. It has only become a hide-and-seek thing, a did-you-see-it-or-did-you-just-imagine-it game. We ask earnestly: Is Trent Lott a racist or did he just misspeak? Did he mean it like it sounded, or was he simply insensitive? Hey, he went on BET to apologize. Shouldn't that count for something?

Our confusion is not hard to understand in an era when racism wears three-piece suits and racists speak fluent PC. More to the point, an era where racist beliefs are hidden in policy, concealed in practice, their effects visible in statistics and studies, but never in anything so crude as a sign that says "Whites Only."

So that racists can always plead innocent. Always throw the rock and hide their hands.

And the rest of us can continue in the self-justifying fantasy that this history ended a long time past.

I am not saying that no hearts changed 40 years ago. Many did, and God bless them. But many only pretended. And some can't bring themselves to do even that.

For proof, go to the Fair. Killen and Barrett are progress' dark reflection, a revelation of what three-piece suits too often hide, a reminder that history does not end.

Remember them next time you're tempted to celebrate that milestone day when hate just disappeared.

JANUARY 31, 2005

DON'T SELL YOUR AMBITIONS SHORT TO 'KEEP IT REAL'

An open letter to African-American kids.

The other day, I used a big word in this column. The word was brobdingnagian; it's from a book called *Gulliver's Travels* by Jonathan Swift, a fantasy about a man whose adventures take him to a number of strange lands. One of those lands was Brobdingnag, where the people were all giants. Thus, "brobdingnagian" is a big word that means, well ... big. (I like using it because it's odd and kind of ugly-sounding.)

Anyway, some guy e-mailed me about it. Here's what he said: "Uncle Tom:

Stop trying to act like the white man and mastering his culture. ... I mean, bro, your [sic] using white man words like Brobdingnabian [sic] or whatever. I never hear talk like that on BET. For us homeys, keep it real. If you want to describe something as big, say 'Shaq-size.'"

My middle son thought it had to be somebody's idea of a joke. And it might be. But there are some rather ... odd people out there, so I'm not sure. Not that it matters. Whether it was meant as a joke or not, it made me laugh out loud.

Then I thought about you.

It occurred to me: You hear stuff like that all the time, don't you? Seems like everybody has an idea of what you can and cannot do, who you can and cannot be friends with, how you ought and ought not speak, where you can and cannot go, if you want to "keep it real." If you want, in other words, to be considered truly black.

I've heard the story a hundred times, guys. I've heard it from your teachers, heard it from my own kids, even heard it from some of you. Like a girl I knew who said black kids ostracized her because she spoke standard English and liked a white boy band.

You know the crazy part? When white people prejudge us, when they say blacks can't do this, that or the other, when they demand that we conform to their expectations of what black is, we have no problem calling them on it. But when black people do the same thing, we're more apt to soul-search about why we don't fit in.

You have to wonder at that. Should it really matter whether it's a white person or a black one who presumes us to be less than we are? Doesn't the presumption stink either way?

I'm going to tell you something you might not want to hear. If you have a goal in this life, something you want to be, you have to realize that the road between here and there might get narrow sometimes.

There may be parts you have to walk alone because there's no space for all your friends; there's only room for one.

Maybe you enjoy opera, maybe you want to be an astronaut, maybe you'd like to be a surgeon. And maybe some black people tell you "we" don't do those kinds of things.

They'll say they're keeping it real, but the only thing they're keeping is some old lies that date all the way back to slavery. White people—many, not all—have told us those lies every day for four centuries, told them so constantly and so convincingly that some of us can't help but to believe.

So when black people repeat those lies, when they advise you to dream the kind of dreams black kids are supposed to dream—rap star, basketball player, pimp—you have to recognize it for what it is. You have to know that Marian Anderson sang opera, Dr. Mae Jemison went into space on a shuttle, Dr. Daniel Hale Williams performed the first successful surgery on a human heart and all three were black, like you.

Most of all, you have to be prepared, if need be, to walk that road alone.

I won't lie: it's not easy. People—black and white—will always have expectations and when you refuse to live by those expectations, they'll call you names, they'll shut you out. It's not easy, but I guarantee that if you stay with it, you'll find that it is worthwhile.

I guess what I'm telling you is this: Please have the guts to be who you are. And to dream brobdingnagian dreams.

FEBRUARY 28, 2005

DON'T LET THIEVES STEAL THE LEGACY OF THE HOLOCAUST

Dear Ariana Schanzer:

I hope you won't mind being called out like this. It's just that I saw your picture Feb. 21 in the *Herald* and it made me want to talk to you.

In the photo, you're smiling a giddy smile, dancing cheek to cheek with this equally delighted older man who looks to be about 60 but who is, the caption tells us, actually 90. Which makes your grandfather, Samuel Schanzer, exactly 80 years older than you.

It would have been a touching image under any circumstances, but the thing that made it stand out for me is that it was taken at a reunion of Holocaust survivors. It occurred to me, Ariana, that you are a blessing your grandfather would have found too absurdly wonderful to hope for back when he was young and the world was burning down around him. You are a miracle he would not have known how to dream.

I'm certain he understands how lucky he is. I'm hoping that you, even at your tender age, understand, too. And that you will cherish the gift of these years you have with him.

Not just because he is your grandfather, but because it is important that his story survives him and is passed to generations not yet born.

I'm concerned about what has become of the Holocaust in recent years, Ariana.

It's not just the people who deny it ever happened that I refer to, though heaven knows that bunch is scary enough. To the degree anyone can erode the hard edge of historical certainty, to the degree the Holocaust can be made a "controversy," they spit on ashes and bones and make themselves thieves of legacy.

Still, I think the clearer and more present danger isn't those who deny the Holocaust but, rather, those who trivialize it, who make it a thing undeserving of our reverence.

I'm thinking of the people who opened a disco a few years ago near—or possibly in—one of the outbuildings of Auschwitz. And of a painting that made headlines in 2002 because it depicted a man standing among a bunch of death camp Jews holding up a can of Diet Coke. And of a cartoon a student magazine ran last year. It showed a bearded man sitting on the edge of an open kitchen stove. The caption read, "Knock a Jew In The Oven! Three Throws for a Dollar." The headline read, "Holocaust Remembrance Week."

And I'm thinking of the people who say they don't care about the Holocaust because it happened to other people in other places at another time.

We have these delusions about history, Ariana. We tend to regard it as a closed book. We like to insulate ourselves from its atrocities and injustices, to say that, yes, those were awful things, but they were done by unenlightened people in an unenlightened era, so they have nothing to do with us, here, now. Slavery, lynchings, the mass murder of people whose only offense is difference ... these things could never happen again, we say.

But Ariana, that's foolish. Did you know that there is slavery right now, this minute, in Mali?

Did you know a man was lynched in Texas seven years ago because he was black?

And mass murder has never left us. In just the past few years, we have seen it in Rwanda, in Bosnia-Herzegovina and in Sudan—people still killing for the offense of difference.

So we owe it to your grandfather—and mine—to stand in the gap for them, to tell their stories when they no longer can.

And to shatter the self-satisfied smugness that allows some of us to believe the past is finished business. As a writer named William Faulkner once pointed out, the past isn't even past.

Remember that when people try to make the Holocaust abstract, Ariana. Remember, when they try to make it absurd. Remember the warmth of your grandfather's cheek against yours, remember how small your hand was in his.

Remember, and pass it on.

APRIL 18, 2005

FOR ONE STUDENT, A LESSON IN THE POWER OF IMAGES

It was a sunlit moment.

For the past couple of weeks, I've had students in my pop culture class talking about African-American images in entertainment media. As part of that discussion, I showed them a movie—Spike Lee's 2000 satire, *Bamboozled*.

It is in some ways a deeply flawed film. But it derives an undeniable power and poignancy from its evocation of a century's worth of African-American stereotype. A bad taste parade of Aunt Jemimas, Sambos, pickaninnies and minstrels shuffles across the screen and you can't help but feel overwhelmed—saddened and sickened at this coarse slandering of black people and black life. When the movie went off, the room was sullen, silent and maybe a little shell-shocked.

Then I showed them a rap concert video. Lots of swagger and threats of violence. Lots of crotch-grabbing, lots of motherbleep this and motherbleep that, lots of street gang shout-outs and every other word the N-word for an audience that was predominantly white and delirious with enjoyment.

One student said that, had she never seen *Bamboozled*, she would never have thought twice about that video. But having seen it, the rappers seemed—and she said this with some surprise—"ignorant."

That was the sunlit moment—one of those rare instances when you can actually see your point getting across.

It came against a backdrop of big news from the hip-hop community. Meaning last month's cease-fire between 50 Cent and The Game, two rival rappers who make their livings with images of violence. The two shook hands at Harlem's historic Schomburg Center for Research in Black Culture, agreeing to squash a squabble that culminated in February with gunfire between their entourages outside a New York City radio station. One man was injured.

Afeni Shakur, mother of the murdered Tupac, pronounced herself "proud" to see peace break out. A New York rapper who calls himself Cormega said it was "a beautiful thing."

With all due respect, let me just say that my own response is decidedly more mixed.

I keep trying to put this in a context I can understand, keep trying to imagine people loyal to Al Green shooting it out with those loyal to Marvin Gaye. Or Gladys Knight and Aretha Franklin holding a news conference, like Middle East potentates, to announce a cease-fire.

I find myself wondering how African-American culture, that old sweet song of strivers and lovers, blues and rhythm and how I got over, ever came to this. Is this how the present generation of African-American entertainers builds upon the opportunities secured for them by the sacrifices of those who came before? Is this why Nat Cole was attacked onstage by white racists and Paul Robeson was blacklisted? Is it why the Temptations endured segregated ballrooms and Sammy Davis Jr. put up with death threats? So that two petty thugs with a reported 14 bullet wounds between them can get rich off coonish stereotypes that would make Sambo blush?

Most of all, I wonder this: How in the world did we ever reach a point where all of this came to seem normal?

The questions are not about music. They are, rather, about the willingness of black people to lift black people. About whether it is still true that more is required from those who are given more. About whether this "more" is something we who are African American have the right to expect and the will to demand. About whether we still give a damn about we.

I felt good leaving school last week, felt warmed by that sunlit moment. Then I stopped at a newsstand where the cover of *Vibe*, a hip-hop magazine, showed a striking image. Three murdered icons of rap—Jam Master Jay, Notorious B.I.G. and Tupac Shakur—standing in a graveyard among the tombstones.

I took it as a reminder that the need is urgent to find answers to those questions. And that until we do, sunlit moments will be few and far between.

JULY 18, 2005

A FATHER'S HOMOPHOBIA TURNED DEADLY

Ronnie Paris and I had the same father.

At least, that's the way it felt reading the news reports out of Tampa last week. They told of how Ronnie's dad—his name is also Ronnie Paris—used to hit the boy, throw him around, bang him up. According to testimony from the man's wife and sister-in-law, he did this to toughen the boy up, make a man out of him. Paris' fear was that, otherwise, his son would grow up to be "soft," a "sissy."

Or gay.

There are only three differences between this little boy's experience and mine.

One, the word "gay" wasn't a common synonym for homosexual when I was a child. My dad's word was "punk," which meant the same thing.

Two, in all fairness to my old man, he was nowhere near as harsh to me as Ronnie Paris was to his son. My dad never left me with broken bones, internal bruising or brain swelling.

The third difference is the most important. I am alive. Little Ronnie Paris is not. He died on Jan. 28, 3 years old.

Last week, a Tampa jury found the toddler's 21-year-old father guilty of second-degree manslaughter and aggravated child abuse.

Afterward, Ronald Paris Sr.—father of the killer, grandfather of the victim—protested his own blamelessness to a reporter from the *Tampa Tribune*. "I raised my son in the right way," he said. "We played football, went fishing, went to wrestling matches, boxing, all that."

It's one of those "Lord, give me strength" quotes, because it manages to be earnest, self-justifying and clueless all at the same time. To put it another way, it's telling what the eldest Ronald Paris doesn't say about raising his boy right.

He doesn't say he ever talked to him. Doesn't say he ever hugged him. Doesn't say he ever taught him.

Don't get me wrong. There is nothing wrong with fishing, football and other "manly" pursuits.

But while you're tossing the pigskin around, maybe you should explain to a son that the measure of a man is more than the ability to summon or endure violence. And the strength of a man has to include the strength to be tender sometimes, especially when confronted with a tiny life that looks to you for protection and guidance.

Maybe it's not too much to ask also that a father teach his son that "gay" is not something you can knock out of a child. Nor should you want to.

A story by way of illustration. I have a younger brother. By the time he was a toddler, my father had given up on me, resigned himself that his bookish and unathletic oldest child was doomed to punkdom.

So Dad decided he would save my brother from that fate. He took him under his wing and taught him every manly heterosexual art and vice he could.

I'll give you one guess which of my father's sons went to the gay pride beach party a few years back.

It's probably a sign of God's mercy that our father did not live long enough to learn.

Too bad there wasn't a little mercy for the youngest Ronnie Paris. Too bad his mother—now facing charges of felony child neglect—did not call authorities. Too bad the state, which took the child out of the home in 2002, did not leave him with the foster mother who loved him. Too bad he was returned to his birth parents in mid-December.

Too bad he was in a coma by Jan. 22.

It is said the Parises could not wake him that day after he fell asleep on the couch in a neighbor's home. His folks had gone there for Bible study. Apparently, "Thou shalt not kill" was not among the verses on the agenda.

Maybe you can tell that I take this one personally. It's hard not to. Ronnie Paris was terrified his child would grow up gay. Now the boy won't grow up at all.

And I'm left to choke on the irony. Paris thought he was going to teach his boy how to be a man when clearly, he didn't know himself.

OCTOBER 7, 2005

BENNETT'S QUIP TOUCHES ON TACIT RACE, CRIME TIE

My youngest son was arrested last year.

Police came to my house looking for an armed robbery suspect, five-feet eight-inches tall with long hair. They took my son, six-foot-three with short braids. They made my daughter, 14, fresh from the shower and dressed for bed, lie face down in wet grass and handcuffed her. They took my grandson, 8, from the bed where he slept and made him sit on the sidewalk beside her.

My son, should it need saying, hadn't done a damn thing. In fact, I was talking to him long distance—I was in New Orleans—at the time of the alleged crime. Still, he spent almost two weeks in jail. The prosecutor asked for a high bail, citing the danger my son supposedly posed.

A few weeks later, the prosecutor declined to press charges, finally admitting there was no evidence. The alleged perpetrator of the alleged crime, a young man who was staying with us, did go on trial. There was no robbery, he said. The alleged victim had picked a fight with him, lost and concocted a tale. A surveillance video backed him up. The jury returned an acquittal in a matter of hours.

But the damage was done. The police took a picture of my son the night he was arrested. He is on his knees, hands cuffed behind him, eyes fathomless and dead. I cannot see that picture without feeling a part of me die.

So I take personally what William Bennett said. For those who missed it, Bennett, former education secretary and self-appointed arbiter of all things moral, said last week on his radio program that if you wanted to reduce crime, "you could ... abort every black baby in this country, and your crime rate would go down. That would be an impossible, ridiculous and morally reprehensible thing to do, but your crime rate would go down."

The comment has been widely denounced. Bennett says critics are quoting him out of context, leaving out his denunciation of the idea and the fact he was criticizing a thesis that holds that making abortion readily available to low-income women in the '70s led the U.S. crime rate to drop in the '90s.

Fine. I get all that. But see, my anger doesn't stem from any mistaken belief that Bennett wants to practice eugenics on black mothers. No, what bothers me is his easy, almost casual conflation of race and crime. Not class and crime, not culture and crime, but race and crime. As if black, solely and of itself, equals felony.

It's a conflation that comes too readily to too many. The results of which can be read in studies such as the one the Justice Department co-sponsored in 2000 that found black offenders receive substantially harsher treatment at every step along the way than white ones with similar records.

They can also be read in that picture of my son, eyes lifeless and dull with the realization of How Things Are.

I once asked a black police officer who was uninvolved in the case how his colleagues could have arrested a six-foot-three man while searching for a five-foot-eight suspect. They were looking for a black man, he said. Any black man would do.

So how do I explain that to my son? Should I tell him to content himself with the fact that to some people, all black men look alike, all look like criminals?

Actually I don't have to explain it at all. A few months back, my son was stopped by police and cited for driving with an obstructed windshield. The "obstruction" was one of those air fresheners shaped like a Christmas tree.

So my son gets it now. Treatment he once found surprising he now recognizes as the price he pays for being. He understands what the world expects of him.

I've watched that awful knowledge take root in three sons now. In a few years, I will watch it take root in my grandson, who is in the fifth grade.

The conflation of black and crime may be easy for William Bennett, but it never gets any easier for me.

OCTOBER 24, 2005

PERSONAL FOUL CALLED ON THE GANGSTA LOOK

I am trying to feel Marcus Camby's pain. I am also trying to keep a straight face. I cannot do both.

Camby, for those who never read the sports page, is a very tall man who is paid $8 million per annum to play basketball for the Denver Nuggets. You'd think life would be good, but Camby is feeling put upon.

This is because last week the National Basketball Association instituted a dress code for its players. No more sunglasses worn indoors, no more sleeveless shirts, no more headphones during news conferences, no more caps cocked to the side, no more do-rags, no more rumpled sweats, no more chains bearing gaudy pendants the approximate size and weight of a small child. Business casual dress is now required of every player while on team business.

Camby feels this is an unfair burden. He told a reporter that if the NBA wants to impose a dress code, it should give each player a clothing allowance.

Did I mention that Camby is paid $8 million a year?

Of course, not every NBA player who opposes the dress code has cited financial hardship as his reason. At least two—Stephen Jackson of the Indiana Pacers, Paul Pierce of the Boston Celtics—have cited race. They think the code is aimed at ridding the league of the hip-hop "gangsta" look that is so popular among young black men.

"...I think that's part of our culture," said Pierce. "The NBA is young black males."

Does he have a point? Is race a factor here? Having given the matter considerable consideration, I have an answer. In fact, I have three:

1) No. The new dress code will also require a wardrobe upgrade for such noteworthy white slobs as Dirk Nowitzki and Steve Nash.

2) Maybe. Given that over 75 percent of its players are black, the NBA can hardly avoid being a microcosm of racial issues.

3) Who cares?

Actually, No. 3 is my favorite. Let us assume that NBA commissioner David Stern is indeed motivated by a perception that basketball fans find it increasingly difficult to relate to a league of Scary-Looking Young Black Men—especially after last year's brawl between players and fans.

So what? This is business. Stern is entitled—obligated—to use any moral means to protect his multi-billion-dollar corporation. If you earn a lavish living from that corporation you should also be concerned.

As for race: Let's grant that for some, all young black men, indeed, all black men, are scary-looking. Still, to believe the dress code is racist, you must ignore that the gangsta look is not popular among middle-aged blacks, but is often embraced by young whites. Point being, this is less racial than generational.

Meaning a generation of young black people choosing a style of dress that connotes criminality and street values. And it's childish to say, as Camby did, that "You shouldn't judge a person from what they wear." Unlike skin tone, unlike nationality, unlike sexual orientation, clothing reflects a conscious choice.

So, judging people by what they wear is fair. One has an absolute right to dress in a lime green suit with red shoes and an orange tie. But one has no reasonable expectation of being treated seriously as a candidate for the executive position while so attired. Because the company also has rights, including the right to ensure you represent it well.

Clothes, we used to say, make the man. The man, if he has a lick of sense, realizes this. The African-American man—so often scorned simply for being—should understand that better than anyone, particularly if he is fortunate enough to be lavishly compensated for playing a game.

So it's hard to muster sympathy for Marcus Camby. Poor baby thinks he's being mistreated? I can think of eight million reasons he's wrong.

OCTOBER 28, 2005

THE LESSONS, MYTHS, REALITY OF ROSA PARKS

"Noncooperation with evil is as much a moral obligation as cooperation with good."—Martin Luther King, Jr.

Her feet were not tired. At least, no more so than usual.

She always hated that legend so let us, in this, the week of her death at age 92, set the record straight. And while we're at it, let's correct another misconception: It's not precisely true that she refused to give up her seat to a white man. The seats next to her and across the aisle were empty, vacated by black people who had already heeded the bus driver's command to get up. So there were places for the white man to sit.

But under the segregation statutes of Montgomery, Ala., no white man was expected to suffer the indignity of sitting next to a black woman or even across from her. So driver J.F. Blake asked again. And Rosa Parks, this soft-spoken 42-year-old department store seamstress just trying to get home from work, gave him her answer again. She told him no.

Her feet were not tired. Her soul was exhausted.

On Dec. 1, it will be 50 years since that drama played out in Court Square. Fifty years since police took her away. Fifty years since black Montgomery protested by boycotting the buses. Fifty years since community leaders tapped as their leader the new preacher at the Dexter Avenue Baptist Church, Martin Luther King Jr.

That moment in Court Square was the birthplace of the 13-year epoch called the Civil Rights Movement. You could make a compelling argument that it was also a birthplace of the modern world.

None of which Rosa Parks could have foreseen that December evening half a century ago. All she knew was that she was tired, sick of acquiescing, accommodating, accepting foolish white laws and white people who said she wasn't good enough to occupy a bus seat. Something had gotten into her that wouldn't let her go along any more, something that turned a lifetime of yes into an electric moment of no.

In the world born from that moment, it is not uncommon for white men to sit next to black women, to work for them, be married to them, get arrested by them. Indeed, any list of the most powerful women in America is likely to have two black women—Oprah Winfrey, Condoleezza Rice—at the top.

Racism that was once brazen enough to demand a black woman's bus seat is covert now, a throw-the-rock-and-hide-your-hand charade, its effects as visible as ever, its workings mostly hidden. But for all that, it is now only the second most worrisome threat to African-American life.

African Americans are the first. Because many of us have internalized the lies of inferiority so deeply as to make racism superfluous. We don't need white people to destroy us; we happily destroy ourselves. Destroy our families by exiling fathers from them, destroy our futures by declaring education something only white people do, destroy our spirits with a culture that celebrates all that is seamy, soulless and material.

This is the threat that troubles most, simply because while racism strangles aspiration, nihilism renders it stillborn.

And in the face of this threat, too many of us do what Rosa Parks got sick of doing: acquiesce, accommodate, accept.

Indeed, let a white man call our children fatherless, ill-educated thugs and we will, justifiably, rip him an orifice God never intended. Let our children say the same thing of themselves and many of us call it music and look the other way.

The lesson of Rosa Parks' life is that you don't have to look the other way. That night on the bus, she wasn't a movement, wasn't an icon. She was just a woman, one woman who'd had enough, who refused to comply any longer with a system that dehumanized her.

Her death reminds us that there is no number more powerful than one, no word more potent than no. And no force more compelling than a soul grown exhausted enough for change.

SEPTEMBER 18, 2006

BLACKS CAN OFTEN SHARE BLAME FOR POOR SELF-IMAGE

"Can you show me the doll that looks bad?"

The two baby dolls are identical except that one has pale skin, the other is dark. The little black girl, maybe 5 years old, has been holding up the pale doll, but in response to the question, she puts it down and picks up the other.

"Why does that look bad?" the interviewer asks.

"Because it's black," the little girl says.

"And why do you think that's the nice doll?" asks the interviewer, referring to the light-skinned doll.

"Because she's white."

"And can you give me the doll that looks like you?"

The dark-skinned girl reaches for the light-skinned doll, jiggling it as if she really wants to pick it up. In the end, with palpable reluctance, she pushes the black doll forward.

You might be forgiven for thinking you have happened upon one of the "Doll Tests" conducted by Dr. Kenneth Clark beginning in the late 1930s, tests that helped persuade the Supreme Court to strike down segregation in its *Brown v. Board of Education* decision.

But this is a new doll test, conducted by Kiri Davis, a 17-year-old student from New York, for *A Girl Like Me*, her short film about black girls and standards of beauty. Be warned: If you have a heart, the new doll test will break it.

Hard upon mourning, though, will come outrage. How is this possible? How can this still be true? How in the hell, a lifetime after a little boy in Arkansas pointed to the black doll and said, "That's a nigger ... I'm a nigger," can we still have black children who think black and bad are synonymous?

Some of us were born of the generation that came of age with a mandate to hurl that thinking back onto history's trash heap. Some of us remember when James Brown sang "Say It Loud, I'm Black and I'm Proud." Some of us knew that when Aretha Franklin spelled out "Respect," she wasn't just talking to a feckless lover. Some of us piled Afros high on our heads and sprayed them with Afro Sheen till they shone. Some of us clenched our fists and cried "Black is beautiful" in the face of a nation that had always told us you could be one or the other, but never both.

And for what? So that 40 years later, our children would still parrot media-derived lies of their own worthlessness? What's appalling is that many of the lies now originate with black people themselves.

That's not to let white people off the hook. The simple arithmetic of majority/minority means that under the best of circumstances, a child of color will always see fewer images of people like her in media. And the white makers and gatekeepers of those fewer images have historically weighted them toward ineffectuality, hypersexuality, native criminality and plain ignorance.

What's different now is that African Americans are, themselves, often the makers and gatekeepers. And under our aegis, the images have, in many ways, gotten worse.

To surf the music video channels is to be immersed in black culture as conceived by a new generation, a lionization of pimps and gold diggers, hustlers and thugs who toss the N-word with a gusto that would do the Klan proud.

A new generation, afflicted with historical amnesia, blind indifference and a worship of filthy lucre, dances a metaphoric buck and wing, eyes rolling, yassuh bossing, selling itself out, selling its forebears out. Most of all, selling the children out.

And it's little excuse to say we're only buying lies we have internalized, lies that become self-fulfilling prophecy. That's all well and good, but the moment you're able to understand that you've been lied to is the moment you bear responsibility for promulgating some truth in reply. That too few of us are willing to accept that responsibility is driven home every time one of those black children chooses a white doll.

We've spent 387 years in this country trying to get white folks to love us. Might help if we first learned to love ourselves.

SEPTEMBER 25, 2006

RADICALS ARE THE ONES WHO SHOULD SAY THEY'RE SORRY

I'm probably going to have to apologize for this column, so let's get that out of the way:

I'm sorry. I did not intend to offend Islam or its followers. I respect Islam and, indeed, all the ways humanity worships and seeks its Maker.

With that taken care of, let us get right to the point: Would somebody tell the pope to stop explaining himself?

We are, for those of you who haven't been keeping count, up to the fourth clarification and/or expression of regret from Pope Benedict XVI for comments he made recently that inflamed much of the Islamic world. The apologias began with a Vatican statement issued Sept. 14 which said in part, "It was certainly not the intention of the Holy Father ... to hurt the feelings of Muslim believers." From there, you can trace the evolution of papal regret through headlines from the *New York Times*.

Sept. 17: Vatican Says Pope Benedict Regrets Offending Muslims

Sept. 18: In a Rare Step, Pope Expresses Personal Regret

Sept. 21: For 4th Time, Pope Clarifies Islam Remark

I'm not here to defend the pope. The words that got him in trouble—they came during a speech about faith and reason at Regensburg University in Germany—were indeed ill-considered. The pope quoted 14th-century Byzantine Christian emperor Manuel II Paleologus as saying, "Show me just what Mohammed brought that was new, and there you will find things only evil and inhuman, such as his command to spread by the sword the faith he preached." Religious conversion at sword point is contrary to reason, said the pope, and thus, contrary to God.

His use of the emperor's quote infuriated much of the Muslim world. In Somalia, a radical cleric reportedly called for the pope to be killed. In Iraq, a terrorist group vowed war against "worshipers of the cross." In the West Bank, churches were firebombed.

All of which could and should have been foreseen. Though he called the emperor's comments "brusque," Benedict did not take time to otherwise disassociate himself from them. That was foolish. And yes, there was something rather weaselly about the papal apology: "I am deeply sorry for the reactions in some countries to a few passages of my address, which were considered offensive." In other words, I'm not sorry for what I said; I'm sorry for how you responded to it.

For all that, though, I've had my fill of papal genuflection. In the first place, clumsily framed as it was, Benedict's point was clear and unassailable: True religion and violence are mutually exclusive.

In the second place, the violent response of some Muslims not only makes the pope's point but also slanders their religion more effectively than some centuries-old quote ever could. What is the Arabic word for irony?

Between this latest controversy and the rioting earlier this year over cartoon depictions of the Prophet Mohammed, there seems something pathetically reflexive about some Muslims' reaction to perceived religious insult. It's as if they are addicted to the faux power to be found in throwing a tantrum, threatening violence, demanding attention, forcing apologies.

Of course, faux power is, by definition, not real. Real power effects change. Faux power makes noise and changes nothing. When they behave like this, Muslim radicals highlight the difference—and the fact that they don't know the difference.

Ultimately, this latest episode speaks less to papal error than to the fact that Islam is being hijacked by ignorant thugs who use violence—both threatened and real—as a conduit to power. Not justice, power. And fake power at that. In the process, they make Islam seem synonymous with bombings, beheadings and blood.

If anybody owes Muslims an apology, it's them.

OCTOBER 9, 2006

AN OPEN LETTER TO THE KILLERS OF MR. LAWRENCE

Good morning, gentlemen. I don't know your names yet, but I want to talk to you about the man you killed.

I read about it in the *Miami Herald*. How Lemroy Lawrence walked out of his house in Miami Gardens at about 9 p.m. Tuesday to get some papers from his truck. How you approached him out of the darkness. How there was a struggle. How he was shot in the back.

Police put out a description of the suspects they're looking for, a description of you: young, black and male. Maybe you'll be in custody by the time these words see print. Maybe it'll take longer. But you'll be caught. For some reason, I have no doubt.

Afterward, you'll show up in court and they'll have your picture on the news, and you'll be wearing one of those jail jumpsuits and giving that scowl of hard-as-calculus and dead inside that young men like you like to show the world as a way of saying nothing matters to you and you can't be touched. Inside, you'll be puking your guts out.

They're going to give you life. Or maybe death. Either way, you'll have a long time to contemplate what you've done. You'll turn 30 in jail, 40 in jail, maybe grow old in jail, and the person you are now will be a distant memory, a stupid young punk you'll wish you could reach back in time to slap, scream at, shake by the shoulders and beg to turn his life around, not do this terrible thing. Maybe you'll find Jesus. Maybe you'll find remorse. Maybe you'll read books, become educated, change your life.

And all the while, Lemroy Lawrence will still be dead.

Moreover, the ironies of that death will still be sharp as razor blades. Lawrence was a husband, father, high school shop teacher, yes. He was also a mentor in the 5000 Role Models of Excellence program, a program that exists to save young black men at risk. Young black men like you.

I spoke at one of their assemblies years ago. They made me an honorary member. Somewhere in my closet, I still have the tie they gave me, the tie that is the uniform of the program: against a field of red, it shows hands reaching out.

It was all the brainchild of state Sen. Frederica Wilson. According to Role Models literature, 95 percent of the boys who graduate from the program get in no further trouble with school officials or police.

Point being, you destroyed a man who had dedicated his life to saving yours.

It's painful but hardly coincidental to note that in May, Wilson herself was mugged—outside the Role Models office—by a young black man.

In a very real sense, of course, it's a waste of time talking to you. You stood in the endless moment before the awful act, the moment when all things were still possible, and you made your decision. You pulled the trigger. You crossed a sacred line, and there's no going back.

But I find myself thinking about the young black men for whom there is still time, the ones who stand at that line but haven't crossed it yet, the ones who still live in the moment before, and thus, still have time to reclaim their futures, redeem their lives.

With any luck, they will learn from this. With any luck, they will understand that they are both the hope and the despair of the African-American nation and that we've known too little of the one and far too much of other. We are a people who are killing themselves, one heartbreak at a time. So maybe those young men will look at what you did and realize they need to be better than this. We all need to be better than this.

Better than drugs. Better than guns. Better than ignorance. Better than fear. Better than handcuffs. Better than poverty. And yes, Lord, better than death.

It's too late for you. But I think of all those other young brothers out there walking the edge of that sacred line, and I hope they step back before it's too late for them.

Before it's too late for us all.

NOVEMBER 13, 2006

A TWISTED VIEW ON 'FLAUNTING' GAY IDENTITY

Today's topic: flaunting homosexuality. Exhibit A: Doogie.

Meaning Neil Patrick Harris, who, in another life, was the title character in *Doogie Howser, M.D.,* the tale of a boy genius who becomes a doctor. Recently, Harris was outed on a gossip website. His response in a statement to people.com said in part:

"I am happy to dispel any rumors or misconceptions and am quite proud to say that I am a very content gay man living my life to the fullest."

That was it. No muss, no fuss. The world continued spinning, the seas did not boil and the clouds did not bleed.

Still, one suspects that the news was greeted less than warmly in those bastions of social conservatism where, as one gentleman indicates in the new movie *Borat: Cultural Learnings of America for Make Benefit Glorious Nation of Kazakhstan,* they hope to make it legal to string homosexuals up by the soft parts. Indeed, one suspects that the most—pardon my language—liberal response in those parts would be something along the lines of, "Fine, he's gay. Why couldn't he keep that to himself? Why do they have to flaunt it? I don't go around announcing that I'm straight!"

Put aside that Harris was forced into his announcement by an individual who called him out online. Put aside, too, the fact that one "flaunts" one's heterosexuality whenever one publicly canoodles with a sweetie of the opposite gender.

Concentrate, instead, on this notion many social conservatives have that homosexuality is best dealt with by being ignored, denied, kept from public view. Why, they ask, in letters to editors and websites done up in red, white and blue, must homosexuals "flaunt" their "deviant behavior"? "Flaunt" meaning to acknowledge in any way, no matter how small, their sexual orientation.

Which brings us to Ted Haggard. Until earlier this month, he was senior pastor of New Life Church in Colorado Springs and president of the National Association of Evangelicals, an influential preacher who had George Bush's ear. Neither the church nor the NAE has been known for its friendliness toward gay people. So there was quite an uproar when Mike Jones, a gay prostitute, dropped the bombshell allegation that he'd had a three-year sexual relationship with the preacher. Haggard initially denied even knowing Jones but then recanted, admitting that, on at least one occasion, he sought a massage and bought meth from the gay hooker.

On Nov. 2, Haggard stepped down from the NAE presidency. Two days later, his church fired him. He has confessed to "sexual immorality" and will spend the next three to five years in "restoration," a process that reportedly involves confrontation, counsel and—you can't make this stuff up—rebuke from "godly men."

This all raises two questions. One: Between this guy, the late gay-bashing former Spokane mayor, James West, Pat Robertson biographer Mel White, and Michael Bussee and Gary Cooper, leaders in the "curing homosexuality" movement until they fell in love with one another, can't we now safely assume that any conservative who rants about the homosexual agenda is a lying hypocrite gayer than a Castro Street bar?

And, two: Wouldn't you much rather be Neil Patrick Harris than Ted Haggard just now? In other words, wouldn't you rather be a content gay man living life to the fullest, than a closeted gay hypocrite living lies to the fullest? Especially since lies are so frequently found out.

That's the fallacy social conservatives miss. In a culture that allows gay people room to be gay people, there is no need of lies. In a culture that does not—i.e., theirs—lies are rampant. And that's unfortunate, not simply for the person in question, but for all the people in his or her life.

And here, I'm thinking of Gayle Alcorn. She and Haggard have five children. They've been married 28 years. That's a long time to sleep next to a lie.

I bet she wishes he had "flaunted" his homosexuality a long time ago.

DECEMBER 15, 2006

MY FREEDOM LINKED TO OTHERS— INCLUDING GAYS

This is for a reader who demands to know why I write about gay issues. His conclusion is that I must secretly be gay myself.

Actually, he doesn't express himself quite that civilly. To the contrary, his e-mails—which, until recently, were arriving at the rate of about one a week—evince a juvenility that would embarrass a reasonably intelligent fifth grader. The most recent one, for example, carried a salutation reading, "Hi Mrs. Pitts."

We're talking about the kind of thing for which delete buttons were invented. So you may wonder why I bring it to your attention, especially since acknowledging a person like this only encourages him. It's simple, actually: He raises an interesting question that deserves an answer.

If from that you conclude (or fear) you're about to read a stirring defense of my manly male masculinity, no. The guy is free to believe what he wishes; I really don't care. And here, let me digress to confess that, though I refer to him using masculine pronouns, I actually don't know if he's a he because his notes have been anonymous. Still, I assume it's a guy because the level of sexual insecurity the e-mails suggest strikes me as—boy, am I going to get in trouble for this—rather guy-specific.

Anyway, to get back to the point, I'm not here to argue sexuality. I just find myself intrigued by the idea that if you're not gay, you shouldn't care about gay rights.

The most concise answer I can give is cribbed from what a white kid said some 40 or so years ago, as white college students were risking their lives to travel south and register black people to vote. Somebody asked why. He said he acted from an understanding that his freedom was bound up with the freedom of every other man.

I know it sounds cornier than Kellogg's, but that's pretty much how I feel.

I know also that some folks are touchy about anything seeming to equate the black civil rights movement with the gay one. And no, gay people were not kidnapped from Gay Land and sold into slavery, nor lynched by the thousands. On the other hand, they do know something about housing discrimination, they do know job discrimination, they do know murder for the sin of existence, they do know the denial of civil rights and they do know what it is like to be used as scapegoat and boogeyman by demagogues and political opportunists.

They know enough of what I know that I can't ignore it. See, I have yet to learn how to segregate my moral concerns. It seems to me if I abhor intolerance, discrimination and hatred when they affect people who look like me, I must also abhor them when they affect people who do not. For that matter, I must abhor them even when they benefit me. Otherwise, what I claim as moral authority is really just self-interest in disguise.

Among the things we seem to have lost in the years since that white kid made his stand is the ability, the imagination, the willingness, to put ourselves into the skin of those who are not like us. I find it telling that Vice President Dick Cheney hews to the hard conservative line on virtually every social issue, except gay marriage. It is, of course, no coincidence that Cheney has a daughter who is a lesbian. Which tells me his position is based not on principle but, rather, on loving his daughter.

It is a fine thing to love your daughter. I would argue, however, that it is also a fine thing and in some ways, a finer thing, to love your neighbor's daughter, no matter her sexual orientation, religion, race, creed or economic status—and to want her freedom as eagerly as you want your own.

I believe in moral coherence. And Rule No. 1 is, you cannot assert your own humanity, then turn right around and deny someone else's.

If that makes me gay, fine.

As my anonymous correspondent ably demonstrates, there are worse things to be.

JANUARY 8, 2007

KORAN DEBATE ANOTHER REMINDER OF INTOLERANCE

On Thursday, Keith Ellison took his ceremonial oath of office as a Democratic representative from Minnesota using Thomas Jefferson's Koran. From this, we learn the following surprising fact: Thomas Jefferson owned a Koran.

Which probably shouldn't surprise us at all. Jefferson was renowned for his restless intellect and wide-ranging interests. Still, one hopes the tacit reminder that this Founding Father and author of American values did not fear the Koran will silence those who have condemned Ellison's decision to use that book for his swearing in. One hopes, but one does not expect.

After all, the objections raised by the congressman's critics are not exactly steeped in logic.

Take conservative columnist Dennis Prager, who wrote that Ellison's decision "undermines American civilization." Throughout history, he said, people of other faiths have taken their oaths using Christian Bibles. If you can't do that, he said, you shouldn't be allowed to serve in Congress.

Prager was echoed by a blowhard chorus. Virgil Goode, a Republican representative from Virginia, warned constituents that unless we get tough on immigration, we'll see many more Muslim congressmen demanding to use Korans. The American Family Association called for a law requiring the use of Bibles at swearing-in ceremonies. For sheer illogic, though, Roy Moore, he of the Ten Commandments rock at the Alabama courthouse, topped them all. He cited the constitutional principle of freedom of religion "without interference by government" in demanding Congress prevent Ellison from taking the oath on a Koran.

Lord, where to begin?

In the first place, Moore's argument refutes itself so effectively he must have been drinking when he wrote it.

In the second place, what does immigration have to do with it? Ellison was born in Detroit.

In the third place, I doubt his election presages a flood of Muslims in Congress, but if that happened, it would be because a majority of voters wanted it. Isn't that the very definition of democracy?

In the fourth place, contrary to what Prager thinks, this isn't the first time a politician has declined to take his oath on a Bible. Law Professor Jonathan Turley, writing in *USA Today*, reminds us that Presidents John Quincy Adams, Theodore Roosevelt and Herbert Hoover opted not to use Bibles. Jewish lawmakers have used Jewish holy books. President Franklin Pierce declined an oath altogether.

In the fifth place, it's stupid to require a man to take an oath on a book that has no meaning for him.

In the sixth place, what does it tell you that we're even having this conversation?

It tells me—reminds me—that there has always been a strain of intolerance in the American character, a reactionary streak that denies

American values under the guise of defending them. That strain rises periodically, enflamed by demagogues and opportunists like Charles Coughlin in the 1930s and Joe McCarthy in the '50s, but it feels stronger and less abashed now than it has in years.

It is paradoxical that the same nation that speaks seriously of electing Condoleezza Rice or Barack Obama to the presidency can also speak seriously of denying Keith Ellison his office because he is a Muslim. That's just the kind of country we are, I'm afraid. Not always sufficiently brave. So Muslims—doesn't matter whether we're talking Middle East crazies or a Midwest politician—become the latest brand name of our fears. Some people claim to defend American values that they're too faint-hearted to even understand.

And yet for all that, this week, a Muslim put his hand on Thomas Jefferson's Koran and swore to serve all the people of his district. Then he shook Virgil Goode's hand and invited him to have coffee.

Thank goodness we're that sort of country, too.

JANUARY 15, 2007

KING'S DREAM IS SUMMONS TO ACT, NOT JUST TO HOPE

And so Dream season rolls round again.

That's Dream, of course, as in "I Have A ..." We celebrate Martin Luther King Day today, which means schoolchildren dutifully reciting the great 1963 oration, television news dutifully replaying the grainy black-and-white footage—and many people dutifully missing the point.

At least, that's how it often seems to me.

In some ways, King is a victim of his own success. The controversial ideals he championed and for which he was killed—voting rights for all, access for all, liberty and justice for all—have become accepted to a degree he would have found difficult to believe.

The march he led, the one that troubled the president and riled the conservatives, has become revered as one of the signature moments of the American experience. And as a result, that speech he gave, that tough-minded recitation of American wrongs, that preacherly prophecy of American redemption, has become a Hallmark card, elevator Muzak, bland cliché.

I have a dream, the schoolchildren say. I have a dream, the newscast says. I have a dream, the people say. I have a dream. A dream. A dream.

They wax eloquent about the dreamer and the dream and, listening, you find yourself wondering if they realize that it was much more than a dream. That it was not, in other words, some airy-fairy castle in the sky to be reached by dint of hoping and wishing, but a noble place to which the nation might lift itself if people were willing to sacrifice and work. Nor did King counsel endless patience in expectation of that goal.

"We have also come to this hallowed spot," he said, standing at Lincoln's doorstep, "to remind America of the fierce urgency of *now*."

Over and over, he said it: "Now is the time. *Now* is the time."

None of which is to demean "I Have A Dream." To my mind, King's speech trails only Lincoln's address at Gettysburg on the list of the greatest public utterances in American history. But it seems to me that this most revered of speeches is also one of the least understood.

You see, King spoke to an audience that had been working for civil rights—not just dreaming. They were an audience of marchers and sit-in organizers, of boycotters and committers of civil disobedience. "I am not unmindful," he said, "that some of you have come here out of great trials and tribulations. Some of you have come fresh from narrow jail cells." Because these were people who had laid their bodies, their freedom, their time, their treasure, their very lives on the line for a cause they believed in.

I think of them when I am asked by young people, as I often am, "What can I do?" about the war in Iraq or the encroachment of civil rights, or the genocide in Darfur, or the continuing intransigence of racism. They hate these things, they say, but feel helpless to respond. "What can I do?"

It always amazes me that people who command technology their forebears could not have imagined can feel so powerless after those forebears, armed with little more than telephones and mimeograph machines, went out and changed the world.

"What can I do?"

I tell them to start by realizing that they *can* do. When did we become so narcotized, so benumbed and bereft, as to forget that?

As Margaret Mead once said, "Never doubt that a small group of thoughtful, committed citizens can change the world. Indeed, it is the only thing that ever has."

That is one of the most enduring lessons of Martin Luther King's life and career. One hopes that lesson is not lost on all the people quoting his most famous speech today.

It is a fine and noble thing to have a dream. But having a dream is no excuse for accepting an onerous status quo and waiting passively on "someday" to make things right. A dream is not an excuse. It's a responsibility.

And now is still the time.

JANUARY 22, 2007

ASKING MUSLIMS TO DO THEIR JOB ISN'T 'INTOLERANCE'

OK, let's say you fly into Minneapolis-St. Paul. Let's say you're carrying alcohol—rum from the Caribbean, a Merlot you found in Napa Valley. Let's say you try to hail a cab while carrying said alcohol.

Good luck. You're going to need it.

Three-quarters of the drivers serving the airport are Muslims, most from Somalia and, in recent years, many have refused to carry passengers carrying alcohol because Islam frowns on liquor. Dozens of passengers have reportedly been left stranded. Occasionally, even blind people using seeing-eye dogs have been refused passage by drivers citing Islamic teachings that the saliva of dogs is unclean.

After simmering for years, the issue has come to a boil. Last week, the local airport commission scheduled a public hearing to discuss stiffening penalties for the wayward cabbies. As things now stand, a driver who refuses to carry you and your booze has to go back to the end of the cab line and wait hours for another fare. According to a report in the *St. Paul Pioneer Press*, new rules have been proposed that would require a 30-day suspension for a first offense and revocation of a cabby's airport license for two years after the second.

Sounds good to me, but Khalid Elmasry disagrees. He's the spokesman for the Muslim American Society of Minnesota. Here's the society's idea: Color-code the taxis according to whether the drivers accept alcohol.

Yeah, because flying is not enough of a hassle already.

"We will not see this perfect solution," Elmasry wrote last week in *USA Today*, "even though it meets everyone's needs. In an environment of fear and misunderstanding of everything Muslim, tolerance has become too much to ask."

In a word: baloney. Out of deference to religious sensibilities, we'll make it all-beef baloney but still: baloney.

This is not intolerance. It's not Minnesota Rep. Keith Ellison, a Muslim, taking his oath of office on a Koran and being tortured for it by xenophobes.

Rather, it is a group of men who refuse to do their jobs because of a perceived conflict with their religious beliefs. You're entitled to your religious beliefs. You're not entitled to require your employer or customers to go to extraordinary lengths to accommodate those beliefs.

This was a particularly dubious fight for the cabbies to pick. In the first place: if this were as critical a religious issue as they would have us believe, why aren't Muslim cabbies all over the country refusing to haul liquor-bearing passengers?

In the second place: in the atmosphere of "fear and misunderstanding" Elmasry cites, it is foolish to needlessly invite negative attention. Why write Rush Limbaugh's script for him?

If this all sounds familiar to you, it's because we've seen this movie before. Two years ago, the news was full of Christian pharmacists who cited religious reasons for refusing to fill prescriptions for the "morning after" contraception pill or provide birth control to unmarried women. Different religion, same hubris, same eagerness to impose one's own moral standards upon others.

And what's next? Will the drivers refuse to serve gays or Jews or women without veils? Will they decline to ferry a customer to a bar or barbecue joint? Will we let everybody in every profession reject any customer whose race, culture, religion or moral choices offend?

No. Because that is anathema to this nation's ideals. And the sooner certain Muslim cabbies—and Christian pharmacists—understand that, the better. To stand shivering in a Minneapolis winter waiting on a color-coded taxi would prove "tolerance" only of religious extremists who think the world must accommodate itself to their beliefs.

You want a "perfect solution?" Fine, here it is: Muslim cabbies should do their jobs. Period.

APRIL 9, 2007

AFTER THE FLOOD, THE BIG EASY IS STILL A TARGET

Your home is a FEMA trailer.

There was a time when your home was a home like anybody else's, but that was before Hurricane Katrina drowned everything. Now your home is a trailer, where late at night you fix yourself a drink and talk to the dog about how it hurts to see your city in ruins, how frustrating it is trying to navigate a rebuilding process the local newspaper calls "nightmarish."

So one day, you are invited to appear on a panel in late March before a convention of newspaper editors in Washington. You were one of the most memorable voices in Spike Lee's HBO documentary, *When The Levees Broke*, and you and other survivors have come to exhort the editors to stay with the story, follow the rebuilding of a major American city at least as closely as they do Anna Nicole Smith, Britney Spears and other important newsmakers.

Afterward, this guy comes up, identifies himself as a columnist with the *Miami Herald*. You give him your card. It identifies you as Gralen B. Banks, managing director of a New Orleans consulting firm.

The columnist wants your response to something that's been circulating on the Internet. It was supposedly written by an emergency manager in Colorado, though different versions carry different points of origin.

The e-mail describes how the area has just recovered from a blizzard of "Biblical proportions"—44 inches of snow, winds up to 90 miles an hour, utility poles down, roads closed, communities cut off.

And yet, says the e-mail writer, 'George Bush did not come. FEMA did nothing. No one blamed the government. ... Jesse

Jackson or Al Sharpton did not visit. ... Nobody demanded $2,000 debit cards. No one asked for a FEMA trailer. No one looted. We did not wait for some affirmative action government to get us out of a mess created by being immobilized by a welfare program that trades votes for 'sittin at home' checks."

What's your response? Your response is to smile. A tolerant smile. A Lord-give-me-strength smile. You point out patiently, calmly, that no snowstorm compares to Hurricane Katrina. "When the snow melted," you say, "your city was still there, so you're comparing apples to transmissions."

But it is hard to stay patient and calm. It just gets to you, how niggardly, stupid and flat-out cold some of your own countrymen can be. Why, you ask, do they play this game of Whose Disaster Was Bigger? "What's the f------ point of that? We have a disaster and we expect help. Are we arrogant, are we wrong for expecting it? Why are you pissed off with us? What did we do other than ask for what anybody else would quite naturally ask for and in all likelihood get quicker than we did?"

People were not this nasty toward Miami after Hurricane Andrew. So what is it about you?

"New Orleans," you say, 'has always been known as the place where anybody can come. You're an accountant in real life and you want to be Marilyn Monroe? Do your thing. We ain't gon' say nothin'. But what did we do to you that would make you turn on us, that would make you say something like, 'We had 10 feet of snow, f--- 'em.' What were we, other than citizens in a position where something happened to us same way something could happen to you?"

You cannot take it in. It does not compute.

You are the son of a funky little river town once known as the place the world went to hear jazz and taste beignets and walk where Satchmo walked. But all that is part of another world now, another world 19 months gone and so five minutes ago.

Now you live in this new world of government forms and empty places and fools who think a snowstorm compares to the loss of everything you've ever known. So you smile ("Lord, give me strength") and you try to be patient and you try to explain it to them.

At night you go home. And home is a FEMA trailer.

APRIL 13, 2007

FIRING OF IMUS REMOVES LEADER OF SORRY BAND

Obviously, someone has put crack in the nation's drinking water.

What else can one think after the spasms of bigotry to which Mel Gibson, Isaiah Washington, Tim Hardaway and Michael Richards have treated us over the last nine months? That's a lot of stupid in a short period of time.

And then there's radio shock jock Don Imus who, as even polar bears must know by now, last week leveled racist and sexist insults against the Rutgers University women's basketball team, most of whom are black. Until then, the team was best known for a gritty season that brought them within a game of the championship. Now they are famous as the objects of a misbegotten attempt at banter between Imus and producer Bernard McGuirk.

"That's some rough girls from Rutgers," says Imus. "Man, they got tattoos ..."

"Some hard-core hos," observes McGuirk.

"That's some nappy-headed hos there," says Imus.

The resulting firestorm cost Imus many of his sponsors and his MSNBC simulcast. Thursday, CBS canceled his show outright.

And there are a few things that need saying here:

One, it is beyond pathetic that two grown men would use the reach and power afforded them as members of the media to mock the looks of a bunch of college girls.

Two, while it is fitting that Imus' slur has angered and energized the African-American community, one hopes we'll see this same indignation next time some idiot black rapper (paging Snoop Dogg) refers to black women in terms this raw or worse. Indeed, it's doubtful Imus would have even known the word "ho"—black slang for "whore"—had idiot black rappers not spent the last 20 years popularizing it.

Three, to make this about Don Imus is to miss the point.

There is something entirely too precious about all this, particularly the expressions of shock and disappointment by Imus' media friends and his corporate partners. To put it another way: What did Imus do last week that he has not done repeatedly? We're talking about a man who has built a career on verbal diarrhea. He has slurred women and gays and blacks and Jews. He once referred to Gwen Ifill as "the cleaning lady."

Yet none of that was enough to keep him out of radio's Hall of Fame, nor to keep such VIPs as Tom Brokaw, Chris Matthews, Tim Russert, John Kerry and John McCain off his show. So what's it mean that Imus finally is paying the piper, given that he has danced so long without paying a dime?

What's it mean, all this sound and fury about one stupid remark, when he is an avatar of a school of "entertainment" that stretches far beyond him to video channels and bookstores and TV screens? In this school, coarseness is its own justification, rudeness its own reward. One pushes boundaries of propriety not to enlighten, not to say something vital, not even to make people laugh. One pushes the boundaries because they are there. And the willingness to do so gets mistaken for courage and authenticity.

Don Imus ought to be ashamed of himself, but no more so than Kerry, Matthews, Brokaw, Biden and anybody else who lacked the wit to understand that the willingness to offend in and of itself represents neither courage nor authenticity. The question is, what are you offending for? If you are pushing boundaries, what are you pushing them toward?

It is painfully clear that Imus was pushing toward nothing, unless you count the gratification of his own ego and misanthropy.

What's sad isn't that he was willing to lead in that direction. What's sad is that so many of us were willing to follow.

AUGUST 12, 2007

REPLYING TO THOSE E-MAILS ABOUT VICK

You wanted to read my Michael Vick column? Sorry, that's not going to happen.

Let me be clear: If Vick sponsored dog fights and brutally killed canines who did not perform as he is alleged to have done, he's a despicable man. It wouldn't break my heart to see him caged up with a rabid dog while wearing raw sirloin strapped to his tender parts.

Problem is, that's pretty much all I have to say on the subject, and there's no way to get 615 words—about the length of a column—out of that. Actually, I hadn't planned to comment at all on the NFL star's indictment last month. That's not to say it's not an important story or that the allegations aren't sickening. Still, it's not, so far, a topic to which I think I could bring any particular insight.

So I'm not here to talk about Vick but, rather, about why certain of my readers so dearly *want* me to talk about him. I get these e-mails, you see. Anybody who's been a black columnist longer than 15 minutes knows the kind I'm talking about. They arrive reliably as the tides any time some African American gets in trouble. Inevitably, some Caucasian gentlemen will dare you to lay into this individual the way you "always" do white guys.

I'm not talking about the polite requests ("What's your take on this?"), but about the sneering demands. The "reasoning" seems to be that black malefactors get a pass from black pundits who'll tear a white guy a creative new orifice when he misbehaves. So the black pundit must prove himself to the white guy by tearing some black embarrassment to humanity a hole exactly equal in size and shape. That reasoning is long on smugness, long on entitlement, long on everything except, you know, fact.

Frankly, I doubt Jesse Jackson, Louis Farrakhan, Whitney Houston, Tim Hardaway, Isaiah Washington, New Orleans DA Eddie Jordan, Ray Nagin, the NAACP, Ice Cube, 50 Cent, Ludacris, the family of Martin Luther King, Jr. and other black folk who have been ripped and ridiculed in this space would agree that I give black folks a free ride. But again, we're not talking about facts here. For that matter, we're not talking about me, nor even about journalism.

No, what we're talking about is that some white people—emphasize: *some*—seem to feel they have a perfect right to demand, overtly and repeatedly, that a black professional prove himself to them. We're talking about the realization, as a black professional, that for them, you will forever be on probation, your mastery of your profession, your right to be there, constantly subject to demands for verification.

We're talking about the black lawyer second-guessed by the client who never spent a day in law school. About the black money manager whose clients won't accept her advice until it is seconded by her white partner. About the black cardiologist whose diagnoses are rejected by patients unwilling to accept them from a doctor of her gender and race.

And yes, I know some people would argue that this is only to be expected, that the very existence of affirmative action entitles white people to question the competence of black ones. That's a cop-out. I've said it before, I'll say it again: If affirmative action is defined as giving preferential treatment on the basis of gender or race, then no one in this country has received more than white men.

Still, though the rationalization is lame, it serves a purpose: It deflects us from thinking too hard how it must feel to learn that, even after years of education and apprenticeship, after the hard slog of working your way up and waiting your turn, some people will still find it problematic to accept you as a professional. Will still raise a hoop and regard you with an expectant stare.

They think I should prove myself to them by trashing Michael Vick? No.

I could not prove half as much in honoring that request as they prove in making it.

SEPTEMBER 26, 2007

ADD CONTEXT TO JENA DEBATE; IT'S IGNORANT TO EQUATE THIS SITUATION TO THE O.J. AND DUKE TRAVESTIES

Please indulge me as I answer an e-mail I received last week in response to a column decrying unequal justice as represented by the controversy in Jena, La. A fellow named John wrote:

"Your columns usually merit reading. But this time, You sound like the typical Black guy crying 'victim.'

"Leonard, you list instances of Black injustice and I'm sure there are many. However have you forgot about O.J.? He got away with murder Leonard. He killed his white wife! Or how about Sharpton and the Brawley case? Or the Duke case. I could go on and on. You want more respect for you and your race? Stop sounding like a nigger and start sounding and acting like a Black man. You'll get respect and justice. Try being a Black man all the time, not just when it fits your agenda."

John, thank you for writing. Here are a few words in response.

That column you disliked argued that Jena, where six black kids were initially charged with attempted murder after they gave a white kid a black eye and knocked him out, is part of a long pattern of the justice system being used to keep blacks in line.

You were one of a number of readers who wrote to remind me of Simpson. If the point of your reference to him, Tawana Brawley and the Duke lacrosse case was that the justice system has repeatedly and historically mistreated whites, too, on the basis of race, I'm sorry, but that's absurd. Not that those cases were not travesties. They were. And if those travesties leave you outraged, well, I share that feeling.

But, here's what I want you to do. Take that sense of outrage, that sense of betrayal, of having been cheated by a system you once thought you could trust, and multiply it. Multiply it by Valdosta and Waco and Birmingham and Fort Lauderdale and Money and Marion and Omaha and thousands of other cities and towns where black men and women were lynched, burned, bombed, shot, with impunity. Multiply it by the thousands of cops and courts that refused to arrest or punish even when they held photographs of the perpetrators taken in the act. Multiply it by a million lesser outrages. Multiply it by L.A. cops planting evidence. Multiply it by the black drug defendant who is 48 times more likely to go to jail than the white one who commits the same crime and has the same record. Multiply it by Abner Louima and Amadou Diallo. Multiply it by 388 years.

And then come talk to me about O.J. Simpson.

You may call all that "playing victim." I call it providing context. Jena did not happen in a vacuum. So this false equivalence, this pretense that the justice system as experienced by white people and black ones is in any way similar, is ignorant and obnoxious.

Much like your turning to a racial slur to describe how you think I "sound." I found that word interesting coming near the end of an e-mail whose tone, while critical, had, until that point, been reasonable. I suppose you just couldn't help yourself.

It says something about the intransigence, self-justification and retarded self-awareness of American racism that a man who uses the language you do would, in the same breath, offer advice to black folks seeking "respect and justice." Appreciate the effort, John, but I'm afraid you can't solve the problem.

See, you *are* the problem.

OCTOBER 14, 2007

YOU CALL IT A 'PRANK,' BUT I CALL IT TERROR

This will be a history of rope.

It strikes me that such a history is desperately needed just now. It seems the travesty in Jena, La., has spawned a ghastly trend. Remember how white students at Jena High placed nooses in a tree last year to communicate antipathy toward their African-American classmates? Now it's happening all over.

A noose is left for a black workman at a construction site in the Chicago area. In Queens, a woman brandishes a noose to threaten her black neighbors. A noose is left on the door of a black professor at Columbia University. And that's just last week. Go back a little further and you have similar incidents at the University of Maryland in College Park, at a police department on Long Island, on a Coast Guard cutter, in a bus maintenance garage in Pittsburgh.

Mark Potok, the director of the Intelligence Project of the Southern Poverty Law Center, told *USA Today*, "For a dozen incidents to come to the public's attention is a lot. I don't generally see noose incidents in a typical month. We might hear about a handful in a year."

The superintendent of schools in Jena famously dismissed the original incident as a "prank." It was an astonishing response, speaking volumes about the blithe historical ignorance of people who have found it convenient not to peer too closely at the atrocities of the past lest they be accidentally ... moved.

But watching this trend unfold, it occurs to me that maybe what we need here is the opposite of ignorance. Maybe what we need is information. Maybe what we need is a history of rope.

A history of rope would have to include, in 1904, Luther Holbert and his wife, who had their fingers chopped off and handed out as souvenirs. Holbert was beaten so badly one of his eyes came out. It hung by a thread. A large corkscrew was used to bore into the couple's flesh. It tore out big chunks of them each time it was withdrawn. A rope was used to tie them to the tree.

A history of rope would have to include, in 1917, Rufus Moncrief, who was beaten senseless by a mob. They used a saw to cut off his arms and otherwise mutilated him. The mob hanged Moncrief. Then, for good measure, they hanged his dog. Ropes were used for both.

A history of rope would have to include, in 1918, Mary Turner, burned alive in Valdosta, Ga. A man used a hog-splitting knife to slash her swollen stomach. The baby she had carried nearly to term tumbled out and managed two cries before the man crushed its head beneath his heel. A rope was used to tie Turner upside down in a tree.

A history of rope would include thousands of Turners, Moncriefs and Holberts. It would range widely across the geography of this nation and the years of the last two centuries. A history of rope would travel from Cairo, Ill., in 1909 to Fort Lauderdale in 1935 to Urbana, Ohio, in 1897 to Wrightsville, Ga., in 1903, to Leitchfield, Ky., in 1913 to Newbern, Tenn. in 1902. And beyond.

You might say the country has changed since then, and it has. The problem is, it's changing again.

It feels as if in recent years we the people have backward traveled from even the pretense of believing our loftiest ideals. It has become fashionable to decry excessive "political correctness," deride "diversity," sneer at the "protected classes." Code words sanding down hatred's rough edge. "State's rights" for the new millennium. And now, out come the nooses. Just a prank, the man says.

Mary Turner would argue otherwise. I find it useful to remember her, useful to be reminded of things we would rather forget. To remember her is to understand that there is no prank here.

A history of rope would drown your conscience in blood.

DECEMBER 2, 2007

MURDER IS THE GREATEST INJUSTICE OF ALL

And once again, this is how we die.

Fallen, crumpled, bleeding from a bullet's hole. Woman and child left to wail, left to mourn. Left.

It was, of course, not a "we" who died that way last week in Miami, but a "he," NFL star Sean Taylor, 24, shot in his home by a burglar. But maybe we can be forgiven, we African-American people in general, we African-American men in particular, for placing a "we" where others would a "he," for seeing in the fate of this singular individual all the brothers and sisters we have wept and mourned and given back to the soil. Maybe we can be forgiven for feeling the only difference is that the world knows his name and did not know theirs.

And this is how we die. We die in profligate numbers. Just under 15,000 Americans were murdered in 2006. Roughly half of them—7,421—were black. African Americans are 12 percent of the nation's population.

And this is how we die. We die young. Of the 7,421 African-American murder victims of 2006, more than 40 percent—3,028—were Taylor's age or less.

And this is how we die. We kill one another. Of the 3,303 African-American murder victims whose assailants are known to authorities, 92 percent were killed by other blacks.

It's easy to make too much of that last statistic. After all, murder, like other violent crime, tends to be a segregated thing. About 82 percent of white murder victims owe their demise to another white person, yet one never hears lamentations about the scourge of "white on white" crime. Violent crime is, more than anything, a matter of proximity and opportunity.

Still, with all that said, that difference of 10 percentage points of likelihood whispers a soft suggestion that sometimes, we don't much value us, that some of us have learned to see our lives the way the nation historically has: as cheap and lacking in worth. Note that even before three people were detained Friday, it was being taken for granted by some Internet posters and at least one African-American columnist that Taylor's assailant would prove to be black. That is a dangerous, and potentially embarrassing, assumption. But at the same time, no one will exactly be shocked if police end up parading disheveled black kids past television cameras.

Because this is how we die.

We die shot in the head and shot in the gut and shot in the back and shot in the chest and shot in the thigh. We die on asphalt and on concrete, and lying in bed and slumped against refrigerators and prostrate on gurneys in the back of ambulances hurtling down city streets and quietly inside, too, in the soul a little, at the carnage our communities become.

We die and it goes unremarked, die so much it's hardly news anymore. A child dies from random bullets or a famous man dies at a burglar's hand and the media are all over it, yeah. But 12 percent of the nation is 50 percent of the murder victims, and it's mainly business as usual. No government task force convenes to tell us why this is. No rallying cries ring from podiums and pulpits. Crowds do not march as they did in Jena, demanding justice.

But one could argue that murder is the greatest injustice of all. And life the most fundamental of civil rights.

We ought not—*I* ought not—deny Sean Taylor his singularity, his personhood, in the rush to make him a symbol. So let us say here for the record: No, this is not 7,421 murders. This is one. One heartbeat stilled. One child fatherless. One family shattered. One.

I understand all that. Still, maybe we can be forgiven for feeling that, in the broadest outlines, we've seen this story before. Because this is how we die. And yes, Sean Taylor is one man.

But he's also one more.

DECEMBER 9, 2007

WE MUST ALL LEARN TO LIVE TOGETHER

A few words before I go.

First off: happy holidays. Merry Christmas, happy Kwanzaa, happy Hanukkah. Barring something unforeseen, we won't talk again until the new year. Your humble correspondent is taking a few mental health days.

It probably isn't your idea of an ideal holiday spot, but I plan to spend one of those days at the U.S. Holocaust Memorial Museum in Washington, D.C. It's something I do most years around this time, though I find it difficult to explain why.

I guess if trees strung with light, malls crowded with shoppers and Christmas music filling the air impart a sense of festivity and rightness with the world, the shadowed halls of this monument to human hatred, human hubris and human resilience impart something I find equally valuable this time of year.

Call it a centeredness. Call it a somberness. Call it a sacredness.

If the holidays are about deliverance, those hours spent among the shoes of dead Jews and manifestoes of mass murder are a stark reminder of what we need deliverance from. Our own meanness. Our own smallness. The petty cruelties whispered into us by the worst angels of our nature.

Some of you will know that I had a very interesting spring and early summer. I wrote a column some people disliked, and it led to harassment and death threats from self-styled neo-Nazis under the tired delusion that paleness of skin equals mental, moral or physical superiority. It was a striking, stinking reminder of the seemingly bottomless potential for sheer stupidity that lives within each of us. And by that I mean, each of us.

As Sly and the Family Stone once memorably sang, "There is a yellow one that won't accept the black one that won't accept the red one that won't accept the white one." That's as succinct an encapsulation of the human condition as you'll ever hear.

To walk in the Holocaust Museum is to be reminded of the logical, inevitable result of that refusal to accept, that insistence upon declaring that some racial, sexual, religious or cultural fraction of us must live outside the circle of human compassion. After all, there was nothing terribly new about what the Nazis did. Their sole innovation was to institutionalize hatred and mechanize murder so that 11 million people—six million of them Jews—could be most efficiently put to death.

But this idea that some of us are less than the rest of us, that some of us are roaches, vermin, viruses, parasites, infestations, beasts or subhumans to whom one owes no duty of human decency or commiseration, didn't start with the Nazis. It is as old as Cain. As widespread as the common cold.

Yet we don't learn, never learn. Dead Jews become dead Rwandans become dead Bosnians become dead Darfurians, yet still some of us mouth pious hatreds with a smug certitude and offhand arrogance accessible only to the deeply, profoundly and utterly wrong.

I'm reminded of an older white lady who called me once to thank me for a column decrying some racial insult. She had a grandmother voice, a voice that sounded like cookies in the oven smell and she wanted me to know she admired black people, supported black people. Then she added in a conspiratorial whisper, "It's the Jewboys I can't stand." Because everybody is sure their own hatreds are just.

We've got to live together.

Sly Stone sang that, too, in his song. If that seems, almost 40 years later, a faded hope, it is, nevertheless, a hope, and one you clutch instinctively as shrunken Jews stare out from photos on a wall, across a gulf of 60 years. A reminder. A warning. A testimony.

And meantime, somewhere far away, the trees are filled with light, the air is laced with hymns of joy.

FEBRUARY 6, 2008

REJECTING FEMINISM MAKES NO SENSE

Brace yourself. I'm going to use a word that offends folks. I'm talking the "F" word.

Feminist.

This woman sent me an e-mail Monday, and it got me thinking. See, in describing herself, she assured me she was not "a 'women's libber'"—the late 1960s equivalent of feminist. She also said she was retired from the U.S. Navy. There was, it seemed to me, a disconnect there: She doesn't believe in women's liberation, yet she is retired from a position that liberation made possible.

Intrigued, I asked my 17-year-old daughter if she considers herself a feminist. She responded with a mildly horrified *No*. This, by the way, is the daughter with the 3.75 GPA who is currently pondering possible college majors including political science, psychology and ... women's studies. I asked her to define "feminist."

There began a halting explanation that seemed to suggest shrillness wrapped around obnoxiousness. Abruptly, she stopped. "It's hard to explain," she said.

Actually, it's not. Jessica Valenti, author of *Full Frontal Feminism: A Young Woman's Guide to Why Feminism Matters*, calls it the I'm-Not-A-Feminist-But syndrome. As in the woman who says, "I'm not a feminist, but ... " and then "goes on to espouse completely feminist values. I think most women believe in access to birth control, they want equal pay for equal work, they want to fight against rape and violence against women."

"Feminist," it seems, has ended up in the same syntactical purgatory as another once-useful, now-reviled term: liberal. Most people endorse what that word has historically stood for—integration, child labor laws, product safety—yet they treat the word itself like anthrax. Similarly, while it's hard to imagine that any young woman really wants to return to the days of barefoot, pregnant and making meatloaf, many now disdain the banner under which their gender fought for freedom. They scorn feminism even as they feast at a table that feminism prepared.

Says Valenti, "The word has been so effectively misused and so effectively mischaracterized by conservatives for so long that women are afraid to identify with it. They'll say everything under the sun that's feminist, but they won't identify with it because they've been taught feminists are anti-men, feminists are ugly."

Deborah Tannen agrees. She is a professor of linguistics at Georgetown University and author of a number of books on gender and communication, including *You're Wearing That? Understanding Mothers and Daughters in Conversation*. "The reason, I believe, is that meanings of words come from how they're used. And since the word feminist is used as a negative term rather than a positive one, people don't want to be associated with it."

With apologies to Malcolm X, they've been had, they've been hoodwinked, they've been bamboozled. And it's sad. I've lost track of how many times, visiting high schools or teaching college classes, I have met bright girls juggling options and freedoms that would've been unthinkable a generation ago, smart young women preparing for lives and careers their foremothers could not have dreamt, yet if you use the "F" word, they recoil.

We have lost collective memory of how things were before the F-word. Of the casual beatings. Of the casual rape. Of words like "old maid" and "spinster." Of abortion by coat hanger. Of going to school to find a man. Of getting an allowance and needing a husband's permission. Of taking all your spirit, all your dreams, all your ambition, aspiration, creativity and pounding them down until they fit a space no larger than a casserole dish.

"I'm not a feminist, but ... ?" That's a fraud. It's intellectually dishonest. And it's a slap to the feminists who prepared the table at which today's young women sup.

So for the record, I am a feminist. My daughter is, too.

She doesn't know it yet.

MARCH 2, 2008

ADVICE TO A YOUNG COLLEAGUE

Last week, a fellow journalist wrote to ask me for help.

His name is David Tintner, and he's a senior at Cooper City High, where he's the editor of the school paper. Recently, he wrote a column criticizing those who wear what he regards as "an extremely offensive symbol": the Confederate battle flag. David says a group of students known on campus as "the Redneck Nation" took exception. A gang of them cornered him at lunch to yell at him. They've made threats and tried to stare him down.

Despite this, David writes that he "found it really cool that so many people actually read the paper. One kid who usually associates himself with the 'Rednecks' actually came up to me and said that after reading my column he put all of his Confederate flag attire away and won't wear it anymore. However, the rest of the 'Redneck Nation' seems to have it in for me now."

David added: "I'm sure you deal with this sort of thing all of the time. I mean what's a good opinion piece if it doesn't make someone mad right? I was just hoping you could offer a few words of wisdom, I would really appreciate it."

Dear David:

My first words of wisdom would be, watch your back. It sounds as if some of the folks you're dealing with aren't screwed on too tight.

That said, let me offer you some answers to the arguments typically advanced by defenders of this American swastika.

They will tell you the Civil War was not about slavery. Remind them that the president and vice president of the so-called "Confederate States of America" both said it was.

They will tell you that great-great grandpa Zeke fought for the South, and he never owned any slaves. Remind them that it is political leaders—not grunts—who decide whether and why a war is waged.

They will tell you the flag just celebrates heritage. Remind them that "heritage" is not a synonym for "good." After all, Nazis have a heritage, too.

I wish I could say any of that will do you any good. Problem is, it's logic, and we live in a time where people are less able to accept, understand or respond to logic.

If you approach writing your column as I do mine, you see it as an attempt, not to hammer the other side down, but to persuade persuadable minds. Unfortunately, persuadable minds are an endangered species these days. You and I have the misfortune to live in a time and media culture when people think that the loudness of the argument matters more than the coherence of it, when threats and intimidation substitute for logic and reason, a time of made-up "facts" and ideological "truth," a time when critical thinking is a lost art and ignorance is ascendant.

By way of example: I guarantee you the three lines of argument I gave you above will earn me loud rebuke from Confederate flag fetishists. They will insult my ancestry and intelligence, throw hissy fits of indignation. The one thing they will not be able to do—this matters to me, though it will not matter to them—is refute a single word of what I said.

I tell my column-writing classes that if ever you propound an argument and all the other side can do in response is have a tantrum, you may consider yourself the winner, by default, of that debate. It is, I grant you, small consolation, but I commend it to you anyway. If you insist on trying to be a reasonable person in an unreasonable time, you should get used to small consolations.

You can find another in what you yourself wrote about the young man who disavowed his Confederate gear because of your column. People do still read us, we do still have an effect and, once in a very great while, we can even take credit for change.

And you're right. That is the very definition of cool.

APRIL 2, 2008

CAN YOU SEE THE PROMISED LAND OF EQUALITY?

"I may not get there with you."—Martin Luther King Jr., April 3, 1968

A few words about the Mountaintop and the Promised Land.

On the last night of his life, Martin Luther King Jr. famously told an audience in Memphis that he had stood on the one and seen the other. He did not define the Promised Land, but he did not need to. That audience of striking sanitation workers and their supporters, those long-suffering women and men who erupted in cries and shouts, already knew.

The Promised Land was where you did not have to march for your dignity. It was where you did not have to sing for your freedom. It was where there was no need for speeches to verify your humanity. The Promised Land was that sacred place where all of God's children would stand as equals on level, fertile ground.

Friday marks 40 years since King was killed. And the search for that promised land has shrunken until it fits inside an old riddle, the one that asks whether the glass is half empty or half full.

I'm moved to this conclusion by a column published last week in the *Washington Post* by Shankar Vedantam, who writes on issues of human behavior. Vedantam's piece recounted two studies. The first, by Philip Mazzocco of Ohio State University and Mahzarin Banaji of Harvard, asked white volunteers a question: If they were to be reborn black in America, how much money would they ask for to cover the lifetime disadvantages? Most gave amounts less than $10,000. Mind you, to go a lifetime without television, they wanted $1 million.

When it was explained to them that being black meant that they would earn a fraction of what whites earn, suffer higher rates of infant mortality, be unemployed at a rate nearly twice the national average, be more likely to be poor and live at dramatically greater risk of being jailed or killed, whites raised their asking prices a hundredfold.

That blacks and whites live different realities is hardly news. What's intriguing is the reason, as suggested by the second study. Yale University researcher Richard Eibach found that whites and blacks employ different measures in assessing racial progress. Whites judge it by looking at how far we have come ("How can you say there's still racism when we have an Oprah Winfrey and a Barack Obama?") Blacks judge it by how far we have yet to go ("How can you say there's no racism when police keep stopping me for no reason?")

So each side of America's most intractable debate chooses the path of least resistance, the path that shoves the onus for change off to the other side. Thus, whites can feel justified in noting the incredible progress we have made, and blacks can feel equally justified in feeling still victimized, and it never seems to occur to any of us that both views are true, that they do not contradict one another. We never seem to realize that we are having an argument over how much water is in the glass.

I guess you can't see that from the narrow valley of cynicism and self-interest. But in his last public exhortation, King called us up from there, called us up to the grand view, the big picture, the mountaintop. From there, he said, you could see the Promised Land.

Whites, Eibach told the *Post*, see that promised land—racial equality—as an ideal, something it would be nice to achieve someday. Blacks see it as a necessity, something you work to make manifest here and now. The urgency embodied in the one view, and the luxuriant indolence in the other, speak volumes about the cognitive distance between blacks and whites.

And explain why, rather than being inspired by the possibilities glimpsed from a mountain peak, we trudge through a valley arguing how much water is in the glass. Is it half empty? Half full?

I guess that would depend on how thirsty you are.

APRIL 6, 2008

DETROIT MAYOR: 'YOU SHOULD BE ASHAMED'

Dear Detroit Mayor Kwame Kilpatrick:

So it's a black thing? Not a sleaze thing, not a betrayal of the public trust thing, not a breaking the law thing? Just a black thing?

This would seem to be the message of the recent rally thrown for you at a black church in Detroit. It was, to judge from media reports, quite the shindig. Standing room only, gospel choirs doing that gospel choir thing, posters in red, black and green, chants of "I can make it through the storm!"

The church's Cardinal Ronald Hewitt seems to have caught the spirit of the event when he declared, "Kwame Kilpatrick just happens to be the symbol of bold, uncompromising black power in this city. We're not giving him to you. He is ours."

And there you were, with your bold, uncompromising self, standing in the pulpit proclaiming, "I will humbly serve you till the day I die." O.J. Simpson and Michael Jackson would be proud.

I'm not comparing your alleged crimes to the murder and child molestation the courts say those two brothers didn't commit. All you did—allegedly—was swear under oath that you weren't intimately involved with your chief of staff, until a series of steamy text messages showed you two were getting busy like bunnies. Oh, and fire three cops who had gotten too close to the truth. Oh, and approve an $8.4 million settlement when lawyers produced said text messages.

But the reason I compare you to Juice and Mike is that, like them, when you got in trouble, you came running to us. The African-American community, I mean.

Granted, they had further to run. Before the cuffs went on, Jackson and Simpson couldn't have found black America with a road map. The jock had ensconced himself in chi chi Brentwood where he was said to have built a world in which about the only thing black was the busboys at the four-star restaurants. The moonwalker had—one of his top aides told me this once—peeled his skin the color of bones and carved himself a nose that would not be out of place on Tinker Bell, because his African features were abhorrent to him.

Yet, to listen to Jackson's brother Jermaine and Simpson's lawyer, Johnnie Cochran, during their respective trials, they were some combination of Emmett Till, Rosa Parks and Kunta Kinte, targeted for the color of their skin, not the content of their criminal files.

"A modern-day lynching," said Jermaine, while Cochran said freeing Simpson would be a blow against racism. And black folks cheered the acquittals of these men like the Freedom Train had come.

It has become standard for high profile brothers in trouble (think R. Kelly, Marion Barry, Mike Tyson) to wrap themselves—or be wrapped—in the flag of racial victimization. The claim that someone has been mistreated on account of race resonates powerfully for black people in a nation where the Jena 6, Genarlow Wilson, Marcus Dixon, Hurricane Katrina, and other abominations are both recent memory and ever-present fear. Black folks tend to close ranks first and ask questions later when one of our own is in trouble, because we know the unfairness this country is capable of.

I honor my people for that.

But I'm sick of seeing our generosity cynically abused, our genuine fears manipulated, by brothers who have flat-out misbehaved. How often have we wasted political capital making racial martyrs out of guys like you?

As Public Enemy once said, "Some blacks act devil, too." We ought to remember that and guard our political capital more closely.

Frankly, Mr. Mayor, you remind of me of Eliot Spitzer, but without the class. What he did to a prostitute, you're doing to a people.

For that, sir, you should be ashamed.

JUNE 29, 2008

OBAMA MUST CONFRONT MUSLIM ISSUE

It is not difficult to understand why Barack Obama has a fear of scarves.

In the 17 months he's been pursuing the presidency, the senator has faced a crude and shameless campaign from conservative pundits, GOP functionaries and assorted ignoramuses in the peanut gallery to prove him a secret Muslim—a "Manchurian candidate," as one put it—trained from birth to subvert America from within and, I don't know, make us all eat falafels or something.

On about a half-second of intelligent reflection, the flaw in that theory is apparent: If unfriendly forces had indeed inserted a *secret* Muslim among us, said Muslim would have blonde hair, blue eyes, flag pins out the wazoo and a name like Joe Smith. Too bad intelligent reflection is a stranger to the people in question. With a grim fanaticism, they seize upon every perceived crumb of Obama's "Muslim-ness" to press their case, using everything from his middle name to his disdain for the cheap patriotism of the American flag lapel pin to a photo of him wearing native dress on a trip to Somalia.

So it's easy to see why workers for his campaign barred two women wearing hijabs, Muslim head scarves, from sitting behind him, within range of TV cameras, at a June 16 rally in Detroit. When someone is throwing at you, you don't hand him rocks.

But that doesn't make what the workers did right.

Yes, Obama apologized profusely. Good for him. It would be easier to take the apology seriously, though, if: a) somewhere in the last year of manifold denials that he is a Muslim, Obama had found the time, space or guts to point out that there's nothing wrong with being a Muslim, particularly in a nation that enshrined religious freedom in its founding documents; b) he hadn't spent so much time treating the American Muslim community as one does the carrier of a contagious disease.

Indeed, as the *New York Times* reported last week, members of that community are feeling well and truly snubbed by Obama, who has visited a number of churches and synagogues, but has yet to find his way to a single mosque.

Again, the politics of this are no mystery. Obama has spent the last year and a half being pilloried as the Other, representative of something so alien and strange to American values that even greeting his wife with a simple fist bump is fodder for a week of commentary.

He is required to walk an unprecedented political tightrope, to be one part John F. Kennedy, one part Jackie Robinson. More, he is required to prove his American-ness like no other candidate before him. Pictures of him speaking in a mosque would not, putting it mildly, be helpful.

But see, the thing that has made Obama a phenomenon is this sense that he Gets It, that he won't play the same old games by the same old rules. He comes across as a man brave enough to reason and to expect that voters will do the same, a man brave enough to treat intelligent adults like intelligent adults. His campaign, more than most, is an implicit promise to never put that which is politic above that which is right.

This standoffishness toward American Muslims is a denial of all those things.

Until Sept. 11, 2001, that community was poised for assimilation, poised to submerge itself in the American mainstream like the Jews, Irish and Italians before them. The actions of a handful of their co-religionists on that fateful day wrecked that trajectory beyond recognition and unleashed something base and ugly in the American character.

Muslims were snatched from the threshold of acceptance, painted once again as the alien and vaguely threatening Other. Can you imagine how that must feel? It is galling and painful to see yourself reduced to a caricature based on someone else's fears.

And Barack Obama should know that better than most.

NOVEMBER 5, 2008

'WE' ARE FINALLY PART OF 'WE THE PEOPLE'

"For the first time in my adult lifetime I am really proud of my country. And not just because Barack has done well, but because I think people are hungry for change."—Michelle Obama, Feb. 18, 2008

I always thought I understood what Michelle Obama was trying to say.

You are familiar, of course, with what she actually did say, which is quoted above. It provided weeks of red meat for her husband's opponents, who took to making ostentatious proclamations of their own unwavering pride in country.

But again, I think I know what the lady meant to say. Namely, that with her husband, this brown-skinned guy with the funny name, making a credible run for the highest office in the land, she could believe, for the first time, that "we the people" included her.

It is, for African Americans, an intoxicating thought almost too wonderful for thinking. Yet, there it is. And here we are, waking up this morning to find Barack Obama president-elect of these United States. In a sense, it is unfair—to him, to us—to make Tuesday's election about race. Whatever appeal Obama may have had to African Americans and white liberals eager to vote for a black candidate is, I believe, dwarfed by his appeal to Americans of all stripes who have simply had enough of the politics of addition by division as practiced by Karl Rove and his disciples, enough of the free-floating anger, the holiday from accountability, the nastiness masquerading as righteousness, the sheer intellectual dishonesty, that have characterized the era of American politics that ends here.

But in the end, after all that, there still is race.

And it would be a sin against our history, a sin against John Lewis and Viola Liuzzo, against James Reeb and Lyndon Johnson, against Fannie Lou Hamer and Martin Luther King, against all those everyday heroes who marched, bled and died 40 years ago to secure black people's right to vote, not to pause on this pinnacle and savor what it means. It would be a sin against our generations, against slaves and freedmen, against housemen and washerwomen, against porters and domestics, against charred bodies hanging in southern trees, not to be still and acknowledge that something has happened here, and it is sacred and profound.

For most of the years of the American experiment, "we the people" did not include African Americans. We were not included in "we." We were not even included in "people."

What made it galling was all the flowery words to the contrary, all the perfumed lies about equality and opportunity. This was, people kept saying, a nation where any boy might grow up and become president. Which was only true, we knew, as long as it was indeed a boy and as long as the boy was white.

But as of today, we don't know that anymore. What this election tells us is that the nation has changed in ways that would have been unthinkable, unimaginable, flat-out preposterous, just 40 years ago. And that we, black, white and otherwise, better recalibrate our sense of the possible.

There was something bittersweet in watching Michelle Obama lectured on American pride this year, in seeing African Americans asked to prove their Americanness when our ancestors were in this country before this country was. There was something in it that was hard to take, knowing that we have loved America when America did not love us, defended America when it would not defend us, believed in American ideals that were larger than skies, yet never large enough to include us.

We did this. For years unto centuries, we did this. Because our love for this country is deep and profound. And complicated and contradictory. And cynical and hard.

Now it has delivered us to this singular moment, Barack Obama is president-elect of the United States.

And we the people should be proud.

JANUARY 19, 2009

YEARS OF STRUGGLE, SACRIFICE BRING US TO THIS HISTORIC DAY

"My soul looks back and wonders how I got over."—Clara Ward

And I wish Rosa were here.

She made history by refusing to give up her seat. It was just over 53 years ago, on a cold December night in Montgomery, and something got into her that said, Enough, no more. No more laughing when she was not amused, no more scratching where she did not itch, no more giving up a seat she had paid for with U.S. currency earned from the sweat of her own brow, just because the man who wanted the seat was white and she was not. No more. Call the police, bus driver. Rosa would be sitting there when they arrived.

I wish Rosa could be here to see Barack Obama seated before the U.S. Capitol, waiting for history to call his name.

Call it a lament for the long departed. Ever since that day in November when what could not happen did, I've repeatedly had occasion to catch myself in the act of wishing so-and-so could be here to see what has transpired. Some of the names are personal—a little white girl came up to my mother once and tried to rub off the darkness her grandmother had told her was dirt; I keep wishing Mom could be here.

Most of the names are historical—heroes of the civil rights years, both sung and unsung. I wish Mother Pollard, the old woman who said during the Montgomery bus boycott, "My feets is tired, but my soul is rested" could be here. I wish Fannie Lou Hamer, whose heart, but never her spirit, was broken by Mississippi intransigence, could be here. I wish Emmett Till, Jimmie Lee Jackson, Goodman, Chaney and Schwerner, Viola Liuzzo and all the other martyrs were here.

And I wish Malcolm and ol' Bull were here.

Theophilus Eugene Connor—they called him Bull—was the commissioner of public safety in Birmingham, Ala., who brought tanks, police dogs and high-pressure hoses to the streets because he didn't believe America's promises ever should be extended to all Americans. Malcolm X was a prophet of black rage who rejected racial integration because he didn't think America's promises ever would be extended to all Americans.

I wish those men, who agreed on America's limitations if on nothing else, could be here to see that they were wrong, here for this startling moment when America affirms her defining promise, the one that begins with truths held self-evident.

And yes, on this day we honor his memory and his martyrdom, I wish Martin Luther King were here to see a Dream coming true.

Did he expect this moment? Did he feel it coming as he prophesied from the steps of the Lincoln Memorial? Could he see it from where he stood on the Mountaintop?

I suppose it's only natural to be caught looking back as America plunges forward upon a milestone. Only natural to think of how much and how many and how long it took to get here. Only natural to be thankful for what you have lived to see and to lament those who did not.

All those years of struggle, all those hymns and promises and prayers and days when you didn't know where to go or how to get there but only that you had to move. And now look where it has led.

You mourn those who did not get to see, but you also realize the gospel song is wrong, because your soul looks back and knows exactly how you got over. You got over because of Fannie's grit and Malcolm's rage, because of Rosa's stubbornness and Emmett's blood. You got over because of Martin's dream.

They are dead now, but those things they gave are deathless. They live through you, passing down to generations not yet born—something to keep you moving when you don't know where you're going, or how, only that you have to go. You close your eyes, wishing all those people were here. Then your eyes come open and you realize.

They are.

PART THREE:

FORWARD FROM THIS MOMENT

238   LEONARD PITTS, JR.

BUTCHERING THE BIBLE IS PRETEND PC PROGRESS

(And) God created man in his own image, in the image of God created he him; male and female created he them.

And male and female did, in their turn, create political correctness to be a boon upon the earth and manifest joy and understanding to all the diverse creatures therein.

But lo, political correctness did fail in these tasks, did instead sow division and confusion upon the land. And verily, male and female did see the chaos and woe they had wrought, but did not repent of it and carried it wickedly even unto the very gates of heaven.

Ahem.

Are you ready for the PC Bible?

Ready or not, the folks at Oxford University Press have rewritten the New Testament and the Psalms to purge them of their sexism, racism and social insensitivity. They have enlightened the Lord—an act of presumption that makes me fear standing close to them on a cloudy day. Or even a clear one.

In the new Bible, the Father and the Son become the Parent and the Child. God no longer rules a "kingdom," as that word has a "blatantly ... patriarchal character," according to the editors. They've also cut references to the evil of darkness in deference to African-American sensibilities. Nor will there be any more talk of the "right hand" of God, as this may offend the left-handed.

And so, "Our Father which art in Heaven, Hallowed be thy name. ... Thy Kingdom come" now reads: "Father-Mother, hallowed be your name, may your dominion come."

Really rolls off the tongue, doesn't it?

I confess to selective badgering. I have no beef with rewritings designed to clarify the Bible's arcane language. But clarification is not the aim here. Political correctness is, driven by the underlying assumption that it is possible or even desirable to impose uniformity upon humanity. The Oxford Press' Bible butchery bespeaks a trend toward what I will call petty equality—a cut-rate conformity in which we obsess on meaningless, minuscule details that give us the illusion of social progress. We seem to have stopped pressing for the real thing.

Frankly, I'm less concerned with darkness connoting evil in the Bible than I am with it connoting evil at the ATM.

Less concerned with the "patriarchal character" of God's kingdom than I am with the patriarchal character of the American workplace.

And—insensitive lout that I am—I'm not concerned with the rights of the left-handed at all.

How come there's never a plague of locusts around when you need one?

The first English translation of the Bible was completed in 1388. Can we all agree that a 607-year-old text is likely to contain antiquated references that will surely offend somebody, especially if that somebody looks hard enough? Can we further agree to accept, reject or ruminate upon the book for what it has to offer instead of torturing its language in the name of some grotesque parody of progress?

Are we—blacks, women, lefties—really that thin-skinned?

I am reminded of children—the picky, jealous carping when they think a sister or brother is getting more goodies than they are. So the unwary parent ends up counting out pieces of popcorn by hand, dispensing Kool-Aid with a measuring cup—enforcing a petty equality that has nothing to do with real equality and everything to do with shutting the little beggars up.

I know we live in whiny, sissified times but, really, are we that bad? That insecure? That dumb?

I have to believe we're not. And yet, seeing the makers of this new scripture bestow their demeaning "equality" upon southpaws, blacks, women and anyone else who might feel marginalized by the biblical "bias" of long-dead right-handed white males, I'm not so sure.

I find the new scripture more offensive than the supposed defamations it purports to correct. If heaven is PC, the other place is starting to look a whole lot better.

DECEMBER 6, 1995

DJ'S REBELLION A REMINDER THAT REVOLUTIONARY PEOPLE ARE US

Sometimes, revolution is a quiet sound. As subtle as the jutting of a jaw or the planting of feet. As soft as an explosion in the soul.

Remember the bus? Ordinary bus under an ordinary twilight in an ordinary town? Remember the white man who got on and the black woman who refused to get up? Remember what she said?

No.

Sometimes, revolution is a single word.

Marcel Thornton said it just the other day. A 29-year-old disc jockey from station WERQ-FM in Baltimore, he went to the march of a million men, listened to the cry for personal responsibility, returned to work and said no. No more songs about girls with their legs in the air and boys "hard as a roll of quarters." No more tunes about drug-fueled joys and the romance of violent death. No.

It will not surprise you to hear that Marcel Thornton no longer has a job.

Sometimes, revolution requires sacrifice.

The question is, what are you willing to sacrifice for? Where will you draw the line? It's a very personal thing, choosing the point at which revolution becomes necessary. And rightly so. Revolution is dangerous business. And revolution catches fire sometimes.

It happened 40 years ago on that bus. Ordinary bus under an ordinary twilight in an ordinary town, it gave rise to an extraordinary movement of marchers and martyrs that transfigured the nation and inspired the world.

Yes, revolution fizzles sometimes, too.

Maybe that's what will happen with Marcel Thornton. Maybe he'll reconsider, maybe his employer will have a change of heart, or maybe he'll just sink from public view like a pebble in an ocean— forgotten harbinger of a change that was never made.

But thank him anyway, because he's done us a good deed here. He's reminded us of the nature of revolution.

Lord knows we needed it.

Often someone faces a deplorable condition and asks, "What can I do?" It comes with a shrugging of shoulders and a lifting of brows as if to emphasize, I am ordinary, I am solitary, I am only me. Change is not within my power.

You sense in it not just helplessness, but deferral. Give me someone larger than me, it says, a lightning bolt of a person, and then I will help make revolution.

Of course, revolution does not recruit giants or lightning bolts— it makes them. Some of us have forgotten that. Small wonder.

The Greed Decade and the Information Age have bequeathed us mass anonymity and caused us to forget our own power. We have become taillights in a traffic jam, faces in a shopping mall, citizens of the "virtual" community. We cocoon on the couch with a pint of Haagen Dazs and some rentals from Blockbuster—small in the presence of multinational Goliaths, shadowed in the klieg lights of the stars. And we wonder, some of us, if anybody else is out there and if so, do they feel the way we do?

Isolated. And more, deeply apprehensive about the state of this union: children dying at children's hands, sick cruelty rising in our communities and culture like bile in the throat, Washington playing cynical games of divide and conquer and, most of all, like Dorothy stranded on the road to Oz, the rest of us, lost in a quagmire of "family values" clichés, trying to find our way back to simple decency.

"Give us Perot!" we cry. "Give us Powell!" Give us a leader, a lightning bolt, someone who will make revolution.

But revolution is both simpler and more complex than that.

An ordinary woman on an ordinary bus refused to assent to a system that said she was secondary and so forced a mighty nation to own up to its highest principles and reconsider what it means to be free.

Now an ordinary DJ at an ordinary radio station refuses to assent to music that debases humankind. Maybe some of those who make the music will finally ask themselves why—and, perhaps, exercise some personal responsibility of their own.

Sometimes, revolution is a single word.

Sometimes, revolution is in our grasp and we don't even know it.

SEPTEMBER 26, 1996

HEAR GOD IN WHISPERS, NOT THUNDER

It has become axiomatic that just about anyone who invokes God in public these days is seeking to hijack either your pocket or your politics.

We have created God in our own image, endowed Him with our characteristics. Small wonder that when people come before us claiming to speak with His voice, what we hear usually speaks only of human frailties and fears. God wants a yes vote on Proposition A! God wants you to send $100 to Rev. Jim! God wants you to elect a new school board!

They say they speak with the voice of God, but they don't. This isn't the voice that whispers when raindrops fall. Rather, it's a thunder of insecurity, a roar of self-righteousness, a clamoring racket of religious and political hacks all claiming a hotline to heaven.

I guess that's why Chris Carrier's story resonates. I guess it's why I'm struggling to conceive what seems inconceivable.

You see, Carrier, of Coral Gables, was abducted in 1974, when he was 10. His captor burned him with cigarettes, punctured his skin with an ice pick, shot him in the head and left him to die in the Everglades. The boy survived, though he lost sight in one eye. No one was ever arrested.

Then, recently, a man confessed to the crime and Carrier went to see him. He found David McAllister, a 77-year-old ex-con, frail, blind and living in a North Miami Beach nursing home that reeks of excrement. And Carrier befriended him. Began dropping by every day to visit, read to him from the Bible and pray with him.

No arrest is forthcoming; the statute of limitations on the crime is long past. Carrier says that's fine with him. "When I look at him," he told a reporter, "I don't stare at my abductor and potential murderer. I stare at a man, very old, very alone and scared."

First thought: Is Carrier crazy? Maybe. But if so, it's a good crazy. Or at least, a crazy that gives pause.

The man is serious about God. I don't say that because he has a master's degree in divinity and until recently was the director of youth ministries at his church. Nor because by the time you read this, he will have moved to Texas, where he and his wife and two daughters plan to open a Christian bookstore.

I say it because he bowed alongside a man who tried to kill him.

I know I couldn't do it. The same probably goes for any number of TV preachers and pious politicians. We lack the humility, I think. We haven't the guts or the conviction.

Yet at the same time, those same sellers of sanctimony fill our political and social arenas, preying like hawks upon troubled minds that just want to reach a state of grace.

It's worth noting that Chris Carrier didn't stump for money, a vote, or "family values." Instead he tried against all logic to redeem one weak and dirty little scrap of man. His deed reminds me of something I heard once in a gospel song: Maybe God is trying to tell you something.

It's a quaint notion, I'll grant you. Does anyone still believe the deity speaks in a voice that fills the stillnesses? Isn't that just a conceit we wished up one day out of loneliness, a way of avoiding the idea that we might be unaccompanied in the universe?

I don't offer an answer, only an observation: believing gets hard sometimes. Because we have created God in our own image, and it's not a pretty sight.

So I'm glad Carrier did this crazy deed. It strikes me as an affirmation of things I'd like to believe. That the highest work of a lifetime is to become a truly human being. That courage sometimes disguises itself in unconventional forms. And that divinity often speaks not in the crash of thunder, but in the soft murmur of rain.

JANUARY 16, 1997

CHILDREN DESERVE A CHILDHOOD

Six-year-old girls should not wear makeup. Dirt, freckles and pigtails, yes, but not lipstick, rouge and eyeliner, not outside of fantasy sessions in Mom's makeup mirror.

These are things I believe unalterably. I suspect many people do. But they are things that have gone largely unsaid in the discussion of the death of child beauty queen JonBenet Ramsey, who was found strangled and sexually assaulted in the basement of her parents' Boulder, Colo., home the day after Christmas.

Since then the news has been filled with her pageant pictures. We see this 6-year-old with painted face and tousled hair and it stirs in us something we scarcely know how to voice. We say she was beautiful, we refer, as *Newsweek* did, to the "strange world" of children's beauty pageants, we do everything except come out and say it:

How could they do that to that child?

I don't mean her murder—a separate horror complete unto itself.

I mean the life that came before it.

Are children's beauty pageants inherently bad for kids? I couldn't say. But when it comes to what pageants did to this little girl, the truth seems stark and self-evident. I am unsettled by those pictures of JonBenet in grown woman outfits, troubled by her studied model's smiles and flirtatious mannerisms. I see someone who is not yet adult, yet no longer child. Six years beyond the womb, she is a commodity packaged and sold.

And, if you will, sexualized.

I don't know why we do that to children, why we rush them through their years of greatest mental, physical and emotional growth as though adulthood were a train they had to catch that was already leaving the station. The fact is, adulthood will be there whenever a child arrives. So you'd think we'd let the kids be, let them get there at their own pace.

Sometimes, I swear, I think we really hate children. Or perhaps more accurately, hate childhood.

Maybe it's just that our attention spans have become so short and our cynicism so large that we no longer know how to believe in wonder years. Yes, we talk a good game. When 7-year-old Jessica Dubroff flew a plane into the ground in a misbegotten attempt to become the nation's youngest transcontinental pilot, we bemoaned her fate and consoled ourselves by pretending her situation was unique, an exception to the rule. Truth is, she was less an exception to the rule than an extreme application of it.

The case of poor JonBenet Ramsey isn't even that. Indeed, it seems quite tame when compared to those soft porn Calvin Klein ads that caused such a stir two years ago. One would hardly notice her next to hip-hop and rock acts selling explicit songs to ever-younger audiences or the sitcoms where child actors deliver randy punchlines with a knowing wink and leer. Three years ago on a grimy street in inner city Miami, I watched a line of spindly little girls do a lewd booty-shake copped from gangsta rap videos. It made me sad. There is something creepy and disturbing about the sexualization of children. Some visceral sense of fundamental wrong.

You can rail about sex in the media, but that's a cop-out. This is about what we allow and encourage in our homes. It's about our tendency to nudge kids toward behaviors and activities for which they are physically and emotionally unready.

I know children are not malleable lumps of clay, know that they are smarter and tougher than we often give them credit for. But I prefer to err on the side of caution any day of the week because at the bottom line, they are still children. Not vessels for adult fulfillment, not a second chance for faded parental dreams, not miniature women and men, but children.

That has to mean something. It has to be inviolate.

Sadly, that was not the case with JonBenet Ramsey. So as far as I'm concerned, she was actually the victim of two crimes. On the day after Christmas, she was murdered. But long before that, she was robbed.

JANUARY 23, 1997

RODMAN: NOT A REBEL, JUST A JERK

Dennis Rodman is a punk.

Can we agree on that now? Can we stop pretending he's a misunderstood rebel? Can we accept that he is a jerk, a nitwit, a bum, and find for him some dark hole in the bowels of obscurity?

As you may have heard, the Chicago Bulls forward has been suspended for at least 11 games by the NBA for an incident during a game last week. It's one of the longest suspensions in league history and one of the most richly deserved. It seems that, while struggling for a loose ball, Rodman fell out of bounds. Eugene Amos, a cameraman sitting nearby, turned his lens on Rodman. So Rodman kicked him.

You'd think that, what with his previous rap sheet (assaults on other players, attacks on referees, cursing on television, vulgar gestures, defiance of coaches and generally embarrassing humanity), we would finally understand that the man is just an ass, unworthy of our money or time.

Dream on. A few Rodman apologists have been squealing like stuck pigs over the unfairness of his sentence. And I guarantee you that his return to the court will be one of the biggest sports stories that day. Barnum, it seems, was right about the birth rate of suckers: one a minute.

These days, the cult of celebrity threatens to make suckers of us all.

We support people who betray our trust and spit on our forbearance, stay with them under the delusion that celebrity dysfunction somehow adds up to depth. Joe, the drunk next door, is a jerk. Joe, the drunken movie star, is "troubled." In the court of public opinion, famous people are somehow absolved of blame for their shabby misadventures by the very fact of their celebrity.

I don't mean to suggest that we should be without compassion for or interest in the substance-addicted or emotionally challenged. But there's a fine line between being understanding and giving them free rein to bring boorishness into the sanctuary of our homes. Rodman, among others, has crossed that line like Hitler crossed the Polish border. Why not? We rarely exact any meaningful cost. Indeed, we often reward misbehavior. Rodman knows this. He's built a career on it.

Back in the '80s, he was little known outside of pro basketball. Can it be merely coincidence that, shortly after he began to complain about not getting enough public attention, Rodman suddenly "discovered" previously unknown interests in bisexuality, rainbow hair, body piercing, cross-dressing and public nudity? Or that these things were followed by a book contract, an MTV show and several endorsement deals?

If you think that's just happenstance, see me after the column for a great deal on a beachfront condo in Kansas. Dennis Rodman has adapted the lessons of Barnum to the realities of the '90s. Good is great, but bad is better. Misbehavior enhances marketability.

The cult of celebrity marches on and you could, I suppose, even argue that this is an improvement on the years when celebrities presented wholesome, studiously crafted public faces that often bore little resemblance to their real ones.

But is this lie the only alternative to that one? Aren't we fed up yet with law-breaking football players, tantrum-throwing tennis stars, music-making thugs and drug-addled actors? Don't you sometimes want to say, Hey! You're a guest in my home. Behave!

Understand: I like colorful personalities as much as the next guy. But there's a difference. Charles Barkley is colorful. Dennis is a menace.

I'm not looking for role models here. I'll be a role model for my own child, thank you very much.

But is it too much to ask that pop culture and pro sports not undermine my efforts by selling the message that actions carry no consequences and one can get away with anything? That's neither freedom nor rebelliousness, but a dangerous lie, a prelude to chaos, another slender thread unraveling from the cloak of common cause.

So you'll forgive me if I carry no sign that says Free The Chicago One. The knuckle-dragging numbskull can sit till he grows cobwebs for all I care. He gets no sympathy here.

MAY 1, 1997

TRAGEDY TEACHES US THAT LIFE MUST GO ON

Dear Grand Forks, N.D.:

I was in a cab in Kansas City the other day. Driver points out the Missouri River and starts talking about the flood they had in 1993. He indicates a small structure on a baseball field maybe 200 yards in from the river. That building was underwater, he says.

"Wow," I say. "Sort of like that big flood they're having now."

The driver cocks his head, surprised. "What? What flood? Where?"

I don't tell you this in order to bring you down, Grand Forks—though frankly, if the Red River flood that decimated your community hasn't been able to do it, I guess there's no reason for me to worry.

No, I pass the story along in perverse commiseration and as recognition of a truth you're no doubt discovering for yourself:

For all the earnest prayers that have ascended on your behalf, for all the checks that have been written to the American Red Cross, for all the volunteers who have rushed to your aid from across the country, for all of that, you are, in a very real sense, alone in this.

Nobody who is not there will ever quite understand what you're going through, will ever know the gaping cavity of the loss you've sustained, will ever appreciate the gnawing uncertainty or the little acts of courage. It will be beyond them even to fathom simple things—how desperately one can yearn for plain old ice water, for instance.

You are a headline in the morning paper, a story on the evening news. Nobody knows the trouble you're seeing. Life goes on.

In August 1992, I thought that the cruelest truth of all. It was right after Hurricane Andrew devastated South Florida and I, for one, didn't want to hear about life going on; I wanted to hear about it stopping, about the whole human world pausing out of respect for the pain of my neighbors and me.

But life goes on.

I got my first inkling of that the day we dug out of the house, crossed fallen power lines and downed trees and made our way, dirty and bedraggled, to what remained of a strip shopping mall. As a National Guardsman stood watch against looters, we found a pay phone that was still working. Which is to say, if you held it just right and listened hard through the storm of static, you could make out a faint dial tone.

Certain that my family was worried sick, I called California. My brother-in-law answered the phone and I pressed my grimy cheek into the receiver and fairly screamed the blessed news: "We're alive! We're alive!!"

To which my brother-in-law replied absently, "OK, I'll tell your sister when she gets in." And he hung up. I got the impression he was watching a ballgame.

My sister Linda later told me it had never occurred to them that we might be in the path of the storm. They figured it had struck someplace else—the other South Florida, I guess. But me, I could never get over the idea that my brother-in-law was watching baseball. The very notion seemed a slap in the face, seemed out of whack, off-kilter ... wrong.

Our homes were gone, our children were crying, we had nothing left—and in some part of the country, people were still playing ball?!?

Yup. Life goes on. In '92, I thought it a cruelty. Now I realize it's a comfort.

More, it's a reminder that there is something transcendent and strong in us, some core of iron you never really know is there until circumstance and ordeal strip you to bare essence like the wind strips bark from a tree and you face a choice that's no choice at all:

Keel over and surrender. Or, live through this.

Time after time, we choose to live. Do whatever it takes, but live. Life goes on.

Which is why, as the taxi raced forward, I glanced back one last time and was not surprised by what I saw: On that field that was underwater in '93, a group of children was choosing up sides.

Indeed, I believe the game was baseball.

MAY 10, 1997

CRACKS IN PATH TO SUCCESS NOT JUST STUMBLING BLOCKS

Loath though I am to shill for a multibillion-dollar maker of overpriced athletic shoes, I must say this: You really ought to see the new Nike commercial.

It stars Michael Jordan, nine-time All-Star, four-time MVP, two-time Olympic gold medalist, once-in-a-century icon. Jordan—the man who shackled gravity and courted flight, who made the impossible seem routine and the merely difficult look easy—is seen here arriving at the game, heading to the locker room. His stride is easy, his smile secretive and knowing as he moves down the gauntlet of fans and well-wishers. He walks like a winner.

Yet in the voice-over he says: "I've missed more than 9,000 shots in my career. I've lost more than 300 games. Twenty-six times I've been trusted to take the game-winning shot—and missed. I've failed over and over and over again in my life. And that is why I succeed."

Consider that for a moment. Failure is why he succeeds. Failure is the price of excellence.

Used to be we all knew that. But nowadays it sounds revolutionary.

That's because nowadays, we want it all right now. Nowadays, some of us think children too fragile to sustain the trauma of failure. Nowadays, every mediocre singer is a superstar, every so-so athlete an all-time great. Nowadays, greatness is a cut-rate commodity.

You want to know how far greatness has fallen? A young man told me the other day that Tupac Shakur was another Martin Luther King Jr. or Malcolm X. I asked him to tell me how, exactly, Shakur changed the whole world. He, of course, could not.

Not that it matters. Nowadays, perception is stronger than truth. That used to drive me crazy when I was a music writer. I found myself constantly amazed by the number of singers who weren't and performers who could not, the number of people who, having taken shortcuts to success and back doors to fame, were unready and unsteady when they got there.

But it's not just the entertainment arena that suffers counterfeit greatness. We seem to hear ever more these days about middle managers who arrive at the corner office ignorant and unprepared. About grade inflation, where mediocre academic performances are rewarded with superior marks. About high-school and college graduates who go into the world unprepared to hold down a job.

In so many fields of endeavor, it seems, it has become possible for people to reach the goal without doing the work. We forget that there is a reason to go through ordeal, some value to be found in adversity.

One becomes tougher from those things, learns that failure is not fatal, nor defeat eternal. One gains depth. One becomes ready.

Perhaps one even becomes truly great.

The problem with greatness, though, is that in a society obsessed with perception, it looks too easy. Seen from the outside by those who don't know any better, greatness looks almost like magic. Looks like something anyone could do if he just understood the trick, had the ability, or intercepted the bolt of lightning from God.

How does Angelou write like that, we wonder. How does Hawking conceive such thoughts? How does De Niro act with such conviction and soul?

And how does Jordan fly?

We talk about talent, we nod to luck, but so often, we ignore the most important things. The hard work and many failures. The arriving early and staying late. The rejection of complacency, the refusal of contentment, the unceasing push to be just a little better than the day before.

The results of which were on display in a Jordan highlight clip I downloaded the other day. He fakes left, goes right, elevates to the hoop, finds a man in his path, spins in midair, throws the ball backward over his head and scores.

It leaves the announcers breathless, the crowd roaring. And you wonder again ... how ?

The answer is simple. That moment, seen by millions, was built on a thousand others only Jordan himself will ever know.

You have to pay some dues before you get to walk as winners do.

SEPTEMBER 1, 1997

WE WANTED TOO MUCH, AND PAID A HORRIBLE PRICE

How many pictures of her do you suppose there were? Thousands? Hundreds of thousands? A million?

How many do you suppose would have been enough? How many before photographers and editors and people like us said, this is sufficient. This satisfies our need.

At this writing, the shock of Princess Diana's death in Paris is still fresh. There is still a numbness from this latest cold reminder that life is chance, not guarantee. And yet already, one sorrow surfaces distinct from the others: the manner of her death.

The black Mercedes in which she rode led a high-speed motor chase to escape pursuing photographers. It crashed. And just like that, she was gone. Just like that, she was dead.

It seems a grisly object lesson, its ironies sharp as razor blades. The paparazzi chased to death that which justified their existence, paid their bills and, not incidentally, made some of them wealthy. The goose who laid all those golden eggs lies dead, and there is blood on the hands of her exploiters.

And already, the people are righteous in their anger, outraged at this latest excess of "the media"—a catch-all excoriation that draws no distinction between the *National Enquirer* and *New York Times*. A television newsperson doing a stand-up report hours after Diana's death was called a "scavenger" by a passer-by.

But the hypocrisy of the people is transparent. After all, the photographers who chased Diana into that tunnel weren't badgering her on a whim, bore her no enmity. Rather, their pursuit was based in the sure knowledge that any pictures they took would find favor with magazines and newspapers and thus, with readers around the world who could not get enough of this woman.

Fame makes scavengers of us all, then. Even Diana herself was in on the deal, willing when necessary to use her celebrity toward her own ends. She used it to win sympathy, used it to mold public opinion in her battles with Prince Charles. And yes, she used it, too, to bring attention to the hungry, the sick and the suffering.

She used it, it used her. Her fame was symbiosis and incest, a handshake with the devil.

But she did her best with it, lived her life to the whir and click of the shutters. She entered a room and brought with her a sudden electrical storm, flashes of light and patches of shadow with photographers yelling, leaning in, elbowing one another, trying to capture her. For us.

And you have to wonder, how much more of her did we really need? What amount of pictures would have done the trick? How much closer did we want to be?

We'd attended her wedding, watched her bear children, seen her marriage crumble, heard secrets she whispered to friends. We knew about her eating disorders, her infidelities and insecurities. We saw her sweating in the gym.

We were not this intimate with our own families and friends. Yet we wanted more. Always, more.

Once upon a time, fame seemed one of life's nicer perks, something that raised you above the common run of women and men. Now it is a public body search, the camera lens a proctoscope. We confuse fascination with intrusion, human interest with trespass. Our descent into voyeurism has been so steep and so deep that we now know the underwear preference of the president of the United States and may soon learn about the physical characteristics of his penis and testes.

We know everything about everybody. All it has cost is their dignity. And ours.

Now it seems to have cost one woman her life.

Yet one doubts the object lesson is learned even at that price, even as we remember how a shy, coquettish girl smiling on the arm of her husband became a woman always ducking, running, seeking a lonely place where voyeurs could not intrude. Until finally she fled into a tunnel on the banks of the Seine, still racing for that lonely place she never quite found.

It is said that after the crash, with the vehicle twisted and steaming, with blood leaking, bodies torn and Diana dying, a photographer stood over the mess taking pictures.

Just one more, luv. One more before you go.

MAY 2, 1998

SOMETIMES, JUST STOPPING AND GIVING THANKS CAN FILL THE VOID

One morning last January, a Baptist preacher with a church in a Washington suburb was driving through the city when he was approached by two women.

The preacher hesitated when they approached his window, begging a ride. But then the Rev. Ronald Austin said yes. It was a cold morning, after all. And his parishioners say he's a generous man who finds it difficult to turn away need.

Of course, it's no surprise what happened next. One of the women produced a knife and stabbed the preacher. He scrambled out of the car, but found himself still entangled in his seat belt. The women took off anyway, and Ronald Austin was dragged at high speed for five blocks, the tire constantly rolling over his foot. Finally, one of the women cut the belt and left him lying in the street. He was road-burned, scraped and gashed, his left foot a chunk of raw meat. Doctors had to amputate.

Recently, the reverend returned to the pulpit of Spirit of Peace Baptist Church in Capitol Heights, Md. A newspaper account depicted him as transcendent and triumphant, hopping about crying joy to the rafters. Know what he said? "I have one leg! Thank you, God!"

That's the part that stays with me.

Here's a man made unwhole, incomplete, by an act of useless evil. He ought to be whispering in bitterness. Instead, he's shouting in gratitude. Thank you, God, for what I no longer have. Thank you, for what I still do.

Is it so difficult to make the leap from his life to ours?

We're all incomplete, after all. Whether it be physical, financial, intellectual, emotional or spiritual, we're all missing something. Spend our days looking for that final piece of life-puzzle that stands between us and the finished state of which we dream.

Human nature, isn't it? Only normal that we rush about seeking to fill the hole, close the gap, bridge the distance ... become complete. It's a need as primal as a baby crying for mother's breast, one that rides our keening voices and wounded sighs, pokes itself through in sentences that begin with, "If only ... "

Then, a man with one leg blesses the Maker for leaving him that much, and if it doesn't give you pause, well, maybe it should.

You can distill it to aphorism if you want. The old William DeVaughn song, "Be Thankful For What You Got," might apply. As could the cliché about the half-empty glass.

For me, though, what the reverend said poses a challenge deeper than adages. For me, it raises a defining question: When is enough enough? When do you get to feel complete or at least make peace with the idea that completeness might never come?

The never-finished striving that fills our days is like the proverbial double-edged sword. It gives juice to life, lends it vitality, clarity and edge. But, often, it also leaves a woman or man unable to master the simple trick of standing firmly in one moment and taking all that it has to offer before moving on to the next. Instead, it seems as if we're always straining toward the next horizon, always striking bargains with God for tomorrow's bounties, always waiting on something which is yet to come.

"I need a new house, and then I'll be happy."

"Once I get a raise, life will be great."

"After I find a husband, things will be perfect."

And it never ends, does it? There's always something more. The house inevitably becomes too small. The raise is never quite enough. The husband invariably snores.

So you look in awe upon an incomplete man—a now forever-incomplete man—who doesn't feel or seem incomplete at all. Who gazes upon what life has given him and sings a song of morning joy.

We spend our lives striving to be complete, and this will never change. But sometimes it's good, isn't it, to just stop. Just pause in the fullness of the moment and the stillness of grace.

If a man with one leg can cry jubilation, what excuse is there, really, for a man who has two?

JULY 16, 1998

WHAT DRIVES KIDS TO COMMIT VIOLENT ACTS?

'We don't deserve this. All I want is for it to go away."

That's Amy Grossberg in a letter to her then-boyfriend, Brian Peterson. The "this" and "it" she refers to is their baby boy, the one she was pregnant with at the time. The one the New Jersey teenagers killed moments after its birth. The one that was found in a garbage bin, wrapped in a trash bag, with its skull broken.

Grossberg and Peterson were sentenced to prison last week. With time off for good behavior, they could be out in as little as 18 months. Of course, the baby they killed will still be dead.

The leniency of the sentences aside, the thing that vexes me is the question I've struggled with ever since this all came to light two years ago: How could they have done that?

I find myself asking that a lot lately, especially where the misdeeds of children are concerned. I asked it in 1994 when 10- and 11-year-old Chicago boys dropped a 5-year-old 14 stories to his death because he refused to steal candy for them. Asked it again in 1995, when a group of kids in Silsbee, Texas, chased a horse into a barbed wire fence, clubbed it to death with tree branches and rammed a stick up its nostril. Asked it repeatedly these last months as adolescent maniacs shot up a series of schools.

How could they do that?

I mean, some crimes you can almost understand. Not condone, not excuse, but understand.

Sudden passion caused the murder. Greed and opportunity led to the robbery. Twisted as these motives are, they are not beyond comprehension.

But what causes someone—especially a child—to commit crimes as depraved as these we've recently seen? Crimes where the violence is extreme and the gain minimal or even nonexistent? What is it inside the human conscience that breaks down at such moments?

I didn't get it. Until, that is, I read what Grossberg said: "We don't deserve this. All I want is for it to go away."

And I wonder, could it really be that simple? Could this awful thing have happened just because Amy Grossberg was a spoiled brat?

That's certainly the conclusion of the judge and the prosecutor, who described Grossberg as a vain, egocentric girl, mortified at the notion that her unwanted pregnancy might be exposed to her upper-crust family and neighbors. The baby was an embarrassment, and an intrusion upon her perfect life.

There's something off-putting in the very mundaneness of it, something disconcerting in the notion that so monstrous an evil could spring from so unexceptional a place. But at the same time, there's something about it that resonates, makes me wonder if at least part of what drives some children to acts of depravity isn't as blandly simple as that: They're spoiled.

Not in the sense of material wealth. Rather, spoiled in the sense that they live lives of entitlement, their every waking thought revolving around themselves—their problems, their needs, their wants, their gratification. We blame so many dysfunctions on low self-esteem, but I wonder if some don't suffer the opposite affliction, if some aren't so steeped in self-esteem that they can't see or sympathize beyond the borders of their own lives. Can't begin to respect the needs or feelings of others. Instead, others become objects to be moved—or removed—as necessary.

Of course that is, I'm forced to admit, a description that fits many who are neither young nor murderous. Indeed, one could argue that being spoiled is the all-American affliction. Our culture celebrates acquisition, treats self-interest as the only interest that matters. We live, many of us, in a state of have plenty and want more.

So if Amy Grossberg is a spoiled brat, she's our spoiled brat, an American child right to the top of her selfish, empty little head. And the banality of her motivation fills me with as much recognition as revulsion.

As a precious gift grew in her womb, her best response was, "We don't deserve this."

And you know something? She was right.

MARCH 6, 1999

OUR OUTRAGE IS MUFFLED, WORN AWAY

I'm writing this column because one of my readers dared me to.

Not in words. Probably not even intentionally. She simply sent an e-mail noting her disappointment that most Americans—particularly those who dispense opinion in the newspaper—have chosen to pass without comment an allegation that, 21 years ago, Bill Clinton committed rape.

Funny thing is, I almost never respond when someone challenges me to write something. The tactic usually strikes me as transparently puerile. But this reader—her name is Amy—makes an observation too valid to ignore.

Not that I'm in total harmony with her reasoning. She attributes the relative silence—more accurately, the lack of convulsive outrage—to the nation's indifference to the sufferings of women. I don't think that's what is at work here. I think much of the country feels what I felt upon hearing this news—less indifference than fatigue.

Five years ago when a teenager on an MTV forum asked the President about his preference in underwear, little did we realize that soon we'd all be inquiring about the same region of his anatomy. Little did we understand that the liaison with the lounge singer was just the tip of the edge of the beginning where Clinton was concerned. Little did we know that it would all culminate—at least, I hope it has culminated—in the ordeal through which we just passed. A gauntlet of sex and cigars, inquisition and impeachment, seamy enough to make a maggot gag.

With it finally over, all you wanted was to take a bath. Cleanse yourself and forget that it ever happened.

Except that now, here comes Juanita Broaddrick telling her story of being sexually assaulted in a hotel room by the then-attorney general of Arkansas—Clinton. The tale can't be corroborated, but neither can it be easily dismissed. Broaddrick has no apparent ax to grind, no political agenda to advance, no book deal to push. Worse, the President has yet to personally deny her account—not that his word means a lot these days.

So the question is, what to do with this knowledge?

I chose to put it aside, to store it in the back room of the brain where I keep inconvenient truths and discomfiting information. I decided to un-know it, to pretend it wasn't what it was.

Nor am I the only one. If there's been a public outcry over this, I must've missed it. Could you have imagined even two years ago that there might come a day when a sitting president was credibly accused of rape and the story was deemed unworthy of the cover of either of the two major news magazines?

But my correspondent is right, and this silence is wrong.

Worse, the price of silence is too high, amounting to tacit endorsement of the view that rape is somehow ... acceptable. It is obscene to say that, even by inference.

And yet, if we don't store this knowledge away, if we decide to deal with it instead, what does that mean? What course of action should we demand? What remedy is appropriate? What—to use a buzzword—closure can we find?

Impeachment? It's probably not an impeachable offense and besides, having just left that sewer, I doubt we're ready for another swim so soon.

Criminal prosecution? An attractive option, but the statute of limitations has passed and besides, Broaddrick doesn't want to pursue it.

So what are we left with?

Only the nagging irresolution that is, apparently, the inevitable by-product of any encounter with this president. Even his most infamous paramour, Monica Lewinsky, now speaks of him as "the person that I thought was Bill Clinton."

He is unprincipled, formless, opportunistic—water shaping itself to its surroundings.

Thank goodness that will soon be a problem only for him, his family and his next girlfriend. Our challenge is to see that when he leaves, he doesn't take with him our sense of decency and capacity for outrage.

But the silence that follows Juanita Broaddrick's accusations suggests it might already be too late, that these things might already be gone.

APRIL 22, 1999

TOT'S EMPTY LITTLE BOOTS ARE SYMBOL AT HALLOWED SITE

It is the shoes that stop me.

They are brown and look new, the rubber on the soles still thick, black and unmarked. They are toddler-size boots, made for bouncing in sandboxes and climbing on furniture. They are hanging by their laces from a length of chainlink fence.

I had not planned it this way. Had not made a special effort to be in this particular city during this particular week. Hadn't even thought about it until I was on the way to catch the plane for a business trip. That's when I realized:

Oh, God, that's the city where it happened.

Oh, God, it was right around this time of year.

Oh, God, I have to go to the site.

Which is how I have come to be standing here, staring through chainlinks into an empty space. Used to be, the Alfred P. Murrah Federal Building stood on this spot. But it ceased to exist on April 19 of '95. Came down in a concussive explosion that shattered glass for miles around. Took the lives of 168 women and men. And boys and girls. And babies. Lord, babies, too.

Now there is only a scar in the earth where the building used to be. And construction machines that sit unused, resting from their labors. A memorial is being built upon this site. One hundred sixty-eight empty chairs. A reflecting pool. A blast-scarred tree representing the survivors. All slowly taking shape behind the fence.

In the meantime, the fence itself is the memorial, festooned with teddy bears and rosary beads, poems and caps, name badges and T-shirts. There is a strand of palm, perhaps from someone's Palm Sunday worship. There is a placard bearing a message from a credit-union worker to his slain colleagues. There are dolls representing the icons of joyous childhood—Snoopy and Minnie Mouse are here. So are Chuckie from *Rugrats* and the Taco Bell dog. There are pictures—somebody's nana, somebody's son, somebody's mom, somebody's baby girl, somebody's dad. Somebody that somebody else loved more deeply than they knew while they had the chance to say. All of them dead now. All of them dead now and gone.

And there are shoes. Hanging heavily from a chainlink fence on a windless afternoon.

I am joined by many people. Hundreds, maybe. All filing in soft reverence past the fence, sometimes examining the objects there with a deference ordinarily reserved for religious icons.

For the most part we walk in silence. Indeed, there is a stillness here that seems to swallow sound, to render even footfalls mute. When someone does speak too loudly, it seems an offense against decency itself. Hush, you want to say. This is not a place for talking. This is ground suffering has made sacred.

Besides, even if you talk, what is there to say? What words do justice to the monstrous thing that happened here? What words make it make sense?

Four years later, we've learned so much about the kind of thinking that brought us to this. Learned about a movement of disaffected zealots who take guns into the woods, calling themselves militias and declaring war against the national government. Learned all their crazy theories—black helicopters, U.N. invasion, and God save the white Christian from bowing before the New World Order. We've even met the killer that movement produced, looked into the unfathomable eyes of the crew-cut young man who masterminded this carnage.

But somehow I still can't get my mind around it. Still can't answer the questions that haunt me here at the fence, like ghosts.

What cause could have been noble enough, what anger might have been righteous enough, to justify this willful massacre of innocents? To take all these people away?

I am smiled at by somebody's sister, somebody's uncle, somebody's friend. Just glossy images now. Just memories.

And all I get for my questions is more questions. More raw pain.

Silent mourners shuffle past as I pause at a chainlink fence touching a rubber sole that has never seen a sandbox. It strikes me that there is nothing quite so empty as a child's new shoe that will never once be worn.

AUGUST 21, 1999

ZEALOTS MAKE MONKEY OF 'CREATION SCIENCE'

If I lived in Kansas, I'd be checking plane fares to anywhere right about now. I'd be out of there so fast my shadow would have to catch a later flight.

Not to dump on Kansas. The Sunflower State has contributed much to this country. It has given us spicy jazz and amber waves of grain. Given us American icons like Amelia Earhart, Buster Keaton and Damon Runyon.

Unfortunately, it just gave us something else—a disturbing example of religious zealotry run amok. Meaning, of course, last week's decision by the state board of education to adopt classroom science standards that do not require the teaching of evolution. It seems the religious conservatives on the board are making an end run into Kansas classrooms. Having been told repeatedly by the courts that they cannot force schools to teach so-called "creation science," the Christian right has chosen instead to effectively banish the opposition.

The likely result is that a Kansas education in science will soon be worth about as much as an Iraqi education in diplomacy.

And if this all sounds like a rerun to you, that's because it is. Nineteen twenty-five. The Scopes monkey trial. Clarence Darrow squaring off against William Jennings Bryan over the fate of a Tennessee educator arrested after he dared teach Charles Darwin's theory that humanity evolved from lower animals.

Tennessee won in court, saw the decision reversed on appeal, and has since had to live with the historical black eye of being the state that arrested a science teacher for teaching science. You'd think the lesson would have thus been learned, but evidently they don't teach history so well in Kansas, either. Why else would we be stumbling down this road again toward an unnecessary and unproductive argument over how the world began?

Put aside the fact that it makes the state seem positively medieval. Here's the thing I keep coming back to: Why are those who accept every Bible passage as literal truth so fanatical in their quest to make the rest of us nod assent? If you know what you know, why do you need to be seconded in that knowledge by anyone, much less an agency of the government? If you know what you know, it seems as if you would be serene in the celebration of it.

But in the roughly 20 years since the Christian right coalesced as a political force, in all the time they've sought by hook and crook to make their beliefs the law of the land, serenity is an attribute they have seldom shown. Indeed, it's not too much to say that the characteristic that seems to mark them more, curiously enough, is an abiding lack of faith.

No faith in their ability to survive unaided in the marketplace of ideas. No faith in what they say they know. No faith in their ability to pass that knowledge to their kids. No faith—only the fear that conflicting ideas and competing beliefs pose imminent threat, that they and their children must be kept hermetically sealed, because exposure to opposing views, or even simple questions, is destructive to their convictions.

For what it's worth, I've never perceived evolution theory as incompatible with religious faith. It contradicts the letter of Genesis, yes. But not the essence. For me, at least, it confirms the essence— that we are not accidents, that there is an author to this work.

Think about it. We're told that humans and apes evolved from a common ancestor. We're told that before this there were dinosaurs and before that there were cellular creatures and before that, there was the primordial planet, formed from the debris of a massive explosion, a "Big Bang" that marked the birth of the universe.

And I say, Fine. Who lit the fuse on the bang? What existed prior to the beginning? And what will be here after the end?

Only one name suggests itself to me.

Which leaves me marveling at the weak-kneed creed espoused by some, a belief so flimsy it totters and quails at the first gust of contradiction. Is their God so small that he can be threatened by Charles Darwin?

Mine is not.

SEPTEMBER 2, 2000

A GLIMPSE OF BARBARISM IN A KID'S WORLD

"This is the end of the innocence."—Don Henley

Thank you for setting me straight.

Don't be shy; you know who you are. You read that column of mine about the little girls in Blythe, Calif., ages 5 and 6, who killed Damien Stiffler, the older girl's 3-year-old brother. You saw me hail the decision by the Riverside County DA not to prosecute the girls. You watched me decry the recent trend toward sending juvenile offenders into adult courts to face adult sentences.

And you got me told. Liberal garbage, you said. An attempt to let kid killers off without consequences, you said.

I had argued that treating child offenders the way we treat adult offenders ultimately coarsens us all. Childhood, I said, is a wholly separate time and children creatures of moral innocence.

A naive illusion, you said.

You're right, of course. I don't know why I didn't see it before, but thanks to you, I see it now. Thanks to you, I understand. Now it doesn't even bother me so much to learn that, according to Human Rights Watch, the United States executed 10 juvenile offenders—people who were under 18 when they committed their crimes—

during the '90s. This includes Sean Sellers, a 29-year-old man put to death last year in Oklahoma for murders committed when he was 16. Only five other nations are known to have executed juvenile offenders: Iran, Nigeria, Pakistan, Saudi Arabia and Yemen.

Just being in the company of such forward-thinking countries ought to be a source of pride for all true Americans. But why stop there? What's it say about us that we have only killed 10 killer kids in the '90s? Why are we so squeamish?

Granted, we might eventually need booster seats for the electric chair, but it's nothing we can't work out.

I used to consider youth a necessary barrier to prosecution to the full extent of the law. But you've taught me that we gain nothing from weeping when some useless child gets what's coming to him in an adult courtroom. That we lose nothing—no fundamental piece of our humanity, let's say—by treating such a child with the hardness she has earned.

And that there is no use trying to understand, struggling to figure out, what makes a child come out bad. No use wondering what role our failures, as parents and as a culture, might have played. Better to just get rid of them and move on.

As I'm sure you already know, that sentiment is catching on. Our justice system appears to be moving slowly away from one of its guiding tenets: that children should be treated differently. That belief was the reason we gave kids separate courts, separate penalties, separate places of detainment. Now the wall of separation seems to be crumbling.

Why stop there, though? Why even stop with the death penalty? Brazil and Colombia made international headlines in the '90s for their so-called "death squads," which summarily executed street children, exterminated them like roaches, while the government apparently looked the other way. Perhaps we can try something like that on the hard cases we have here. Can you imagine the kind of nation we'll have once we finally start getting tough on bad children? A better and stronger nation, don't you think? A nation where kids will finally know that we mean business.

How can they not know when they see a 10-year-old sent away for the rest of his life or a 9-year-old having her head shaved and electrodes applied? And yes, some will mourn the kind of people we have become, that we can do these things and call it justice. That's all right, though.

Because we'd make them see that this was necessary. That bad children are without worth and beyond redemption. That, left to the vagaries of the old system, they would inflict barbarism upon us.

But when the new system comes, they won't get the chance. When the new system comes, we'll show them what barbarism really means.

SEPTEMBER 30, 2000
CALL TO PARENTS BEFORE KIDS PULL THE TRIGGER

It began, as it often does, with children and a gun.

Police say it was just before noon on Tuesday that 13-year-old Alfred Anderson, already suspended from school for fighting, slipped the weapon through a gap in the locked chain-link gates of Carter G. Woodson Middle School in New Orleans. Thirteen-year-old Darrell Johnson reportedly used that gun to shoot 15-year-old William Pennington in the chest. Whereupon Pennington somehow wrested the gun away and shot Johnson in the back as the younger boy was attempting to flee. Both were critically injured. Both, miraculously, are expected to recover.

I figure the school district will probably get sued, mainly because that's what we do in America when we can't figure something out. But as best I can tell, the school did everything it could to prevent this.

Metal detectors? It used them. School uniforms? It had them. Security guards? It employed them.

Yet, Woodson Middle was still helpless to stop two of its students from shooting one another. And you wonder what, if anything, could have.

Though police are discounting it as a cause of the violence, residents of the neighborhood say the shooting grew out of a turf war. Apparently, there's an ongoing battle between youthful residents of two low-income housing developments that feed students into the school. No one seems to know how the feud got started and at this point, it's probably academic. The fight has become a perpetual motion machine, a thing that somehow moves of its own volition. It moves because it moves. The boys fight because they fight.

Mayor Marc Morial, whose city was one of the first to sue gun makers to recoup the costs of firearms violence, blames this latest shooting on the easy accessibility of deadly weapons. "Without a gun," he told a reporter, "this would have been a fight between a 13- and 15-year-old, a little pushing and shoving on the playground."

There are pieces of an answer in all of the above. This certainly wouldn't be the first time somebody was hurt in an internecine conflict whose origins no one could recall. The mayor's observation seems likewise valid: There's something profoundly wrong with a country where children find it so easy to obtain deadly weapons.

And yet, there's a difference between a turf war and an attempted murder, between having a gun around and making the fateful decision to use it. Point being that the people and their mayor have identified symptoms, but not the disease.

We have a tendency to do that when these tragedies rip our collective conscience. We blame Hollywood, the video game industry, the gun makers, the members of the rival gang. Not that they don't deserve the blame. It's just that if you're searching for deeper answers, you can't stop there. You have to understand that American families are fracturing and many of our children are falling through the gap. And you have to listen to the story Rosalyn Dabney, a parent advocate at Woodson, told a local reporter. It seems there was to be a meeting at the school for parents. She advertised it by posting flyers throughout both housing projects.

Not one parent showed up, she said. Not one.

Therein lies a question not just for the parents of a poor neighborhood in New Orleans, but for parents in all kinds of neighborhoods all over the country:

How can we expect other people to show concern for our children if we do not?

If we haven't gone to the school, shown up for the game, been involved, how can we blame others for not caring enough? It's convenient and self-exonerating to always point to external forces in the moral maiming of our children. But their guilt doesn't prove our innocence.

Consider that, as her son lay in surgery, Johnson's mother complained that "somebody at school should have known ... what was going on."

But how can somebody at school be expected to know what somebody at home apparently did not?

Meanwhile, Rosalyn Dabney watched hordes of angry, frightened parents descend on the school, demanding answers. It was, she said, the first time many of them had ever been there.

FEBRUARY 3, 2001

GOD KNOWS, SUFFERING IS PART OF GAME

So I was hanging out with God down at the park one afternoon, playing our regular game of one-on-one. As usual, He blanked me. It's not widely known, but God is unstoppable once He gets the ball in the low post.

Afterward, I asked if it was true what this Indian guy said about Him. God hadn't seen the paper, so I showed Him the story. It seems this fellow named T. John, an official in the Indian province of Karnataka, was forced to resign over remarks he made in a speech to some students. He told them last week's earthquake was an act of revenge by God for attacks by Hindus on the country's Christian minority. The quake claimed upwards of 12,000 lives.

I asked God again, "Is it true?"

God sighed. A breeze rattled the tree leaves. "Does T. John know anything about these 12,000 people?" He asked finally. "Do you? Can you tell me which ones persecuted Christians and which ones were Christians themselves? Or Muslims or Jews? Can you describe the ones who stole from the poor or mistreated children? Can you name the ones who gave bread to the hungry or read to the blind?"

I shrugged and said, "Of course I can't."

God said, "I can. Those people didn't die for revenge."

"Then why..." I caught myself, remembering how teed off He got with Job for pestering Him with questions.

But to my relief, God smiled. The sun glanced through the clouds. "I know," He said. "You want a world without pain. A world without suffering and loss. But that would also be a world without healing, without joy and redemption. Each one gives meaning to the other."

God stood and went to practice His free throws. "So," I said, "you don't bring calamity on people to teach them lessons?"

"I didn't say that," said God, lining up His shot. "I mean, I thought Chicago needed to learn humility, so I gave them the Cubs." The ball fell soundlessly through the net. "Adam Sandler movies," He continued, "are my way of saying, 'Support your local library.' I'm not above sending messages."

"Well if that's the case," I said, "why are you so bothered by this T. John?"

"It's simple," said God. "People like him irk me because they're always quoting me when I haven't said anything to them. Always ascribing their own petty motives to me. They're forever putting my name into some cockamamie thing that has nothing to do with me.

"It's not just him. It's the people who declare war claiming I told them to do it. It's that TV preacher who said I was going to kill him unless people gave him money. It's the crowd that claims I sent AIDS as a judgment upon some of my children. It's the ones who hate in my name.

"And the worst thing," said God, "is that the things I do say, no one seems to pay attention. I tell you to take care of one another. I tell you to honor your parents. I tell you to stop stealing, killing and coveting. I tell you I love you."

"Yeah," I told Him, "but you said those things centuries ago. People forget."

"I remind you everyday," said God. He threw the ball to me, I threw it back and bodied up on Him as He started His dribble.

"I remind you everyday," He said again. "In sunrises and silences, in breezes and in smiles, in poetry and jazz, in love and even in tears. Even in tears, I remind you of what is good, of how you ought to be.

"You know what the problem is?" He said as He backed me toward the hoop. "You people make so much noise, you hardly ever hear me. You talk so much I can't get a word in edgewise. You need to hush sometimes. You need to listen."

Suddenly He spun off me and put up this hook shot that hung in the air like possibility itself, then fell through the net without moving the cords. As I said, He's unstoppable in the post.

APRIL 12, 2001

DEAR GOD, I OWE YOU AN APOLOGY

Dear Jean:

I'm writing in response to an e-mail I received from your husband, William. He says you're a regular reader of this column who "thinks the world" of me.

William's cooked up a surprise for you, Jean. He's asking your friends to send a card or a note to congratulate you on an important milestone: This month makes five years you've been breast-cancer free. He asked if I'd be one of the people to send good wishes.

Jean, I have a confession to make. The first thing I felt when I received William's request was a tiny pinprick of resentment. There is, you see, a certain symmetry here: Your fifth anniversary as a survivor of breast cancer is my mother's 13th anniversary as one of its casualties. Whenever I meet someone who has beaten the disease, my joy for them is tempered by a little voice shouting up at God from the sub-basement of being. "What about Mom?" it demands. "How come this lady gets to live, but Mom didn't? What's wrong with you, God?"

Small of me, I know.

But I had a heck of a mom, Jean. Brought up four kids in the meanest neighborhoods in L.A. and never lost a one. Having her in your corner was like having the Marines. She was all the love in the world and I grew up thinking no triumph complete, no good news fully celebrated, until I had shared it with her.

Cancer took her life before it killed her. It shrank her and shriveled her, made her too weak to walk unaided. In the end, it confined her to a bed in my sister's house where she lay for hours on end, drifting in and out of consciousness while I sat nearby, praying for miracles that were not forthcoming.

It was difficult, letting hope go. I remember, she caught me staring at her this one time and I must have looked sad, because she winked at me. Can you believe that? She could no longer speak, but she gave me this wink as if to tell me that she was all right. As if to let me know that she loved me. As if to say goodbye.

That was the last thing she ever "said" to me, Jean. She passed two days after. And even now, 13 years later, not too many days go by without me thinking of her, wondering what she'd say in a certain situation. Missing her.

So you see, there's symmetry between us, Jean. I guess that's why William's note hit me in a tender spot. Anyway, I called your husband and he told me about you. About the shock and disbelief when the doctors said they would need to biopsy your breast. About how your mother died of a rare disease when you were just a girl. About your fear of leaving your teenage sons as your mom had left you.

He told me about the mastectomy, too. How he brought his guitar to play for you as you were being prepped. How some days, you drove to the mountains to walk in the woods, maybe hollering at God from a sub-basement of your own. He told me how the two of you left a crowded city, moved to Maine and bought a farm. He says you hope to make it a place to which people with life-threatening illnesses can come and just take ... time.

There was something in his voice as he spoke and it made me ask a question to which I already knew the answer. "You really love her, don't you?"

"She's changed my life," he said.

In the end, of course, love is the binding tie. A husband's wife, a son's mother, a brother's sister, a father's daughter, all threatened by this cancer, this killer and thief. And I still pray for miracles.

So, Jean, God bless you. Please accept my heartiest congratulations. And my thanks. Because meeting you, albeit through William, has convinced me that maybe it's time to quit hollering at God. Time to embrace the symmetry.

April becomes a month to remember love that was lost. And celebrate love that remains.

MAY 12, 2001

WE GUYS DO DUMB THINGS TO IMPRESS WOMEN

In today's column, we'll examine the recent decision by the NBA to allow the use of the zone defense. If there's time afterward, we'll talk about exciting new advances in the prevention of jock itch.

... OK, men, now that women have fled this page like a flock of startled geese let me tell you the real reason we're gathered here today. In two words: Harry Rabin.

He's 77 years old and, according to his lawyer, a decorated veteran of World War II who saw action at Normandy. Recently, Harry was sentenced to three years in federal prison for robbing several banks in Skokie and Glenview, Ill.

You know why he did it?

He was trying to impress a girl. The "girl" was 76.

Ah, the things we do for love. We male men of the guy persuasion, I mean. There's an apparently endless list of Dumb Things We Do as a way of telling women, "I find you attractive. Can we please have sex?"

The details: Harry's sweetheart was rich. And poor Harry was a retired security guard who worried that he wasn't in her league. That a woman from the lobster-and-champagne crowd would soon grow bored with a guy on a beer-and-chili budget. So in the fall of '98, Harry picked up a gun and embarked upon his life of crime. He netted $8,700 in the first two robberies; police nabbed him shortly after the third.

Harry told the judge he can't believe he did something so dumb. For whatever it's worth, I can. I mean, I'm sure there are men who would find it hard to identify with Harry. There's a word for them. Liars.

Because when it comes to doing dumb things to impress the babes, every heterosexual male nitwit in the world has battle scars a mile long. At least that's the finding of a recent survey I conducted by the highly scientific journalistic method of—I'm a trained professional, kids, so don't try this at home—asking around.

My research turned up one guy who rode Greyhound from New York City to Atlanta so he could spend time—all of three hours—

with his girlfriend. Then he hopped back on the bus because he had to get back to work. In New York.

There's a teenager who bragged to his girl about his new car. This kid, who can't even drive, then jumped on his bike and pedaled over to her house. Spent the entire visit praying she wouldn't look outside.

Remember the scene from *Aliens* where the android spreads his fingers on the table and stabs a knife between them with staccato speed to prove his precision? One guy tried to duplicate that for a girl. Like to cut his finger off. And then there's a 36-year-old buddy of mine who tried to prove to his girl how "young and fit" he was by roller-blading off a ramp. Naturally, he took a nasty fall. She thought he should go to the emergency room, but my friend just laughed a deep, manly laugh and told her there was no need.

Ended up driving himself to the ER the next day, using the one arm that wasn't swollen and impossible to lift.

It seems a common characteristic of guyhood, this cheerful willingness to risk embarrassment, disfigurement or disability to please a woman. Not just among us human types. I mean, male frogs sing frog arias, male owls offer dead mice, male bighorn sheep try to butt each other's brains out. And, at least one male human robbed banks. It's all the same when you get down to it.

And right about here, I guess, your humble correspondent ought to confess some of the dopey things he has done in the pursuit of love. But golly gosh, we're just about out of space. Besides, I think the women are coming back.

So in closing, let me just say that there remain serious questions about the effect of the zone defense. But the outlook is good for the elimination of jock itch in our lifetime.

SEPTEMBER 12, 2001

WE'LL GO FORWARD FROM THIS MOMENT

It's my job to have something to say.

They pay me to provide words that help make sense of that which troubles the American soul. But in this moment of airless shock when hot tears sting disbelieving eyes, the only thing I can find to say, the only words that seem to fit, must be addressed to the unknown author of this suffering.

You monster. You beast. You unspeakable bastard.

What lesson did you hope to teach us by your coward's attack on our World Trade Center, our Pentagon, us? What was it you hoped we would learn? Whatever it was, please know that you failed.

Did you want us to respect your cause? You just damned your cause.

Did you want to make us fear? You just steeled our resolve.

Did you want to tear us apart? You just brought us together.

Let me tell you about my people. We are a vast and quarrelsome family, a family rent by racial, social, political and class division, but a family nonetheless. We're frivolous, yes, capable of expending tremendous emotional energy on pop cultural minutiae—a singer's revealing dress, a ball team's misfortune, a cartoon mouse. We're wealthy, too, spoiled by the ready availability of trinkets and material goods, and maybe because of that, we walk through life with a certain sense of blithe entitlement. We are fundamentally decent, though—peace-loving and compassionate. We struggle to know the right thing and to do it. And we are, the overwhelming majority of us, people of faith, believers in a just and loving God.

Some people—you, perhaps—think that any or all of this makes us weak. You're mistaken. We are not weak. Indeed, we are strong in ways that cannot be measured by arsenals.

Yes, we're in pain now. We are in mourning and we are in shock. We're still grappling with the unreality of the awful thing you did, still working to make ourselves understand that this isn't a special effect from some Hollywood blockbuster, isn't a plot development from a Tom Clancy novel. Both in terms of the awful scope of their ambition and the probable final death toll, your attacks are likely to go down as the worst acts of terrorism in the history of the United States and, probably, the history of the world. You've bloodied us as we have never been bloodied before.

But there's a gulf of difference between making us bloody and making us fall. This is the lesson Japan was taught to its bitter sorrow the last time anyone hit us this hard, the last time anyone brought us such abrupt and monumental pain. When roused, we are righteous in our outrage, terrible in our force. When provoked by this level of barbarism, we will bear any suffering, pay any cost, go to any length, in the pursuit of justice.

I tell you this without fear of contradiction. I know my people, as you, I think, do not. What I know reassures me. It also causes me to tremble with dread of the future.

In the days to come, there will be recrimination and accusation, fingers pointing to determine whose failure allowed this to happen and what can be done to prevent it from happening again. There will be heightened security, misguided talk of revoking basic freedoms. We'll go forward from this moment sobered, chastened, sad. But determined, too. Unimaginably determined.

You see, the steel in us is not always readily apparent. That aspect of our character is seldom understood by people who don't know us well. On this day, the family's bickering is put on hold.

As Americans we will weep, as Americans we will mourn, and as Americans, we will rise in defense of all that we cherish.

So I ask again: What was it you hoped to teach us? It occurs to me that maybe you just wanted us to know the depths of your hatred. If that's the case, consider the message received. And take this message in exchange: You don't know my people. You don't know what we're capable of. You don't know what you just started.

But you're about to learn.

SEPTEMBER 29, 2001

TERROR SHAKES FAITH, PUTS GOD IN QUESTION

So how could God have allowed this to happen?

Standing uneasily at the altar, the minister explained that he had come to a conclusion about that, one he didn't expect us to like. Maybe, he said, God allowed the planes to be stolen, and the people to die, because He was helpless to stop it. Maybe He didn't have the power.

The silence was as sudden as it was stunned. No one said Amen. No one stirred. Nothing moved. He went on speaking. Two women quietly gathered their things and left.

My wife and I turned to each other. She wanted to follow them as an act of protest. I wanted to stay as an act of faith.

But as the sermon went on, it became clear that faith would not be rewarded. This wasn't some clever speaker using a daring rhetorical device. This was just what it seemed to be: a man of God publicly struggling with a crisis of conviction. Of all I've seen in the wake of Sept. 11, this was, in some ways, the most dismaying.

It occurs to me that we've spent a lot of time these past days toting up all that has changed in our world as a result of that awful Tuesday morning. Comedy. Sports. Travel. But I get the sense that, in ways as unremarked upon as they are profound, faith was changed as well. In churches, synagogues and mosques, people are left to define and defend what it means to believe in a world where belief suddenly seems either a weapon of war or an act of futility.

After all, the men who hijacked the planes thought they acted at the behest of Allah. And Jerry Falwell, a Christian minister, claims their attack represents God's verdict on the ACLU and other bogeymen of the right wing. Meanwhile, there's a posting on the Internet that asks, plainly and plaintively, "Where Was God?" And now, there's a minister at my church who thinks God was simply not able. We gaze upon wreckage and ruin and struggle to see the hand of the deity.

But maybe that's not the worst thing in the world.

It occurs to me that God, especially in times of crisis, has more spokespersons than Amway. Some simply seek to divine the divine. Others claim to know His mind and motives as surely as if they had read His diary.

But so many times what you discover is that people have created God in their own image. That they interpret Him according to their petty biases and predispositions, attribute to him their political party and ball team, their motivations and hatreds, their timetable and comprehension.

Maybe it's good to be reminded sometimes that mortality can't fathom eternity, nor limitation comprehend endlessness. Maybe it's good that we are sometimes forced to say words we are loathe to say, "I don't know."

So go on, ask me why the terrorists succeeded. Or, for that matter, why the Jews were slaughtered and the Africans kidnapped. Ask why innocents die cruelly while the cruel live long and well. Why pain happens in the name of God. Why the world makes so little sense.

I don't know. I just don't know.

It's a humbling thing to say. Makes you feel less sure of your own powers, less in control of your own world. Makes you feel like a child lying awake in the scary dark, trusting the adults to know what's going on and how to make it better. Which is precisely the point. I'm reminded of the refrain from a little-known rock song: "The less I believe in me, the more I believe in thee."

Some people will never believe. Some people will always believe without question. And some people—most of us, I suspect—will always believe with question.

We shake our fists at God for daring to live outside our imaginings. We curse the skies for raining down unfair misfortunes. We see suffering and wonder why.

Like that child in the dark, we struggle to learn how to rest at peace with things we don't know. And how to rely on the one thing we do.

Always, morning comes.

NOVEMBER 10, 2001

MAGIC TOUCH ENHANCING GAME OF LIFE

It's been 10 years since the roof fell in.

Not my personal roof, though it felt like it at the time. No, the roof that fell in belonged to a basketball player named Magic Johnson.

Let me tell you about Magic and me.

I've never been a big sports fan. Never cared much about football or hockey, boxing or baseball. The only reason basketball is an exception is that one day I happened to turn on the television and see this giant man doing impossible things. Spinning and weaving through a forest of outstretched limbs with balletic grace, looking to his left and somehow—somehow!—delivering the ball unerringly to a man on his right.

I was hooked. Over the next 12 years, I won and lost a thousand games, stored up a roomful of trophies, vicariously, through him.

I remember, in the spring of '91, I was newly arrived in Miami, staying in this flea-trap motel while I waited for my family to join me from L.A. I had no television in that place, and the NBA Finals were on, so I did the only thing I could. Slipped into the TV critic's office after hours and watched the games. Sat there pulling for my team in the darkness of a near-empty newsroom as the clock ticked past midnight.

Of course, that was the year Michael Jordan's Bulls waxed Magic's Lakers, but we won't talk about that. The one thing that assuaged my disappointment was the certainty that next season, Magic would be back and he'd have a new trick or two and then, boy, Jordan would be in trouble.

But as it turned out that was, for all practical purposes, Magic's last season. The following November, he faced the cameras and announced that he was retiring because he had become infected with HIV.

We all thought he was dead.

Remember? It seems strange now, after a decade in which he has un-retired, re-retired, hosted a god-awful talk show and opened coffee shops in every urban community in America, but that's how we thought then. That he would keel over any second.

My colleague, sports columnist Dan Le Batard, irked some readers—and I was one of them—by describing Johnson in print as "a dying man." I thought it was insensitive. I wanted to think it was inaccurate, too, but I worried that I was only fooling myself.

Eleven years, said Dan. That's how much time "the averages" gave him. Eleven years and he would be gone. So there's still time for Dan to be proven right. But every time you see Magic doing a halftime interview on NBC or clowning around with Leno, looking healthier and happier than anybody else you know, it makes you wonder.

I mean, you don't even think of HIV when you see him anymore. It takes an effort of will to remember that it lurks in him still, could kill him still. If not in the 11th year, maybe in the 13th? Maybe the 15th? Or, maybe 30 years from now, he dies after being run over by a bus.

You don't know. You never know. I think that's the moral of the last decade. That you don't foreclose possibility, you don't give up, you don't stop living. You find a way back.

I remember this one game—1989 Western Conference semifinals, Lakers vs. Sonics—when Magic's boys were getting their behinds whipped. Down 29 points in the first half. My oldest son was so disgusted he left the room. As he did, the TV camera panned Magic's face. He didn't look panicked and he didn't look distressed. He looked angry.

"Lakers are going to win this game," I called to my son. He thought I was crazy. They won by two.

If you're wary of sports analogies, I don't blame you. Life is not nine innings or four quarters. But there is, just the same, a lesson to be found in an improbable come-from-behind victory. It's the same lesson you find in watching a "dying man" live, 10 years on.

Namely, that there is no such thing as a foregone conclusion.

That's why you put the ball in play.

SEPTEMBER 8, 2002

WE STAND AS AMERICANS, NOW MORE THAN EVER BEFORE

And so, September comes around again.

In the first days, it seemed appropriate somehow to mark our distance from the awful event in small increments, grateful that each step forward was another step away.

We commemorated the end of the first week, the end of the first month. Now, suddenly, we are at the end of the first year since that late summer morning when two air buses controlled by terrorists were crashed into the towers of the World Trade Center, a third into the side of the Pentagon and a fourth into the Pennsylvania countryside.

One year. And predictably, we keepers of communal memory, we photographers and composers, artists and journalists, attempt now to summon back that day, to offer such context as we can, such meaning as we are able. But the tools of our trades feel inadequate to the task.

Where are the colors on the palette, the words in the dictionary, to explain what it felt like watching those planes impale those towers, the mind refusing to process the things the eyes reported?

What images in a viewfinder or notes on the scale can capture it all? How can you frame the dry-mouth disbelief of seeing people leap from burning skyscrapers and knowing their decision was perfectly logical, of watching dust-caked survivors wander the outskirts of holocaust like some army of the godforsaken, of knowing that your greatest city is suddenly closed for business?

Of praying, "God, why?"

I don't know the words for those things. Can't imagine the pictures or the songs.

I only know that Sept. 11, 2001, is the day the good old days ended. And, paradoxically, the day that made us Americans again.

I'm not talking about patriotism.

Rather, I refer to the fact that we are a people who wear national identity lightly, when we wear it at all. Most days, we choose not to. Most days, we are a nation of fiefdoms defined by markers of race, education, employment, income, religion, gender, sexual identity, age, culture, geography and more. We are soccer moms and angry white men, yuppies and Afrocentrics, Cuban exiles and religious conservatives, and for generations, we've enjoyed the luxury of not having to be anything more.

It's not that we didn't know we were American. It's just that on most days prior to that one day, we were free to define ourselves by other things.

But, as we were brutally reminded, identity is not only a matter of how you perceive yourself. It's also a matter of how you're perceived by others.

The hijackers of Sept. 11 did not see soccer moms or angry white men. They saw something they have always hated, something they sought to kill. They saw Americans.

And the people around the world who mourned the carnage of that day, who offered us money, blood and prayer, did not see Cuban exiles and the religious right. They saw something that has always given them hope. They, too, saw Americans.

You may love that identity or hate it, may embrace that identity or be profoundly ambivalent toward it. But, as the events of that day made painfully apparent, the one thing you cannot do is pretend it doesn't matter, has no bearing on your life.

We got away with that for a long time. Small wonder. One of the perks of being the biggest, the strongest and the most influential is that you can also be the most oblivious, neither knowing nor caring overmuch how you are defined by others. They react to you more than you do to them.

Until, invariably, something happens that forces you to react. Then you stagger about, shocked and indignant, as if betrayed by history itself. That's what occurred on Sept. 11.

Now, September comes back around, and our lives are baseball, back-to-school sales, summer movies and other things it once seemed we might never care about again. Still, there's an empty space in the New York City skyline and soldiers at war on distant mountains. Reminders that we are the same, but also different now.

We've learned that we can no longer escape who we are. The truth is, we never could.

DECEMBER 23, 2002

HOLIDAYS BEG CURE FOR 'AFFLUENZA'

Every year, we take this picture.

It's late on Christmas Eve after the fat man has gone and the last bike has been assembled. We are exhausted, ready to tumble into bed. But before we do, we take a snapshot of the finished product.

It's usually impossible to fit it all into one frame. The loot spills across the floor, covers couches and chairs. A sea of Barbie dolls and remote-control cars, athletic shoes and video games.

I used to like that picture. I'd look at myself or my wife standing before that bounty and I'd feel the distinctly masculine pride of the provider who has once again provided.

But lately, that picture fills me less with pride than with a wistful melancholy. I say to myself: My goodness, look at all that stuff. Stuff that three weeks ago filled Christmas lists and dreams. Stuff whose whereabouts children won't be able to tell you three weeks from now. Stuff.

The lament is not—at least, not solely—about the secularization of a Christian holy day or the gaping distance between children of poverty and those of plenty. Truth to tell, what really gets me is the stuff itself, the fact that no matter how much of it you acquire, you're never sated. There's always something new or next to buy. We run a race with no finish line, play a ballgame with no final buzzer. It's never over.

John De Graaf would call that condition "affluenza." It's a word that refers to the "disease" of affluence, of empty consumerism gone wild. The veteran TV producer has done two PBS documentaries and coauthored a book (*Affluenza*) on the subject.

His cure for the "illness" is simplicity itself. Literally. De Graaf, who lives in Seattle, is a prime mover in what's called the simplicity movement, a grass-roots effort to get Americans to cut back on the stuff that clutters their lives. It encourages us to ask if we really need those $200 athletic shoes or that DVD burner. Or have we simply been convinced that we need them by a commercial culture that does not always fight fair?

As in the marketing meeting he captured in one of his documentaries: "Without any embarrassment," he said, "they used terms like 'owning,' 'capturing,' 'branding' children. They talked about how to stir up in kids these anti-parent attitudes in order for them to want to get around parents" by nagging them into surrender.

Many years ago, says De Graaf, he worked on a Navajo Indian reservation where the average annual income was $600. Yet, the kids seemed never to be bored. Always seemed to find ways to amuse themselves. Then De Graaf came home for Christmas to a younger brother who kept complaining that he had nothing to do, even though his room looked like an explosion at a Toys 'R' Us. It was an awakening.

De Graaf sees affluenza in environmental, business, labor and quality-of-life dimensions. For me, though, the most alarming thing about affluenza is its effect on the spirit.

If life is a search for wholeness, then that search must by definition be at odds with consumer culture. The advertiser's job, after all, is to make us feel unwhole, incomplete, until we own his or her product. "You gotta go shopping!" says one ad. "It's all inside," promises another.

Acquisition becomes an end unto itself. Some people go to malls looking for no particular product. They go, they say, because it makes them feel good. The mall becomes the church of consumerism, the purchase an act of sacrament.

We breathe, therefore we buy. But somehow, we can never buy enough to feel whole.

Every Christmas morning the camera flashes, freezing in time a sea of plastic things and shiny boxes bought to bring happiness. And you wonder if this is not, in the end, the very antithesis of prosperity. Maybe wealth begins the day you are finally able to want what you have. Finally manage to say something that none of us, rich or poor, ever seem able to say.

I have enough. I don't need anything more than this.

JANUARY 17, 2003

LOGIC TELLS US: NO DEATH PENALTY

Forgive me, but I'm about to speak heresy.

Blame the outgoing governor of Illinois, who last week emptied his state's Death Row. George Ryan commuted to life in prison the death sentences of 167 condemned criminals.

The result: a firestorm of criticism, much of it from those who have lost loved ones to violent crime. Our instinct is to give great weight to what those people have to say. To listen with great reverence.

But—and here's the heresy—it occurs to me that maybe we've already listened with too much reverence.

I bow to no one in my empathy for people whose lives have been affected by violent crime. You see, I live with one. My wife's brother Ted was killed in a random shooting 10 years ago.

I still remember her saying, "What? What?" over and over again into the receiver when we got that awful 3 a.m. phone call. It was as if words had suddenly ceased to have meaning.

I have stood with her at his grave. I have awakened in middle night to find her wide awake. I have held her helplessly as she wept.

So I know a little something about this. And one of the things I know is that there's nothing I would not have done to spare her that pain. Or to get justice for her.

That's the problem. Because we all feel that way, don't we? We all empathize, we all suffer with them, we all feel there's nothing we would not or should not do for people whose grief is so immense. And if they want, if they need, to see a killer killed, so be it.

In the face of their demands on our collective conscience, it can seem insensitive or even uncaring to voice doubt about that process. Yet, if you are intellectually honest about it, how can you not?

The answer is simple: Avoid intellectual honesty at all costs.

Consider the recent study indicating that the state of Maryland has been choosing whom to execute based on color of skin and place of residence.

You'd think that would give a fair man pause. Yet incoming Gov. Robert Ehrlich has shrugged it off, keeping an ill-advised campaign promise to lift a death penalty moratorium imposed by his predecessor.

The difference between George Ryan and the Robert Ehrlichs of the world is this: Somehow, Ryan reached a point where conscience would no longer allow him to ignore what he saw.

Three years ago, Ryan, a former death penalty supporter, suspended state executions. He was stung by the fact that since 1977, 13 people had been freed from the Illinois death house after they were found to have been wrongly convicted.

Now the other shoe drops. "I no longer shall tinker with the machinery of death," Ryan said last week.

Surely that makes sense. If you owned a machine—a car, a computer, a microwave oven—that was as prone to failure as capital punishment, you would have ditched it a long time ago. Yet we insist that this broken hunk of junk can somehow be made to function properly if we are just persistent and ingenious enough. And never mind all the people who are freed from Death Row because a cop lied, a witness erred, a lawyer bungled, the system failed.

Killing killers illustrates our respect for the sanctity of life, death penalty advocates argue with oily, Orwellian rhetoric. And you look at this poor slob who just spent 20 years under sentence of death for something he didn't do and you wonder, what about his life? Doesn't it have sanctity, too?

By any logical standard, life without parole should be the highest punishment in our legal arsenal. It's less expensive than the death penalty and it is reversible in the event of error.

So where's the logic in state-sanctioned executions? There isn't any. There's only the blinding emotion that says if we don't kill killers, we betray the victims. We show ourselves to be soft.

And how silly is that? By sentencing 167 people to the slow death of the five-by-12 cell, George Ryan did not save killers from justice.

But he just may have saved us from ourselves.

JUNE 6, 2003

NO CAUSE JUSTIFIES PLANTING OF BOMBS

Ronald Smith lost an index finger and part of one thumb. Emily Lyons lost an eye. Fallon Stubbs lost her mother.

The losses came not because of anything they did, nor anything they said. It was just happenstance. Just the result of being in the wrong place when bombs exploded.

It has been a few years and chances are you've forgotten their names, if you ever knew them at all. I came across them while doing a computer search to see how many times the name of accused serial bomber Eric Rudolph and the word "sympathy" have appeared together in news media since his arrest last Saturday in North Carolina.

I got 49 hits.

Some led to people like Bill Hughes, mayor of Murphy, N.C., who says media have oversold the notion that folks in that area identify with Rudolph because his reputed views (white supremacist, anti-gay rights, anti-government, antiabortion) mirror their own.

It's a fair admonition. The rural South is too often stereotyped as a monolithic backwater of ignorance and intolerance. I refuse to believe that most people who live south of Charles Mason and Jeremiah Dixon's line would find anything admirable in Rudolph.

But many clearly do. They're careful to disavow the violence he's alleged to have visited upon his targets: the 1996 Olympics in

Atlanta, a gay nightclub and abortion clinic in the same town, another clinic in Birmingham. At the same time, they make clear that if Rudolph did it, they can surely understand why.

Franklin Holloway, a retiree, told the *Washington Post*, "I wish they hadn't caught him. Look at those abortion doctors. They kill innocent babies."

His wife Linda added, "If he did that Olympic bombing he should be punished. But as far as those abortion clinics and the gay club is concerned, he shouldn't be punished for that. You see, those things are not right in the sight of God."

One wonders if she recognizes Osama bin Laden's reasoning coming out of her mouth. One doubts it. Religious fanatics are seldom perceptive of irony.

Still, it's fitting that she invokes al Qaeda arguments to justify the bombings. After all, the crimes amount to nothing less than terrorism.

Rudolph is believed to have spent five years hiding in the rugged woods on the southwestern tip of the Tar Heel State. Authorities believe he had help, though no one has confessed. Still, many locals say they'd have been willing to give Rudolph any assistance he needed. Some still are.

One woman, Betty Howard, has a "Pray for Eric Rudolph" sign on the marquee outside her diner. She told the *New York Times* she's starting a legal defense fund. "Bless his heart," she says. "Eric needs our help."

In one sense, there's nothing new here. From Jesse James and Billy the Kid to John Dillinger and Pretty Boy Floyd, people have periodically elevated to the status of folk hero thieves, thugs and killers who supposedly "stood" for something. That doesn't make it any less offensive.

And as for Rudolph's alleged causes: White supremacy and homophobia are indefensible and anti-government paranoia—the so-called "patriot movement"—is just flat stupid. His opposition to abortion is the one issue that carries any moral heft, the one about which decent people can, and probably always will, disagree.

Which is why antiabortion activists ought to be the least forgiving of all. If authorities are right, Rudolph has soiled their moral authority with his hypocrisy. I don't care where you stand on the issue: It's impossible to see reverence for life in the act of planting bombs. Much less a cause for sympathy.

Meantime, Fallon Stubbs grieves her mother, Emily Lyons still has nails embedded in her body and Ronald Smith is hoping a recent surgery will allow him to finally walk without a brace.

I'll reserve my sympathies for them.

JUNE 9, 2003

CHRISTIAN'S ARREST TWISTS ARGUMENT

The story is almost certainly apocryphal, but here it is for what it's worth:

Shortly after the Sept. 11 terrorist attacks, Muhammad Ali was supposedly visiting ground zero when someone asked a barbed question: How did Ali, the most famous Muslim in the world who is not a terrorist, feel about sharing his religion with Osama bin Laden? The champ shot back, "How does it feel to share yours with Hitler?"

As I said, the story—it began circulating shortly after the attacks—is probably not true, but it ought to be. It's valuable for what it says about our tendency to demonize the unfamiliar and overlook the obvious.

Which brings us to Eric Rudolph, alleged Christian terrorist.

And, to this question: Is that a fair term to describe the accused serial bomber? Some observers have begun debating that since Rudolph's recent arrest in North Carolina, among them the *Washington Post*, which raised the issue in a story last week, and Arsalan Tariq Iftikhar, Midwest communications director for the Council on American–Islamic Relations, who tackled it a few days ago in the *Herald*.

The question is, to say the least, provocative. After all, the crimes of which Rudolph stands accused—the bombings of a gay nightclub, two abortion clinics, and an Atlanta park at the 1996 Summer Olympics—can fairly be described as terrorism. And he is indeed believed to have been motivated by Christianity, albeit that perversion of it found on the extreme right end of the political spectrum. In that perversion, love of Jesus somehow translates to the conviction that Jews are diabolical, blacks subhuman, and explosive devices a valid expression of faith.

So does that make him a Christian terrorist? And if not, why? What is the substantive difference between him and all the "Muslim terrorists" who plant bombs out of their supposed devotion to Islam?

If you're a Christian, as I am, your reflexive response is likely to resent being lumped with this guy whose beliefs reflect no Christianity you've ever known or practiced. And perhaps you're self-aware enough to realize in the process that this is the argument moderate Muslims have been making for years, to limited effect.

Granted, the comparison is inexact.

For one thing, Christianity is, by a sizable margin, the largest religion in America. Its ubiquity makes it unlikely that Rudolph could ever be seen as "representative" of the followers of Christ. So it's difficult for most Christians to fully appreciate how the term "Muslim terrorist" must resonate with Muslims who are not.

There's another reason the comparison is flawed. Namely, that fundamentalist extremists have managed to hijack Islam to a degree most of us find unfathomable.

In this country, it is considered newsworthy and a cause for concern that a few people in the hills of North Carolina have expressed sympathy for Rudolph. But in the Middle East, "sympathy" for terrorism is general, often taking the form of government support, institutional anti-Semitism and the lionization of suicide bombers. Fairly or unfairly, the damage that behavior has done to Islam in the eyes of the world is incalculable.

For all its imperfections, though, the comparison is a valuable one. It requires the majority to walk in the minority's shoes, demands that we grapple with issues of fairness and sensitivity we might otherwise never consider. It serves to the goose the sauce prepared for the gander.

Is Eric Rudolph a Christian terrorist? If Osama bin Laden is a Muslim terrorist, then isn't the unavoidable answer yes?

Not that we'll ever call him that. As history is written by the winners, so perception is shaped by the majority. And I doubt that any mainstream news outlet will ever use "Christian terrorist" to describe Rudolph. People will say it's provocative and unsettling, and it is.

I'm just not convinced that's a bad thing.

JULY 18, 2003

HIGH COURT NEEDS SUPREME GUIDANCE

Hi, God, it's me, Pat Robertson. How's everything in Heaven?

Clear skies, warm sun and a gentle breeze, eh? Well, it's been raining cats and dogs here in Virginia. But I guess You already knew that, didn't You?

Listen, God, the reason I'm calling: I'm sure You saw in the paper where I've asked the viewers of my TV show, *The 700 Club*, to join me in a "prayer offensive." You've probably heard from them already; they're more responsive than Pavlov's dogs.

Little joke there, Lord.

Anyway, what we want is, we want You to change the Supreme Court. Frankly, your people have had it up to their keisters—excuse the rough language, God—with the Court. First, they said schoolchildren couldn't be forced to pray to You. Then they said a woman had the right to "choose" whether she wanted to be a mother. Now, the court has struck down an anti-sodomy law in the state of Texas. Left-wingers are calling it a great victory for so-called "gay rights."

But Lord, all us real Americans are terribly concerned. I don't mind telling You, I trembled as I thought about what this awful ruling will lead to. Homosexuals will be allowed to get married. Prostitution will be legalized, and bestiality will be mandatory. Even incest will be tolerated—and I'm not just talking about in your trailer parks either.

Then I realized that the solution is simple: Why don't You just get rid of three of the liberal justices? That way, our president can replace them with good, You-fearing conservatives? As I told my viewers, it shouldn't be too hard, given that one liberal justice is 83 years old, another has cancer and another has a heart condition.

Now, I know what you're thinking, Lord, and no, I'm not exactly asking You to kill them. That's the same thing that darn liberal media has been saying. They've been having a field day at my expense ever since this all began. That twit Paula Zahn treated me like a moron on CNN. Some guy from United Press pretty much called me an idiot.

But God, You and I know You wouldn't have to kill them to get them off the court. All You need to do is nudge them a little. Let's say maybe one of them has a recurrence of cancer, not even cancer in a vital part. Cancer of the fingernail, maybe. Or another has a little heart scare. The old ticker just misses a beat or two. Or maybe one falls and breaks a hip. I'm not asking for a compound fracture, Lord. Just a little break. Just enough to convince him to hang up the robe.

Is that really so unreasonable? I don't think so. Not if it allows our president to stack the court with conservatives.

Frankly, Lord—and I'm not being critical—I don't know why You never thought of this before. I mean, everybody knows you're a Republican. After all, aren't conservatives made in Your image? Says so right there in the Bible.

So I can't figure out why You've put up with liberal shenanigans for so long. It's been going on for decades now. Sensitivity training, political correctness, diversity. And don't even get me started talking about rights. Black rights, women's rights, Latino rights, homosexual rights. Everybody wants rights.

What I want is to get back to the good old days when we didn't have to worry so much about rights. The days when Beaver Cleaver was still on the air and Doris Day was still on the radio. The days when, if the president said you were going to war, darn it, you didn't stand around debating the matter, you went to war.

If pushing three Supreme Court justices out the door is what it takes to get back to those days, I don't think it's too high a price.

And while you're at it, could You also do something about that liberal media? I'm serious, Lord, they're a gosh-awful pain in my neck.

Again, I'm not looking for anything fatal or excessively bloody. Maybe just a plague of frogs in the newsroom of the *New York Times*. Or locusts could fly out of Dan Rather's backside. Something simple.

Anyway, I leave it to your judgment. Thanks for listening. And tell Jesus I said hey.

SEPTEMBER 29, 2003

FAITHFUL OFTEN GIVE RELIGION A BAD NAME

This is how you stone a woman to death.

You bury her up to her neck. Then you heave stones at her head. One imagines her face slowly obliterated, her skull repeatedly broken. One imagines the process takes a long time.

One finds it hard to imagine a crueler way to die.

Last Thursday, a court in Nigeria spared Amina Lawal that grisly fate. She is a 31-year-old peasant who had been convicted of adultery under sharia law, a religious code based on the Koran. The chief evidence of her "crime": her 2-year-old daughter, Wasila.

Lawal has long claimed innocence, saying Wasila's father promised to marry her. But the man she identified turned out to be married already and denied fathering her child. Three male witnesses corroborated his claim that he never had sex with Lawal.

An outsider is at a loss to understand how a man's friends can authoritatively testify that he did not have intercourse. But their word was enough under sharia law, and the man was acquitted.

Lawal's exoneration was less sweeping. Judges relied largely on technicalities in setting her free. Their ruling also took into account interpretations of sharia law that hold that an embryo can gestate for up to five years as opposed to the more widely accepted nine months.

Something else an outsider finds hard to figure. Still, that fanciful time frame allows for the possibility that Lawal's ex-husband fathered the child, thus contributing to her acquittal.

I am not a scholar on the Koran, but I'm sure it contains passages to justify throwing rocks at Amina Lawal. Nor would I be surprised to hear that it also contravenes its own harsh justice by passages requiring mercy, compassion, forgiveness.

In this, it would be much like the Christian Bible, which also requires death by stoning for people who commit adultery. Yet, when a group of men brings to Christ an adulterous woman with a demand that the penalty be enacted, he just kneels and doodles in the dirt.

When they press him, he stands and says, "Let he who is without sin cast the first stone." Then he kneels and doodles some more.

One by one, the men slink away.

And isn't that always the way? People are always pleased to indulge their religiosity when it allows them to stand in judgment of someone else, licenses them to feel superior to someone else, tells them they are more righteous than someone else.

They are less enthusiastic when religiosity demands that they be compassionate to someone else. That they show charity, service and mercy to everyone else.

Consider that last month thousands of people wept on the steps of an Alabama courthouse in support of a rock bearing the Ten Commandments. And watching, you wondered: What hungry person gets fed because of this? What naked person is clothed, what homeless one housed?

It seemed a fresh reminder that religious people are often the poorest advertisement for religious life.

How much more convincing an advertisement, how much more compelling a testimony, if people of faith were more often caught by news cameras demonstrating against healthcare cuts that fill our streets with the homeless mentally ill. Or confronting the slumlord about the vermin-infested holes he offers as places for families to live. Or crusading to make the sweatshop owner pay a living wage to workers who are treated little better than slaves.

Problem is, this would require more than the ability to feel self-righteous and aggrieved. It would require putting oneself on the line. Small wonder many people of faith prefer to content themselves with spiritual busywork.

Sometimes, piety is just an excuse to throw rocks at somebody's head.

NOVEMBER 17, 2003

READY-MADE SANDWICH JUST TOO CONVENIENT

How long do you figure it would take you to make a peanut butter and jelly sandwich?

Not trying to set a land speed record, mind you. Just working at a normal pace, slapping jelly on one slice of bread, peanut butter on the other. How long do you figure it would take, start to finish? Thirty seconds? Forty-five?

Do you really have that kind of time to waste?

PJ Squares is betting that you don't. So the company, born— it swears!—in Sandwich, Ill., is offering a solution for time-pressed Americans. A PJ Square, you see, is a two-sided slice of "peanut butter flavor layer" and a second, jelly-like layer made of fruit juice. It comes individually packaged like that shiny fake orange cheese in the dairy case. You slap one down between bread or crackers and presto! Not a PB&J, but an incredible simulation.

PJ Squares are said to be available in "select" supermarkets and Target stores nationwide, but I didn't have to go that far to find one. A co-worker—let's call him "Bob," since that's his name— brought some in the other day, whereupon some of us spent a few minutes not putting out the newspaper. Instead, we had an im-promptu taste test.

The consensus? They are not disgusting. If you were trapped on a desert island and had to choose between one of these or shoe leather, you would pick the Square in a heartbeat.

And yet by their very existence, PJ Squares raise a question of pressing concern: How lazy do you have to be to need a shortcut to a peanut butter and jelly sandwich?!

I'm sorry. Did I say lazy? I meant, "time-pressed." Granted, some of us are too effort-challenged to fan away the flies, and I'm sure PJ Squares will find a nice market among those folks, assuming they can make it to the store. But for most of us, the issue is simply time and the lack thereof. We stagger through sleep-deprived days trying to figure out how to do the same things in fewer minutes.

As the PJ Squares website puts it, "[I]f you only have a few min-utes to give the kids a snack, find the missing soccer shorts and get to a game, you can grab a box of PJ Squares and get on the road." In other words, they're convenient.

Heaven help us.

I mean, when "convenience" became a Madison Avenue mantra 50 years ago, the idea was that it would give us more leisure time.

Instant coffee, instant oatmeal, hands-free mops and wrinkle-free slacks, self-propelled lawn mowers, frozen foods and microwave ovens ... the promise, sometimes implicit, sometimes stated, was that they would make life's mundane chores a breeze, that they would free us to read and chat, to paint or play the piano or just pause and sniff those darned roses. Life would be better.

So here we are, a half century later. What are you doing with all your extra time?

Yeah, that's a good one, isn't it? We get the same 24 hours previous generations did and yet ours seem to have been shortchanged. You want to demand a recount. While their days seemed merely busy, ours feel ... crammed. Stuffed to the breaking point with deadlines, demands, presentations, Net surfing, business trips, soccer practices, things that all have to be done right now.

And there is never enough "now" to go around.

I blame convenience. Because with more time has come an implicit expectation of more accomplishment. What excuse is there for lingering over the morning meal when breakfast is a bar you can munch in the car? How can you justify relaxing with a book in the airport lounge when the big report can be downloaded to your PDA?

Woe unto the unstructured moment, the moment not spent planning, racing, rushing, doing. The moment you spend just being.

The paradoxical thing is, we had more of them when life was less convenient.

Yeah, maybe I exaggerate, but this much I know: If you're too busy to make a peanut butter and jelly sandwich, you're too busy.

DECEMBER 15, 2003

O COME ALL YE FAITHFUL
TO FIND JOY AT THE MALLS

An excerpt from the Gospel according to St. Luke, revised and updated for the 21st century:

"And there were in the same country shepherds, abiding in the fields, keeping watch over their flock by night. And lo, the angel of the Lord came upon them, and the glory of the Lord shone round about them and they were sore afraid. And the angel said unto them, 'Fear not: for, behold, I bring you good tidings of great joy.'

"Wal-Mart is having a sale on DVD players. Just $29 apiece. And five megapixel digital cameras are also available for $344 and up. This be a Wal-Mart exclusive. In addition, ye shall find the Bratz doll with the Funky Fashion Furniture set for a mere $28.88 apiece.

"Rejoice, ye humble tenders of sheep! I bring ye news of plentiful shopping and bargains abundant. Gleaming temples of commerce await thee, open long hours for thy convenience. And their shelves are heavy laden with wonders that shall beggar thy poor imaginings.

"Consider ye these bargains: Circuit City doth present thee a discount of $50 to $400 on all manner of large televisions, including flat screens. Free delivery doth be available. JCPenney doth sell 14-karat gold chains for half off, while Cingular doth offer 500 bonus rollover minutes on select cellphone calling plans. And at Toys Doth Be Us, ye may obtain a 35th Anniversary Elmo doll for only $5, with a purchase of $75 or more. The offer be good only so long as supplies endure.

"Truly there be an awesome bounty of material treasures offered unto thee.

"But be ye warned: to claim and hold these treasures shall require of ye great sacrifice and exceeding diligence. Ye shall rise before the sun to catch the early bird specials. Ye shall traipse throughout the day, returning wearily to thine abode long after the sun has fallen from the sky.

"Ye shall find parking for thine ass and thy cart exceedingly limited, forcing thee to circle the parking lot, hunting for the man who is about to remove his ass and his cart to another place.

"Ye shall compete against thy fellow shoppers, who seek the same must-have items at the same bargain prices. This shall require of ye sharp reflexes. Also, sharp elbows.

"Nor shall this be the end of thy testing. For once all these things are done, it shall come to pass that the bills come due. And on this date, there shall be wailing and moaning and gnashing of teeth throughout the land and ye shall eat naught but beans and buy naught but generic brands until well after Mother's Day. Spouses shall bicker with one another and fathers shall wander the abode turning off lights and air conditioning, muttering that they be not made of money.

"All this and more shalt thou endure. But thou shalt bear this burden gladly in the hope and longing that it shall lead ye to the ultimate prize: That thou shalt find in thy striving and straining, in thy going and coming, in thy frenzied acquisition of things, a measure of peace, some proof of love. Thou shalt seek ownership of things in the expectation that this will make ye what ye are not, give ye what ye have not, that it will fill thee as sod does a gaping hole and make thee finally and fully, complete."

And when the angel had said these things, the shepherds looked from one to the other with upturned palms and confused demeanor. Finally, one of their number hesitantly raised his hand and spake.

"Forgive us, herald of the most high," he said. "Truly ye bring us word of strange and marvelous things. Yet we cannot help wondering: Is that all there is to thy good news? Just ... shopping?"

Whereupon the angel stroked his chin, then looked up and snapped his fingers in the manner of one chagrined.

"Oh yes," the angel said. "There was one other thing I almost forgot. A savior was born to you down in Bethlehem."

JANUARY 9, 2004

LEAVE GOD OUT OF THE RACE FOR ENDORSEMENTS

I had to go to the market to do some shopping. God went along to keep me company.

He was examining the fine print on some ice cream when I told Him about a news story I had seen. It said that Howard Dean has decided to mention God more often in his campaign appearances.

"What's a Howard Dean?" God asked.

"He's a presidential candidate," I said. "A Democrat."

"What's a Democrat?"

"Well, you see," I stammered, "there are like, these two political parties, and—"

God laughed. "Gotcha," He said. "You are so easy."

"Oh. So you know what a Democrat is."

"I read the papers," said God. He held up the ice cream. "Have you ever read the back panel on one of these? You need a chemistry degree to understand it. What's a diglyceride, for goodness sake?"

"You think I should go to the natural food store?"

God shrugged. "I gave you free will," He said. "Make up on your own mind. So anyway, you were asking me about this Howard Dean fellow, who has decided to give me a plug."

"Yeah," I said as we wandered over to the cereal aisle. "He says he intends to be more open in talking about You from now on. Voters like that, like to know that their presidential candidates are religious. He said he wasn't comfortable talking about You in public before because he's from New England. They like to keep that kind of stuff to themselves up there."

"I've noticed that," said God. "Up North, they act like I was a bad secret, something you don't mention in polite company. Down South, you can't shut 'em up. They call me out for every high school football game."

"You don't sound like you're too impressed either way."

God had been reading the side panel on a cereal box. "Trisodium phosphate," He muttered dubiously.

I tried repeating it. "You don't sound like you're too—"

"I heard you the first time," said God, not turning around. "Why is it, you people always think if I don't respond in the first nanosecond it means I didn't hear you? I hear. And to answer your question: I'm more concerned with what people are than with what they say or don't say."

"What do You mean?"

Now He looked at me. "Mouths lie, hearts don't," He said. "Come on, let's go to the produce section. You should buy some fruit. I don't like all these chemicals you eat."

"What about free will?"

He spread His hands. "Just a suggestion."

"You said, 'Mouths lie, hearts don't,'" I said. He was inspecting an apple. "That's fine for you. You can read hearts. We can't. So why shouldn't we ask a politician to tell us how he feels about You?"

A sigh. "I am not a prop," said God.

"Beg pardon?"

"For years, the conservatives have tried to make me their mascot: 'God wants a Yes vote on Prop. 13. God wants a tax cut.' Now this Dean fellow wants to show that I'm on his side. I am the author of creation and the painter of every sunset. I was here before the first and will be here after the last. I am not a political prop. I am the Lord thy God."

He tore a bag off the roller and dropped the apple in. "And the Lord thy God says you're buying some fruit," He said, picking through the bin for more. "You say 'free will' to me and I'll give you a wart so big ...."

"No, that's fine," I said. "I'm confused, though. I don't understand what You want us to do."

"I told you a long time ago. Look after one another. Call your parents. Take one day out of seven and get some rest. What's so hard about that? I mean, you personally don't seem to have any trouble with it. You do just fine. In fact, sometimes I wish everybody would just be more like you."

My heart leapt. "Really?"

God handed me a bag full of apples and shook His head. "You are way too easy," He said.

FEBRUARY 6, 2004

FLASH BY JANET REVEALS ONLY LACK OF WISDOM

It was a week in which the president agreed to an investigation of pre-war intelligence failures, a Massachusetts court affirmed gay marriage and ricin was found in a Senate mailroom.

So naturally, everybody is talking about Janet Jackson's right breast.

As you surely know, Jackson "unleashed the breast" (credit the phrase to a student of mine) during a Super Bowl halftime duet with Justin Timberlake. As the song ended, Timberlake ripped away Jackson's bustier and an audience of 90 million people got a flash of Jacksonian bosom, full exposure of which was prevented only by a nipple shield.

Both singers have since issued apologies, blaming the strip show on a wardrobe malfunction. CBS, which televised it, has pronounced itself angry and embarrassed. MTV, which produced the performance, says it is as shocked as anybody. And FCC Chairman Michael Powell, deploring what he calls a "classless, crass and deplorable stunt," has launched an actual, no-fooling federal investigation.

Powell might be serious. But if you tell me you're buying the rest of it, I will personally come to your house and slap the taste out of your mouth. You're too gullible to live.

In the interest of my not getting arrested for assault, please take a few things into consideration:

In the tune in question, Timberlake vows to "have you naked by the end of this song";

The network could have, but apparently did not, broadcast on a delay, allowing ample time to omit the objectionable;

In a post-performance interview, a laughing Timberlake told Pat O'Brien of *Access Hollywood*, "Hey, man, we love giving you all something to talk about";

I'm no expert, but I'm pretty sure a woman doesn't wear a nipple shield unless she's expecting to bare the breast.

What you have here, then, is not an accident, but a stunt designed to do exactly what it did: get people talking. From my perch, though, we're talking about the wrong thing.

People have framed the episode in terms of pop culture's explicitness. I believe it speaks more to the culture's emptiness, its shiny artificiality.

Once upon a time, back when Elvis wobbled his leg, shock was a natural byproduct of artistic expression. Elvis used to say he wasn't trying to offend anybody; he was just doing what the music dictated, doing what came naturally.

But we are less innocent now and it is increasingly the case that shock is no longer a byproduct of expression; rather, it has itself become the expression. And there is nothing "natural" about it.

So it's no accident that you have Madonna planting a wet one on Britney and Janet baring her mammary gland for the world to see. Shock has become its own reward, has become both means and end.

It has become a tool of people who have nothing to say, but are ever more aggressive about saying it.

Jackson, you must remember, is 37—an ancient crone in pop years—and has an album coming out soon. She needs attention, so she uses her breast. What else can she use? Her talent? Ha and ha.

Tuesday morning on *Today*, Katie Couric expressed the wan hope that we could now stop talking about this. She was mindful of the irony of saying that after having spent long minutes talking about it before an audience of multiple millions. And yes, I'm aware of the same irony in bringing it up in this more humble forum.

But if you have any appreciation of how exhilarating, revelatory and dangerous pop culture has been and can be, if you understand its power to upend our understanding and rock the castles of complacency, this kind of cheap, calculated shock has to make you sad. Janet's was an act both tinny and tiny, the kind of idea you get when you have no ideas.

So the headline here is not that a woman exposed a breast. It is, rather, that a breast exposed a woman.

FEBRUARY 9, 2004

SHIFTING EVENTS LEAD TO APOLOGY TO THE PRESIDENT

Let me tell you how President Bush ruined my weekend.

But first, a little background.

I write two columns a week, one of which has a Friday deadline for publication the following week. It's a tricky proposition; you're tasked with writing something that will still be relevant three days later. So you look for subjects that are timely but not fluid, not likely to change too much over the weekend.

I figured I'd found such a subject Friday before last when I wrote about former U.S. weapons inspector David Kay's testimony before a Congressional panel. Kay said that he and the Bush administration "were all wrong" in believing Iraq had weapons of mass destruction. The existence of said weapons was, you will recall, President Bush's chief rationale for invading that nation.

Kay thought there should be an independent investigation into whatever intelligence failures led our government to believe there were weapons where there are probably none. Aides to the president promptly dismissed the suggestion and as late as Friday, the president himself was refusing to support it. So I wrote a column sharply critical of his position.

Sunday comes. And with it, news that the president, under pressure from political foes and allies alike, has reluctantly changed his mind and will now support an investigation. He has decided, of all the dirty tricks, to do the right thing.

This is where the weekend turns sour, because I know what's going to happen Monday. And it does. Most newspapers kill the column, but a few run it. So on one page, I'm blasting the president for not supporting the investigation and on another, he is supporting the investigation.

This leads to a handful of nasty notes from diehard Bush fans. Some make reference to an "affirmative action" columnist. Some suggest that I now owe the president an apology.

Which is a real jaw-dropper. He had to be dragged into this like a toddler to a doctor's office, but I ...

Owe him.

An apology?

Very well, then. Here it is.

Mr. President, I apologize for writing that column. I should have realized that even the most mulish obstructionism has its limits.

While I'm at it, allow me to express contrition for a few other things that are probably somehow my fault.

I apologize that some of your supporters are so ignorant as to think criticism of your war has to do with affirmative action or, more frequently, lack of patriotism. I should have done a better job educating them.

I apologize that over 500 Americans have died defending a cause that is apparently not what they were told. I should have protested more vigorously.

I apologize that thousands of other people have died and been maimed. I should have cried out a little louder.

I apologize that much of the world hates us. I should have warned you more insistently.

I apologize that a minority of voters, some hanging chads and the Supreme Court got you into this mess. I should have voted twice.

Finally, Mr. President, I apologize that you rammed through laws making it possible to lock up American citizens indefinitely without trial, charges or access to attorneys. I should have fought you harder. But I was scared.

Funny thing is, I'm still scared. More scared, in fact. I fear terrorist fanaticism, of course. But I also fear what my country has done and become in response to it.

Unfortunately for me, Mr. President, this is another column written on a Friday. Meaning I run the risk that by the time it is read, the world will no longer hate us, your supporters will have stopped questioning the patriotism or credentials of dissenters, the Patriot Act will have been repealed, the Supreme Court will have reversed itself, and all those people will no longer be dead.

I apologize in advance.

JUNE 11, 2004

MEDIA'S PICTURE OF REAGAN ERA IS INCOMPLETE

The Reagan Revolution began in 1980 in Philadelphia, Miss.

Philadelphia, a speck of town north and east of Jackson, is infamous as the place three young civil rights workers were murdered in 1964 for registering black people to vote. Now here came Ronald Reagan, Republican presidential aspirant, opening his campaign at a fair that for generations had served as a forum for segregationists, and offering thinly veiled support for their cause.

"I believe in state's rights," he said.

His death this week has to it, as you might expect, a sense of national moment. Flags at half staff, long lines snaking into the Capitol to pay final respects. His widow weeps, his supporters grieve and I'd have been content to leave them their space, to watch it all in respectful silence.

Except that it's getting kind of deep around here, if you catch my drift. Any deeper and we'll all need hip boots.

I refer, in case my drift goes uncaught, to the fulsome media tributes that have attended the former president's death. Not just fulsome, but uncritical, bereft of balance, lacking perspective. If all you knew of Ronald Reagan is what you saw on newscasts or read in the initial coverage from *USA Today*, the *New York Times*, the *Washington Post* or the *Miami Herald*, you'd think him a cross between Wilford Brimley and John Rambo, a twinkle-eyed grandfather with a fondness for jelly beans who single-handedly saved America, kicked the Commies in the butt, and maybe even found a cure for the common cold while he was at it. You'd never know about what he said in Mississippi.

It's hardly uncommon to speak well of the recently departed. And there is certainly much about the former president's tenure that merits celebration. He restored "can do" to the American lexicon, his vibrant optimism a jolt of adrenaline after the dour Carter years and the criminality of the Nixon gang. He pushed communism to the breaking point. He famously called the Soviet Union what it was—an empire of evil. He changed the political landscape.

But my point here is that some of us also knew another Reagan, and he is conspicuous by his absence from much of this week's coverage.

Some of us remember his cuts in federal lunch programs for poor children and his claim that ketchup is a vegetable.

Some of us remember his revival of the old canard that Martin Luther King was a communist.

Some of us remember Americans dying by the thousands from AIDS while their president breathed not a word.

Some of us remember finding homeless people sleeping under freeways.

And some of us were there when the cities imploded, rent by a cheap and insanely addictive new drug called crack. It turned our mothers into prostitutes, our fathers into zombies, our children into orphans, our communities into killing fields. We looked to the White House for help and received in response a ruinous "war on drugs" and this advice from the first lady:

"Just say no."

To the degree those things are missing from their analyses, news media have embarrassed themselves this week. They have rewritten history and slapped on a happy face.

It's not an issue of respecting the deceased. It is, rather, an issue of telling the whole truth, fulfilling our obligation to write history's first draft. Imagine analyzing a recently departed Bill Clinton and leaving out Monica Lewinsky or memorializing Richard Nixon and forgetting Watergate. That would be what this is: dishonest. Lies of omission.

So let me say this for the record: Some of us watch these proceedings with the sober respect you'd have for any loss of life, but also with dry eyes. The media have sold us a fraudulent version of history. Everybody loved Ronald Reagan, it says.

Beg pardon, but "everybody" did not.

OCTOBER 4, 2004

ALL IS GOING WELL IN BUSH'S IRAQ— WHEREVER THAT IS

"Don't nobody bring me no bad news."—from The Wiz

Evidently, there are two Iraqs.

One exists here on our Earth, the other occupies a parallel space-time continuum perceivable only by a select few individuals, one of whom is the president of the United States.

If you've got a better theory, I'm open to it. All I know is that in recent weeks, we've seen that nation go from awful to whatever comes after awful. Yet, to hear the president talk, the situation is actually a lot better, more hunky and/or dory, than anybody really knows. We're moving forward, he says. We're getting the job done.

Two Iraqs. That's got to be it. That must be why the Iraq the president describes bears so little resemblance to the one described by, well ... just about everybody else in the world.

"It's Worse Than You Think," reads a headline in *Newsweek*, accompanying a picture of a wounded man who seems to be in shock.

A *Wall Street Journal* correspondent sends colleagues an e-mail saying that in Baghdad, it is unsafe to talk to strangers, eat in restaurants, shop for groceries, take a drive, speak English, be an American.

The *New York Times* reports that 2,300 insurgent attacks took place in Iraq during a recent 30-day period—that's 76 car bombs, land-mine explosions, rocket-propelled grenade assaults, shootings and mortar strikes every day in a place roughly the size of California.

Yet Bush describes an Iraq where children go peacefully to school, their parents peacefully to work. "Freedom is on the march," he says.

Two Iraqs.

"[P]rogress is being made," says the president.

"It's getting worse," says Secretary of State Colin Powell.

"I'm optimistic we'll succeed," says the president.

"Right now, we're not winning," says Sen. Chuck Hagel, Republican from Nebraska.

"The Iraqi citizens are defying the pessimistic predictions," says the president.

"The situation has obviously been somewhat deteriorating," says John McCain, Republican senator from Arizona.

Two Iraqs.

The *New York Times* reports that in July, the National Intelligence Council issued a 50-page report representing the consensus of the U.S. intelligence community on the likely course of things in Iraq. It foresaw continuing instability and possible civil war.

The president brushes it aside, saying, "They were just guessing as to what the conditions might be like."

There are two Iraqs. There must be. Because the alternative is profoundly troubling, suggesting a president divorced from reality, holding with such a death grip to his version of truth that nothing can shake him from it. Not news reports, not members of his own party, not his secretary of state, not the intelligence community.

If there are not two Iraqs, we ought to be scared, because a man who filters out information that challenges his beliefs is a man ill-equipped to adapt to new circumstances, unable to formulate new strategies, slow to make necessary change. If there are not two Iraqs, it means such a man has ultimate responsibility for stewardship of American foreign policy in an increasingly volatile world.

Ergo, there are two Iraqs. Otherwise, how can we sleep at night?

I do wish the president had publicized his ability to pierce the space-time continuum. It would have saved a lot of confusion.

I also wish that from time to time he'd talk about the Iraq on this planet. You know, the one where they're planning an election in which maybe a quarter of the population won't be able to participate because it's too dangerous. The one where dozens of children were blown to shreds last week. The one where people we "liberated" hate us. The one that's dissolving into chaos.

But I guess I can't blame Bush for his silence. Why mention the bad Iraq when you have another to talk about?

Unfortunately for the rest of us, we have just the one.

OCTOBER 25, 2004

A FEW ANSWERS FROM ABOVE SHED LIGHT ON TRAGEDY

I threw down the newspaper in disgust. God, who was sitting in the recliner next to mine watching the baseball playoffs, glanced over.

"Relax," He said, "the campaign will be over in a few days."

"It's not that," I said.

"Then what?"

I handed God the newspaper. He put on his reading glasses and spent a few minutes studying the page.

Finally, He shook His head. "Oh," He said, as He laid the paper aside.

"'Oh?' Is that all you can say? Didn't you read the story? These rebels in Uganda, they're kidnapping children and forcing them to be soldiers and sex slaves! It says here they've killed 100,000 people, displaced 1.6 million over the last 18 years. Doesn't that bother you?"

"It bothers me," God said.

"I would think so. Especially since ..."

God arched His brow. "Especially since what?"

It took me a second to gather my courage. "Especially since they're doing it in your name," I said finally.

"It's bad enough they call themselves the Lord's Resistance Army, but did you see this part here? According to the United Nations, these monsters say they're kidnapping kids in order to set up a new government based on the Ten Commandments," I said.

"They forgot No. 8," God said.

"Beg pardon?"

"No. 8," God said. "'Thou shalt not steal.' Also, No. 6, of course. 'Thou shalt not kill.'"

"Why don't you stop them then? Send a plague. Destroy the rebels."

"Is that what you think I should do?"

"You weren't shy about it in the Old Testament."

God sighed. "You send a little too much rain one time and they never let you forget."

"It's not funny!" To my surprise, I shouted it.

"You're angry with me," God said.

I swallowed hard. "I guess I am. It shouldn't be this way. It doesn't have to be."

"Well, we agree there."

"Then make it stop. You could."

"I could," He agreed. "Maybe I will. But it will just start again somewhere else. You know that, don't you? That's the problem with that free will thing I gave you all."

"Yeah, yeah," I said. "We can choose to do right, or we can choose to do wrong. I know all about that."

"Don't give me, 'Yeah, yeah,'" God said sternly. "And for the record, that's not what I meant. What I'm saying is that you people, you're all like that Jim Carrey fellow in that *Bruce Almighty* movie. You all think you can be a better God than I can.

"Some awful thing happens to you, or some bad person isn't instantly struck down by lightning bolts and you figure it must be because God is slipping. You figure He needs your help.

"So you decide to play God. And you use my name to sanction your meanest and most narrow impulses, like I'm a moral Get-Out-of-Jail-Free card or something. You say you're doing my will; then you steal babies and make war. You say you're doing what God said; then you kill one another. I told you to love one another. How do you get from 'love' to 'kill?'"

"But how are we supposed to have faith in you when you let so many bad things happen?" I asked.

"I could ask you the same question," God said.

"You know why I gave you free will? I wanted you to surprise yourselves sometimes. Surprise me, too. I knew you'd do things that disappointed me, but I thought you'd make me proud more often. I thought you would find more opportunities to do good. Instead, you find opportunities to break my heart.

"And yet I keep giving you chances, don't I? Keep giving you sunrises, keep giving you babies, keep giving you breath, waiting for you to surprise me," He said.

I picked up the paper and looked at the awful story again. "Lord, have mercy," I said.

God gave me a wan smile. "I know," He said. "You think it's hard believing in me? Think how I feel, trying to believe in you."

NOVEMBER 8, 2004

WHERE'S THE MORALITY IN BUSH'S POLICY?

I have to thank Jimmy Carter for saving my sanity.

Granted, his was not a presidency one looks back to with fondness. Gas lines stretched forever, Iran took our people hostage, and there was disco, besides.

But Carter's ex-presidency has been a model of that unofficial institution. He has built homes for the poor, mediated wars, helped feed the hungry in Africa, fought disease in Latin America. In so doing, Carter, a deacon of Maranatha Baptist Church in Plains, Ga., has obeyed a directive that Jesus issued one of his disciples.

Do you love me? He asked Simon Peter.

Peter said Yes.

Feed my sheep, said Jesus.

Remembering Carter's example, his very public embrace of that command, is what has gotten me through the last week without a facial tic. Or to put it another way: If one more person tells me that "morality" guided their decision to vote for President Bush, my head's going to pop like a balloon.

Beg your pardon, but one is hard pressed to find much evidence of morality in Bush's ineptly prosecuted war, his erosion of civil rights, and the loss of international credibility that his policies have caused. Unless, of course, one has been quaking in one's boots at the prospect of same-sex couples making a commitment that straight couples have avoided like SARS. In that case, the vote probably reflects one's morality just fine.

More's the pity.

No political tactician am I, but I think Democrats made a fundamental mistake when the Christian right rose as a political force: They watched it happen, ceded God to the GOP without resistance, without so much as a beg your pardon. Democrats, fearful of unsettling the secular West and Northeast, only shrugged as the Almighty was packed up and shipped South, where He is to this day routinely trotted out to endorse various would-be governors, senators and school-board members.

Small wonder faith has come to seem inextricable from voting the straight Republican ticket.

And if you are, as I am, a Christian who remembers what Jesus told Simon Peter, it is galling to see Him reduced to a GOP shill, wrapped in a flag and used as a prop to advance a conservative agenda—which, by the way, stands the Bible on its head.

After all, the Book says that Jesus consorted with lepers and prostitutes. It says He talked with women—which was beneath a man of His time and place—and washed the feet of his followers.

And it tells us He said things that seemed to make no logical sense: If someone takes your shirt, let him have your cloak as well. If someone hits you on the right cheek, offer him the left. Love your enemies. This was crazy talk. There was nothing conservative about this man.

So I look at the success that conservatives on the so-called Christian right have had in claiming Him as their exclusive property, and I wonder, where in the heck is the Christian left? Where are the people who preach—and live—the biblical values of inclusion, service, humility and sacrifice, and why haven't they coalesced into an alternative political force?

Instead of a movement like that, we have an old peanut farmer building houses for the poor.

You wish there were more. You wish there were Christian people shouting from the rooftops that these other people, with their small minds and niggardly spirits, do not represent all of us. And that the faith exemplified by the politics of exclusion is not the faith that the rest of us celebrate, not the faith that lifts us and settles us and makes us whole.

But nobody's shouting these things. It occurs to me that maybe they're all too busy building houses for poor people. And that maybe I should be as well.

God bless you, Jimmy Carter, wherever you are.

APRIL 1, 2005

LESSONS IN KEEPING FAITH, FACING REALITY

"Though he slay me, yet will I trust in him"—Job 13:15

The tears surprised me. I pulled over, blinded by them.

The incident is sharp in memory because it was a turning point: the moment I finally accepted the unacceptable. My mom was going to lose her battle with breast cancer. She was going to die.

My sisters and brother had already come to terms with it. I was the one still clinging, stubbornly and defiantly, to an expectation of miracles. To do otherwise felt like a betrayal of my mother. And of my faith.

But that day back in 1988, acceptance finally forced itself on me. Cancer had made her a stick figure. It had clouded her mind with hallucination. And it had reduced her to a toddler, her hand feather light in mine as she tottered down the hall.

I left her bedside at a trot. Got in the car and drove until I couldn't see.

As you've probably guessed, I'm writing about Terri Schiavo, who died Thursday. And I'm doing what I guess we all do when we contemplate her tragedy. I am personalizing it.

How can you not? On the one side, there is Michael Schiavo, ordering removal of the feeding tube that sustained his wife for 15 years because, he said, she would not have wanted to live in a vegetative state. On the other, there are the parents, Robert and Mary Schindler, begging in tears for their daughter to simply live, in whatever state she could.

It is only natural to run such a painful conundrum though the filter of experience—or imagination—and try to tease out truth you can live with.

Here's mine. Acceptance is hard. Acceptance hurts like hell.

For as much time as we've spent discussing spousal rights, political opportunism and the meaning of life, I think that's the signature lesson here: Conceding the inevitability of death is one of the hardest duties of life. And maybe the longer you put it off—the Schindlers and Michael Schiavo have been fighting for seven years—the more difficult it becomes.

Which is why the denouement of this drama has been painful, even for those of us who were not directly involved.

Watching the increasingly naked desperation of the fight to keep Terri alive came to feel intrusive and voyeuristic. You wanted to turn away, but there was no place you could go.

So you watched as the Schindlers strained credulity with claims that their daughter tried to say "I want to live" even as her feeding tube was removed.

And never mind that, five years ago, according to a report in the *Herald*, the couple openly conceded that Terri was insensate, her brain destroyed.

You watched as the Rev. Jesse Jackson, in a stunning illustration of the axiom about politics and bedfellows, spoke out on behalf of the Schindlers, a boogeyman of the liberal left making common cause with the religious right.

You watched as House Majority Leader Tom DeLay denounced as "barbarism" the removal of Terri's feeding tube and trampled on the constitutional separation of powers with extraordinary legislative maneuvers to keep her alive, yet neglected to mention that he raised no similar objection 17 years ago when his father suffered a massive head injury and the family decided it was best that the elder DeLay be allowed to die.

You watched as people went just a little bit nuts.

And maybe, if you were the praying type, you said, Hey, God, how about a little help here? When should we stop waiting on the miracle? When is it OK to give up hope?

But God, as far as is known, kept His own counsel.

Maybe He felt He'd said what He had to say 15 years ago.

Terri Schiavo's death, hard as it was, feels like mercy. For her and for us. Once again, we can avoid confronting our irresolute feelings and fears.

There is, however, wisdom here, for those who care to seek it. Roughly distilled, it goes like this: To face reality is not to betray faith.

God answers every prayer, a preacher once said.

Sometimes, the answer is no.

JUNE 3, 2005

CHRIS CECIL, PLAGIARISM GETS YOU FIRED

Dear Chris Cecil:

Here's how you write a newspaper column. First, you find a topic that engages you. Then you spend a few hours banging your head against a computer screen until what you've written there no longer makes you want to hurl.

Or, you could just wait till somebody else writes a column and steal it. That's what you've been doing on a regular basis.

Before Tuesday, I had never heard of you or the *Daily Tribune News*, in Cartersville, Ga., where you are associate managing editor. Then one of my readers, God bless her, sent me an e-mail noting the similarities between a column of mine and one you had purportedly written.

Intrigued, I did a little research on your paper's website and found that you had "written" at least eight columns since March that were taken in whole or in part from my work. The thefts ranged from the pilfering of the lead from a gangsta rap column to the wholesale heist of an entire piece I did about Bill Cosby. In that instance, you essentially took my name off and slapped yours on.

On March 11, I wrote: "I like hypocrites. You would, too, if you had this job. A hypocrite is the next best thing to a day off. Some pious moralizer contradicts his words with his deeds and the column all but writes itself. It's different with Bill Cosby."

On May 12, you "wrote": "I like hypocrites. You would, too, if you had this job. A hypocrite is the next best thing to a day off. Some pious moralizer contradicts his words with his deeds and the column all but writes itself. It's different with Bill Cosby."

The one that really got me, though, was your theft of a personal anecdote about the moment I realized my mother was dying of cancer. "The tears surprised me," I wrote. "I pulled over, blinded by them." Seven days later, there you were: "The tears surprised me. I pulled over, blinded by them on central Kentucky's I-75."

Actually, it happened at an on-ramp to the Artesia Freeway in Compton, Calif.

I've been in this business 29 years, Mr. Cecil, and I've been plagiarized before. But I've never seen a plagiarist as industrious and brazen as you. My boss is calling your boss, but I doubt you and I will ever speak. Still, I wanted you to hear from me. I wanted you to understand how this feels.

Put it like this: I had a house burglarized once. This reminds me of that. Same sense of violation, same apoplectic disbelief that someone has the testicular fortitude to come into your place and take what is yours.

Not being a writer yourself, you won't understand, but I am a worshiper at the First Church of the Written Word, a lover of language, a student of its rhythm, its music, its violence and its power.

My words are important to me. I struggle with them, obsess over them. Show me something I wrote and like a mother recounting a child's birth, I can tell you stories of how it came to be, why this adjective here or that colon there.

See, my life's goal is to learn to write. And you cannot cut and paste your way to that. You can only work your way there, sweating out words, wrestling down prose, hammering together poetry. There are no shortcuts.

You are just the latest in a growing list of people—in journalism and out—who don't understand that, who think it's OK to cheat your way across the finish line. I've always wanted to ask one of you: How can you do that? Have you no shame? No honor or pride? How do you face your mirror knowing you are not what you purport to be? Knowing that you are a fraud?

If your boss values his paper's credibility, you will soon have lots of free time to ponder those questions.

But before you go, let me say something on behalf of all of us who are struggling to learn how to write, or just struggling to be honorable human beings:

The dictionary is a big book. Get your own damn words. Leave mine alone.

AUGUST 29, 2005

MEDIA FEED US SUGAR: ADDICTIVE, LACKING NUTRITION

And then Bob Costas said no.

Maybe you didn't hear about it. There's so much news to keep track of, after all, what with Paris Hilton maybe or maybe not getting married, Angelina Jolie maybe or maybe not sleeping with Brad Pitt, and Sean "P. Diddy" Combs announcing to a breathlessly waiting world that henceforth he will be known simply as "Diddy," because the "P" was "getting between me and my fans."

So maybe you missed Costas' modest stand for principle. It seems he was scheduled to guest-host Larry King's program on CNN one recent Thursday when the agenda included yet another discussion of Natalee Holloway, the Alabama teenager who disappeared in Aruba.

When he found out the program's planned focus, Costas asked the producers if they would find another topic. They refused, and Costas declined to do the show.

"I didn't think the subject matter of Thursday's show was the kind of broadcast I should be doing," he said in a written statement. That's as specific as Costas has chosen to be in explaining why he wouldn't do the show, which leaves plenty of room for conjecture. You'll pardon me if I take advantage of it.

See, I like to think Costas was mindful of the racial and sexual bias inherent in the news media's recent fascination with missing persons cases. If you are not white, young, female and pretty, you can go missing all you want and CNN won't come looking for you. There will be no anchor people setting up camp at the place you were last seen, no morning-show interviews with your tearful parents, no urgent updates even when there is nothing to update.

But most missing persons don't fit the media's preferred "pretty white damsels in distress" profile. Most are men, a large percentage are black, and the majority, like the majority of any group, are of average appearance.

LaToyia Figueroa is the exception that proves the rule. She's the pregnant Philadelphia woman—later found murdered—whose disappearance received a measure of media attention after Internet bloggers pressured media to address the institutional bias of their missing persons coverage. Figueroa was, glory hallelujah, black. She was also young, female and pretty.

You might call that progress. I'd choose other words.

But for all that, I hope Costas was thinking about more than bias when he declined to do the show.

I hope he was also passing judgment on the "movie of the week" mentality that has overtaken TV news, this obsession with news as story arc, complete with thrilling premise, attractive protagonist, surprising plot twists and satisfying denouement.

It has always been part of the news business, I suppose, this thing of making people's miseries into soap operas for the rest of us.

But it feels as if it's reached a suffocating zenith in recent years, as if between Laci Peterson, Elizabeth Smart, JonBenet Ramsey, the runaway bride and dozens of others made famous because they were victims or fools, between a new trial of the century every week and constant bulletins on troubled Hollywood marriages, news media are drowning us in a tide of tabloid triviality.

"Pure white sugar, addictive and without nutrition." That's what Marty Kaplan, associate dean of the University of Southern California Annenberg School for Communication, called it last year in the *Washington Post*. I can't improve on that.

Hey, I like an occasional Twinkie as much as the next guy. But can we really live on them?

Shouldn't the news be about the things that affect us, instead of just those that titillate us? Shouldn't it satisfy more than our need to gape at car wrecks?

I like to think Costas would say yes and that's why he told CNN no. Not that it made a difference. They got another host and the show went on as planned.

SEPTEMBER 6, 2005

FAIRNESS NO FACTOR IN FURY OF THE STORM

KENTWOOD, La.—Take Interstate 55 north from Hammond, get off at Highway 1057 traveling east and after a few miles of upended trees and power lines sagging to the blacktop, you come across Lensly Warren sitting out in front of a store eating a bag of peanut M&Ms. The sign that identifies the place as the Country Quick Stop is gone with that wind. The shelves are empty. The below-ground gas tank that once fed the two dilapidated pumps is dry.

And seven days after the storm blew his livelihood away, Warren sits there immobile and disgusted, a living monument to the elemental harshness of this life.

We lie about that. We say that life is fair, that good is always rewarded and that there is available to all of us a place called Happily Ever After. We tell our children to believe this and we even believe it a little ourselves.

Then a hurricane rips to tatters this most cherished of our conceits, landing like a hammer on the just and the unjust alike, not caring that this one cheats on his wife and kicks his dog, but this other one is a good man, oh Lord, a decent sort who just needs for once in his life to catch a break. The storm doesn't care. It blows them both away.

Of course, Warren knew how mean life could be long before Hurricane Katrina roared through this rural community about 50 miles northwest of New Orleans. In the first place, he's a farmer. When you're a farmer you become an expert in the malice heaven sometimes holds toward Earth.

But it's more than that. It's the surgery he had in 2002 to remove nine inches of his colon. It's the seven months of recuperation while the bills kept rolling in. It's the polyps he has developed, the ones doctors think might be precancerous. It's the fact that, "I was supposed to go back for a check-up on the first of October—in New Orleans."

It's the fact that his mother died a month ago.

And now, after all that, here comes the storm, scouring the land like some old Testament plague, like retribution for unguessed sins. It shut off the electric fences that kept the deer out of his peas. He was down in the field this morning, he says, and the animals had been feasting. Might as well let them have it. The people who would ordinarily pick his peas when they ripen in a couple of weeks are trapped in Mississippi by the storm. And even if he could harvest his peas, who would buy them? His buyers were in New Orleans.

"That'll be a loss," he says. "I put up 3,000 square bales of hay. Sell it to the dairy farmers and stuff. And the top blowed off the barn. So I lost that." People from the Federal Emergency Management Agency—FEMA—finally showed up Sunday, he says. They brought water and meals ready to eat, military rations. They've promised to return soon with ice. Warren has no idea when or if they'll return bearing answers.

So he sits in front of his store eating M&Ms. Maybe he'll move in a few minutes, maybe not. But for now, he has been brought down by gravity, claimed by inertia, unwilling to move. Maybe even unable.

Ask him what's going to happen now, how he's going to make it to Happily Ever After, what he's going to do when he gets up, and he says the same thing each time: "Have no idea."

Seven days and counting, and he is still shaking his head. Still disgusted at how life can do you sometimes. "I'm a poor farmer," he says. "I have no money to do this."

His life, says Warren with an exhausted sigh, has hit a downhill grade.

"But I'm blessed," he says. "I could have lived in New Orleans."

SEPTEMBER 8, 2005

JOURNEY SHOWS NATURE'S STRENGTH AND OUR OWN

BILOXI, Miss.—James Edward Bates, a photographer for the *Sun Herald* newspaper, tells me a story as we drive through what's left of his town.

It seems that earlier in the day, he shot pictures of one Carmen Stepanek, a Czech immigrant he found sweeping up hurricane debris in front of her house. In her imperfect English, she asked if he had ever seen *The Karate Kid*. Yes, he said. "How many Karate Kid movies there were?" she asked. "One, two, three?" He said there were at least three.

At which Stepanek, a gray-haired woman of a certain age, folded a black bandanna into a headband, tied it on her brow, struck a fighter's pose and declared, "I Karate Mom Six."

"I fight," she said. "I fight for my life."

Bates, a soft-spoken man, tells me this story as we ride through twilight. We are at the end of a long afternoon spent touring a moonscape of destruction.

That word is purposeful. What you encounter on the tourist strip that runs along the beach is not "damage," but destruction: asphalt buckled, sewage standing in reeking pools swarmed by biting flies, debris piled higher than houses, buildings reduced to their wood skeletons, here and there a shred of wall or roof still clinging to the structure. Bates uses the verb "was" a lot as he pilots his car carefully down the broken highway. As in, "That was a Waffle House ... a new condo under construction ... a Ruby Tuesday ... a Wendy's ... a nightclub ... an RV park." That's what a 28-foot storm surge will do to you. It turns "is" into "was."

I lived through the 1971 Sylmar earthquake that wrecked a freeway interchange and left over 60 people dead in Los Angeles. I am a veteran of Andrew, the 1992 hurricane that ripped roofs from buildings and killed dozens of people in South Florida.

This is the worst I have ever seen.

On Highway 90, a casino barge—a floating building, you understand—sits in the parking lot of a hotel, having been lifted by an angry ocean and deposited there. A few blocks down, we are walking through mud and debris when the sudden smell of natural gas chokes me.

We find Kenny Vallia Jr., retired staff sergeant, USAF, lugging home provisions a taxi driver friend has taken him to Mobile to get. Vallia's home is a second-story apartment in a doomed building. To get there, you hike up uncertain stairs and walk along a balcony whose supports move if you push them lightly. The apartment is fly-swept and dark. But Vallia sees no cause to bemoan his misfortune. "The Lord brought me through the storm for somethin'," he says. "And it wasn't to sit around and wallow in self-pity."

A few minutes later, a few miles away, Jayne and Maury Davis explain how they had to walk across debris that stood 12 feet high and four blocks deep to reach the concrete slab where their home used to be. On the slab, they found a cast-iron cross that used to hang in a downstairs bathroom. It was, says Maury, a message from heaven, "a sign that you're going to be OK, that you're not alone in all this, and keep your faith."

It's after we have seen and heard all of these things that Bates tells me the Carmen Stepanek story. The sun is sinking to a placid ocean and we are returning to the *Sun Herald* building, where RVs are parked in rows and people for whom the loss of homes and loved ones is a fresh wound go about putting out a daily paper.

In other words, his timing is perfect.

An hour later, Bates presents me with a picture of Stepanek. I plan to frame it and put it someplace where I will see it everyday and be reminded. That winds will howl and waters rise and our possessions and lives be twisted into pretzel shapes. That rack and ruin are part of the human condition. But stubbornness is, too. Faith is, too. Defiance is, too.

We fight. We fight for our lives.

SEPTEMBER 16, 2005

KATRINA SHOWS BUSH JIHADISTS HAVE BLIND FAITH

Apparently, Brownie wasn't doing such a good job after all.

You remember Brownie: Michael Brown, head of the Federal Emergency Management Agency and, in that capacity, a focal point for mounting criticism of that agency's leisurely response to Hurricane Katrina. Brownie's qualifications for that job have since been revealed: He used to run horse shows and was a friend of a friend of the president. Last Friday, that president offered support for his beleaguered subordinate. "Brownie, you're doing a heck of a job," said George W. Bush.

By Monday, Brownie was out of work. He resigned, having evidently read the writing on the wall.

The next day, having apparently seen that same graffiti, Bush himself said, "To the extent that the federal government didn't fully do its job right, I take responsibility."

I found that shocking, but that's only because I had thought Bush physically incapable of taking responsibility. Having watched him brazen his way through successive botches and bungles here and abroad with an Alfred E. Neumann grin and a maddening insistence that botches and bungles were part of the master plan, I thought Bush's eyes would roll back if he even came close to saying, My bad.

So I have a question for the Bush jihadists, that shrinking but stubborn minority that still thinks Gee Dubya walks on water and calls down rain. What's it going to take to make you folks stop sending me e-mails by the dozens railing at how the great and powerful Bush is being mistreated by that darned liberal media?

320 LEONARD PITTS, JR.

Take, for instance, Tom in Boynton Beach, who says criticism of Bush is a sop to the "America-hating extreme left wing." Or Darwin—I don't know where he's from—who says liberals are playing "the blame game." And on and on.

It is, of course, their standard defense, akin to a child sticking index fingers in her ears and shouting "Lalalalala, I can't hear you!" until you stop committing the sin of reason. In this case, the argument goes that Bush is being blamed for failures that should be assigned to state and local officials in Louisiana and Mississippi. It's their fault, not his.

So to recap: Media say Bush bears responsibility. Much of the American public says Bush bears responsibility. In an unprecedented show of lucidity, Bush takes responsibility.

Bush jihadists say Bush is not responsible.

Seldom has the intellectual bankruptcy, situational outrage and robotic partisanship of that stratum of the electorate been more apparent. I swear, if Bush blew up the White House, they'd praise him for creating construction jobs.

Yes, the apparent failures of New Orleans Mayor Ray Nagin and Louisiana Gov. Kathleen Babineaux Blanco are manifest and manifold. And people are right to criticize them.

But here's why Bush gets the lion's share of attention: He's the bleeping President of the United States. And the miserable performance of the government he captains speaks not simply to our immediate concerns about Louisiana and Mississippi but potentially to our future concerns about Florida, California or some other state that comes under terrorist attack.

Would you trust the gang that couldn't get water to Bogalusa for seven days to be in charge of rescuing you after a nuclear device went off in Los Angeles?

Would you feel secure in devastated, cut-off-from-the-outside-world Miami Beach knowing your salvation relied on some guy who got his job because he had connections?

More to the point, is incompetence so profound it causes actual *death* OK so long as the incompetents are of the right party, possessed of the right values? Apparently, for some of us, the answer is yes.

Never mind integrity, never mind objectivity, never mind simple enlightened self-interest.

Blue to the left, red to the right even now, even here. This is the nation we have become.

Anybody want to take responsibility for that?

SEPTEMBER 30, 2005

SCIENTISTS DON'T SUE TO GAIN ACCESS TO PULPITS

The Ku Klux Klan is a terrorist group.

It was organized in 1865 for the purpose of controlling and oppressing newly freed slaves through intimidation, violence and murder.

Not many people will argue with that. Historians in particular will find the statement uncontroversial.

But 10 years ago in Vicksburg, Miss., I learned an alternate view. Vicksburg was an especially stubborn stronghold of Confederate sentiment during the Civil War—refused to celebrate the Fourth of July again until 1944. Small wonder, then, that a museum there featured an exhibit claiming the Klan was actually formed to save the South from corrupt black governments and that, while "many people suffered, some no doubt innocently," the night riders sought only to "restore some semblance of decency."

It's a lie, of course, but it's a lie some of us believe. So here's the question: When we teach schoolchildren about the Klan, must we give equal time to this view? Are we required to treat it as if it has the slightest credibility?

Or would that not be an affront to scholarship itself?

It's science, not history, that went on trial this week in Harrisburg, Pa., but the questions still apply. Parents are squaring off in federal court over a local school board's requirement that before children can be taught Charles Darwin's theory that humanity evolved from lower animals, teachers must read a statement acknowledging "alternate" theories of human origin. This would include the so-called theory of intelligent design, which holds that living things are so fantastically complex, they can only have been invented by some supernatural creator.

Proponents of the policy deny they are trying to sneak religion into the classroom. It is, they say, a matter of free speech: Students should be exposed to all sides of an issue.

But for that argument to hold water, you must have more than one side. Where science and the theory of evolution are concerned, you do not. It is the overwhelming consensus of the mainstream scientific community that Darwin had it right. So pretending there is another "side" to the question makes about as much sense as pretending there is another side to the Klan. It reeks of false equivalence, no-fault scholarship, judgment-free education, the bogus notion that all points of view are created equal and are equally deserving of respect.

And that just ain't so.

I believe in God. I believe God is the sovereign author of creation. But that is a matter of faith, not science. Faith, as it says in the book of Hebrews, is the evidence of things not seen. Science, by contrast, is founded upon observable phenomena. They are diametric opposites, but both seek the same goal: to help man and woman comprehend their lives and their world. To help them find answers.

I would argue that faith and science are in some ways more complementary than contradictory. But it's telling that where they do conflict, as in the question of human origin, it's always people of faith who beg for validation. I mean, when has any scientist ever sued for equal time in the pulpit? There is an unbecoming neediness about these constant schemes to dress religion up as science. Why are some people of faith so desperate for approval from a discipline they reject?

It suggests an insecurity that belies the bellicose battle cry of Bible literalists: "God said it. I believe it. That settles it." Or in the words of a church sign as related to me last week by a minister in Maine: Reason is the enemy of faith.

That's a sad, troubling and even pathetic mind-set.

We inhabit a universe vaster than human comprehension, older than human wanderings, more wondrous than human conception. And in the face of that, we do the natural thing. We ask questions and seek answers.

That's not a denial of God. It is evidence of Him.

DECEMBER 12, 2005

CHRISTMAS WAR BELITTLES REASON FOR THE SEASON

Let me begin by speaking the forbidden words.

Merry Christmas.

There, I said it. So did the sky crack? Did the oceans turn to blood? Is a horde of angry Jews, Muslims, Buddhists and atheists storming the gates, demanding a retraction? Or does the world look much the same as it did before?

I'm betting on the last.

So forgive me if I don't take up arms in the so-called War on Christmas. In case you hadn't heard about it—in other words, in case you have a life—let me bring you up to speed.

Recently, conservative and evangelical observers have been loudly complaining about what they call a campaign to de-Christianize Christmas, to unmoor it from its origin as the birthday of Christ. They have a litany of complaints, but seem particularly vexed by word that some retailers have been instructing their sales people to greet customers with "Happy holidays" as opposed to "Merry Christmas." This, as a way to avoid excluding people of other faiths and no faith at all.

It's been a heated battle, and the complainers have not been guilty of understatement.

"A secular and atheistic jihad," cries a guy named David Huntwork on the GOPUSA website.

"Frightening," declares a traumatized Bill O'Reilly.

"A war on Christians," says John Gibson, who wrote a book on the subject.

And a writer on the WorldNetDaily website warns of the possible "persecution and outright criminalization of Christianity."

Well, gee golly.

They're putting so much energy into defending Christmas that one feels downright churlish for pointing out that no one's attacking it. All we're seeing here is an ever more pluralistic society struggling to balance the faith of the majority with the rights and feelings of the minority.

Is it an imperfect process? Believe it.

For instance, the 80-foot decorated spruce erected at the U.S. Capitol in early December has been designated the "holiday tree." That's stupid. It's a Christmas tree. And if—big if—it's true, as some conservative groups claim, that a Wisconsin elementary school re-wrote the lyrics to "Silent Night" to make them secular, somebody should be poked in the eye with a candy cane. That's stupid, too.

On the other hand, the American Family Association is boycotting Target stores to force them to say "Merry Christmas" and that's hardly a sign of intelligence. How is the cashier supposed to know whether a customer is Christian?

More to the point, why is pluralism so hard for these people? Why does it make them feel so put upon? Am I the only one who sends "Merry Christmas" cards to his Christian friends and "Happy holidays" cards to his other friends and doesn't find it especially taxing?

What's offensive here is not the imperfect balancing of minority and majority. What's offensive—also surreal and absurd—is the notion that Christianity, a faith claimed by 76 percent of all Americans, is somehow being intimidated into nonexistence. Some of the earliest Christians were stoned for their beliefs. In some parts of the world today, Christianity is a crime punishable by death. And the AFA is feeling persecuted because a sales clerk says "Happy holidays?"

That's not persecution. It's a persecution complex.

And it trivializes what Christians claim to uphold: the baby born of a virgin's womb.

Of what importance is a salesman's greeting if you're one of the 76 percent who believe that? The greeting that matters was spoken by angels. The Book of Luke says they appeared before shepherds in a field: "Fear not, for behold I bring you good tidings of great joy which shall be to all people. For unto you is born this day in the city of David a Savior, who is Christ the Lord."

Linus said it best. "*That's* what Christmas is all about, Charlie Brown."

MARCH 17, 2006

HISTORY WILL SCOLD THOSE WHO STAYED SILENT

"Every generation blames the one before."—Mike + the Mechanics, "The Living Years"

Late last year, John Conyers, Democratic congressman from Michigan, proposed impeaching the president of the United States. The proposal received scant attention in the media mainstream, though it was picked up with glee by liberal bloggers and provided a rallying point for the president's supporters. The lack of notice can be attributed to the fact that the proposal's chances of passage were roughly akin to those of an ice cube's of surviving a steam bath.

Surely Conyers knew that going in, so one wonders why he put the measure forth in the first place. He gives his answer in the current issue of Harper's. He did it, he said, "to take away the excuse that we didn't know." He added that when future generations ask where he was while the president subverted the Constitution, he wants to have an answer.

One senses the same reasoning in this week's call by Democratic Senator Russell Feingold of Wisconsin to censure Bush for domestic eavesdropping in apparent violation of federal law. Feingold must have known that even this lesser remedy was, putting it mildly, unlikely to pass.

So it has come to this. The president's apologists rationalize even his most obvious and egregious illegalities, mendacities and bungling with straight faces and earnest demeanor and the rest of us are left posturing for history, trying to make certain that when the official record is written we are not indicted by our silence.

Any similarity to the rearranging of deck chairs on the Titanic is surely and purely coincidental.

Your humble correspondent, by the by, doesn't mean to cast aspersions when he talks about folks posturing for history. He's been doing the same thing.

People—conservatives, the occasional liberal—sometimes ask me why I bother. Another column on the sins of G.W. Bush? What's the point? What will change? The people who disagree with him already know. And there's not enough evidence in the world to convince his believers—the word is appropriate—that he does not, in fact, walk on water.

Still, I feel that Feingold and Conyers have a point.

You cannot be a student of history without ruminating on some of the more dubious episodes of the American past and wondering how in the world such things were allowed to happen.

Was the whole country napping when Joseph McCarthy's bullying, innuendos and lies cast a pall on this nation and made a mockery of the Constitution? Didn't anybody speak out when Franklin Roosevelt sent Americans to concentration camps? Where were the good people when Americans of African descent were being lynched in horrific numbers and the president and the Congress stood by and did nothing? You read about these failures of will, of courage, of spirit and you keep asking ... how? How could that which is so obviously wrong now have been so quietly accepted then?

From that question, it is only a short hop to another, more pressing one: What will tomorrow say about today?

I think I know. I think tomorrow will ask how we could have shrugged off the very real possibility that the president broke the law. I think tomorrow will want to know how we could have meekly and quiescently allowed our civil rights to be abridged. I think tomorrow will be perplexed by our tolerance of obvious incompetence and brazen untruths. I think tomorrow will wonder how we could have turned blind eyes and disinterested ears to mounting evidence that the war in Iraq was predestined and Sept. 11 just a convenient pretext.

So I understand where Feingold and Conyers are coming from. Where good and frustrated people all over the country are coming from. History's verdict is all we have left. And when tomorrow calls today to account, some of us want to be able to say, we stood up. We called out. We were not silent.

It is small solace, but it is solace, nonetheless.

JULY 10, 2006

DEBUNKING A STORE-BOUGHT SENSE OF SELF

"Don't believe the hype."—Public Enemy

I feel sorry for Shawn Carter.

I know I shouldn't, but I do.

It seems that in recent weeks, Carter, a rap star and music executive known professionally as Jay-Z, has pronounced himself angry with the makers of Cristal champagne. Cristal, you should know, is frequently referenced in rap lyrics as a synonym for the high life, for pimping and drug dealing your way into an existence where the women are always willing, the luxury cars always gassed up, the sheets always satin.

This prompted *The Economist* magazine to ask Frédéric Rouzaud, president of Champagne Louis Roederer, parent company of Cristal, whether it might hurt the brand's image to be associated with such a coarse, outlaw culture. Rouzaud's reply: "That's a good question, but what can we do? We can't forbid people from buying it. I'm sure Dom Perignon or Krug would be delighted to have their business."

To which Jay-Z responded angrily. The rapper, who in his music has done as much as, or more than, anyone to position Cristal as hip-hop's bubbly of choice, issued a statement decrying Rouzaud's "racist" statement and calling for a boycott.

And here, it might be worthwhile to observe two facts.

One: Cristal has managed to thrive for most of 130 years without Jay-Z's endorsement. Indeed, the brand is manufactured sparingly and is perpetually sold out around the world.

Two: Cristal retails for upward of $200 a bottle. How, exactly, do you launch a boycott of something most people can't afford? Might as well ask me to boycott Gulfstream private jets while you're at it.

It is, on both sides, a silly contretemps. Still, there is something poignant in Jay-Z's apparent surprise and hurt at Cristal's blithe rejection of hip-hop's operating ethos: that acceptance can be bought.

There has never been an entertainment form that placed as much faith in the healing virtues of materialism as rap. From the days when Run-DMC first extolled Adidas shoes, rappers have invoked brand names and branded themselves with talismanic fervor. Timberland! Hennessy! Lexus! S. Carter!

They seem to feel that when you can afford these things, it makes you, I don't know ... complete. As if, with Tims on your feet, Hennessy in your glass and a Lexus in your garage, you're good, you're covered, you're in the club.

For an art form whose artists and fans are largely young, largely black and largely from poor, bullet-scarred neighborhoods, it is a powerfully attractive fantasy. But it is a fantasy nevertheless.

Which is, in so many words, what Frédéric Rouzaud just brutally explained to Shawn Carter: that he is not in the club. That no matter how much Cristal he buys, he will never be in the club. Sure, kid, we'll take your money. But don't mistake that for respect. Not while you're young. And black. And reeking of nouveau riche. And representing values that are anathema to our own.

So yeah, I feel sorry for Carter. But at the same time, what's it tell you that he was even surprised?

Among the many lies of hip-hop, this notion that wearing or imbibing or driving the proper brand will make you whole is in some ways the most infuriating. It represents a corporatization of cool that would have made Miles Davis ill. In his era, after all, cool meant being an iconoclast, a visionary threat to the status quo. In Jay-Z's era, it is a brand name, it has a sponsor, it can be bought off the rack.

Rap could have been, should have been, a truth-teller and world-shaker. Instead it has largely contented itself with being free advertising for corporate titans, selling fake cool, sometimes with corporate assent, but often without even a thank-you. Brand names, it says, will make you whole.

It is painful to know that Jay-Z has sold that lie to young people by the millions. What's more painful is that apparently, he also bought it himself.

AUGUST 30, 2006

IN NEW ORLEANS, REMEMBRANCE HITS A HIGH NOTE

NEW ORLEANS—Here is how this city commemorates one of the most wrenching tragedies in history: It dances.

It does other things, too, on this first anniversary of Hurricane Katrina. It prays. It dedicates memorials. It says thank you. At 9:38 in the morning, the hour when the first levee broke and the city began to drown, it rings bells of mourning. But it dances, too, and that is what makes you know you are not in Columbus, Ohio, or Jacksonville, Fla., but New Orleans, by God, Louisiana. Because where else is death a dance and suffering a song?

They round the corner coming from the Superdome, a brass band playing "Just A Closer Walk With Thee," swinging it slow, stretching the notes like taffy till they wallow in a drunken extravagance of grief. But this is a jazz funeral, where grief is allowed to linger only so long. So after a moment, the drummer kicks it up a notch, the horns give out bawdy growls and "Will The Circle Be Unbroken" comes on like unbridled joy. Out in front, the parade's grand marshal, a man named Babatunji Ahmed, dances with a lethal seriousness, his moves economical, yet filled with grace.

Here and there among the crowd that follows the band, there are spontaneous outbreaks of happy feet. If you have toes, they're tapping. If you have a head, it's bobbing. If you have a soul, it sings.

Somewhere in cyberspace, somewhere in the wilds of talk radio, they are damning this city right now. They've been at it for a year, calling it stupid, criminal, unworthy of saving. The way the city drowned, the way thousands of people were left stranded in harm's way, begging for rescue, fits nicely with an old right-wing narrative that says some of us are congenitally inferior to the rest of us. So Katrina gives them a code, allows them to say "white trash" and use the N-word without quite saying the one or using the other.

And somehow, these venal people, these wannabe masters of the universe, conveniently ignore that what happened last year— how many days did it take for help to arrive?—fits even more neatly with another narrative, the one that says the federal regime is so incompetent it could not pour water from a bucket if the instructions were printed on the bottom.

But you know what? All the narratives are white noise on this day. This day is about remembrance. And renewal.

Katrina was a million hurricanes in a million places. It was the hurricane of a 911 operator, helpless to send help, talking to a woman trapped in an attic with water rising to her chest. It was the hurricane of a child crying in the heat and stench of the Superdome. It was the hurricane of a man huddling with his family in the shade of a traffic sign on the Interstate 10 freeway. It was the hurricane of a teenager breaking and stealing, the hurricane of a cop with a gun making him drop his loot, the hurricane of a body, someone's mother, someone's wife, someone's child, floating anonymously in a watery grave.

A million hurricanes. And now, a million recoveries.

Because that's what human beings do, what we always do. Climb out, assess the damage, adapt to the new reality, start to put things right, find a way to live through this. It is courage, it is foolishness, it is faith. Sometimes there's no difference between the three.

The jazz funeral comes to its end in the shadow of a historic church built by black freed men in the 19th century. People are shouting on the high notes, raising palms to the sky, the music representing not just victory over death, but defiance of death, death kicked in the backside by happy feet.

When the song is done, Ahmed talks to the crowd. He speaks of the failure of the levees, of being stranded by the government. He never loses the lethal seriousness, the stoic dignity. Until he does. Until suddenly he is crying.

People close in about him protectively, lead him to where he can grieve privately.

A million hurricanes. A million recoveries.

Live through this.

SEPTEMBER 11, 2006

ON 9/11, INNOCENCE WAS LOST ONCE AGAIN

On Sept. 10, 2001, this nation was over a quarter century past its last real crisis.

This is not to say the intervening years were uneventful: they were not. Those years saw three attempted presidential assassinations, a shuttle explosion, an impeachment and sundry hostage takings, military actions and political scandals. But there had not, since Watergate, been a true *crisis*, no event of the kind that shakes a nation, that stops it cold and takes its breath and makes it anxious about its future.

In this, the quarter century that ended five years ago was an aberration. Previous generations of Americans had come of age with reminders of life's true nature breathing close enough to stir the hairs at the nape of the neck. From the Great Depression that put the nation on the skids in the 1930s, to the sneak attack that plunged it into war in the 1940s, from the 1960s when every day seemed to bring fresh outrage—assassinations, riots, a step to the brink of nuclear war—to Watergate and the subsequent fall of a president, and from there to the Cold War that hung over more than 40 years of American history like a pall of smoke, we were a nation too frequently made to know that life does not play fair.

By Sept. 10, 2001, we had largely forgotten this truth. Or, more accurately, we had enjoyed the luxury of not being reminded for a very long time.

It was the last day of the good old days and we didn't even know. Not that the days were good and old. Not that they were doomed.

But then, you never know the good old days when you are in them. On Sept. 10, 2001, the Cold War was 10 years past, 17-year-olds were becoming Internet millionaires and we thought a crisis was a president receiving oral sex in the Oval Office.

We had not yet seen people jumping from flaming skyscrapers. We had not yet seen office towers crumble to the ground on live television. We had not yet seen dust-caked people wandering the streets of our greatest city. We had not yet seen a gaping wound in the side of the Pentagon. We had not yet seen wreckage in a Pennsylvania field. We had not yet seen men and women in badges and uniforms rushing forward into chaos and smoke and a certainty of death.

We had not yet seen. So we could not yet know.

On Sept. 10, 2001, such sights as those—never mind the attendant feelings of fury and terror—were unthinkable. As in, literally unable to be thought, unless in the context of a Steven Spielberg movie, a Tom Clancy book, some artist's artifice by which we gave ourselves the pleasure of a good, hard scare, a shiver up the back in the heat of a summer's day. But real? Not in a million years.

On Sept. 10, 2001, we were innocent. And that seems a purely strange thing to say because innocence is the commodity we were repeatedly assured we had lost. We were told this in 1963, when John F. Kennedy was murdered, in 1974 when Richard Nixon resigned, in 1993, when the World Trade Center was bombed.

But innocence, it turns out, is a renewable commodity. That's heartening. Also troubling, because if you can have it again, it can be stolen again.

No, check that. It *will* be stolen again. That's the lesson of these past five years, that there is no vacation from history, no finish line you cross where you can raise your arms and lower your guard. Chaos is not the aberration. Respite from chaos is. And being human means molding yourself to that reality, finding a way to live in the spaces chaos leaves.

On Sept. 10, 2001, we had forgotten that we once knew this.

That last day, like every day, the sun came to America first on the rugged coast of Maine and began its slow arc across the country. Down below, we worked, watched television, checked homework, got dinner on. The sun left us in the South Pacific, the sky turning dark above a pendant of American islands.

On Sept. 10, 2001, we went to bed. We slept in innocence.

And then the morning came.

NOVEMBER 17, 2006

SON, THERE'S STILL NOTHING LIKE THAT SWEET SOUL MUSIC

One day, maybe 20 years ago, I ran into Eddie Levert. Eddie, a charter member of the legendary O'Jays, is one of the greats, a singer of thunderous power. Back then, his son Gerald was just starting out as a professional singer but already, people were remarking how much he sounded like his father.

"You better look out," I told Ed. "He's gaining on you."

"Aw, don't tell that boy that," growled Eddie. "It'll go to his head."

For all his feigned indignation, he couldn't hide his pride. You saw it in him whenever they performed together, the son mimicking dance steps he grew up watching from backstage, or egging the father on with vocal dives and climbs and barrel rolls straight from the old man's own playbook.

So my first thought was of Eddie last week when the news came that Gerald had died of an apparent heart attack at the absurd age of 40. I can't imagine what it must be like to bury your son.

Gerald Levert's death wasn't big news in every neighborhood; he was a black R&B singer with little if any profile on white pop radio. But if you are black and of a certain age, it was the kind of bulletin that made you pull over the car.

We live in an era where music is largely impersonal, a cut-and-paste, machine-tooled artifice. Moreoever, we live in an era where black music in particular is often a police blotter or a sex act or a product placement, but, less frequently, a love song. Still, some of us remember when black music was about soul and soul was about truth—particularly the truth of How It Is between women and men.

We used to call them begging songs, baby, baby please songs, for how they promised moon and stars to a woman if she would just give you the time of day or pleaded with breaking voice and teary eyes for another chance after you fooled around and hurt her.

Truth to tell, they weren't just songs, they were relationship how-to manuals. And Gerald sang them like his father's son: "Baby, Hold On To Me," "Mr. Too Damn Good," "Made To Love Ya."

In him, you heard echoes of soul that came before, echoes of Eugene Record of the Chi-Lites asking, "Have You Seen Her?" and Lou Rawls vowing "You'll Never Find Another Love Like Mine" and Wilson Pickett promising good loving "In The Midnight Hour." You heard the ghost of Luther Vandross singing "Here and Now," Ray Charles swearing "I Can't Stop Loving You" and Barry White, smooth and chocolate like a human Dove Bar saying, "I've Got So Much To Give."

These days, black music produces fewer songs that cherish women. Oh, there are plenty of sex songs, plenty I love your butt songs. But baby, please is becoming a lost art.

I'm reminded of a talk I had with my middle son a few years ago. The Temptations had come on the radio singing "Ain't Too Proud To Beg," David Ruffin swearing to sleep on the woman's doorstep if she would just give him another chance. My son shook his head. Didn't matter how bad he was hurting or how much wrong he had done, he said, he could never sing a song like that. As far as he was concerned, he would be too proud to beg.

I told him that sometimes begging is the best part. I told him that sometimes making up justifies breaking up. I told him that love requires vulnerability. Me, I think things were better in black communities when there was more baby, please on the radio, when we held one another and sheltered one another from the vicissitudes of life. But those days are going: Every singer I referenced above has died within the last three years. And now, Gerald Levert has died, too.

I saw him in concert last year. At one point he came out into the audience and women went crazy, flying at him, wrapping themselves around him with a need deeper than sex. Baby, hold on to me, he sang. And boy, they did.

My son doesn't know what he's missing.

JULY 4, 2007

CAN IDEALS SAVE AMERICA?

Is America great?

We were on a road outside Freetown, Sierra Leone, en route to the tiny village of Yoyema when Saido Kamara asked me that. The drive to Yoyema, they told me, was about 75 miles. Getting there would take us half the day. Sierra Leone has few highways worthy of the name; just craters separated at intervals by a poorly-maintained road. It also has crushing poverty, epidemic corruption and many amputees maimed in a civil war that ended only a few years ago.

Is America great?

I've written before about the question my 22-year-old translator asked when I visited West Africa back in 2004. I resurrect the question now because it seems an apt one for a troubled nation that today marks the 231st summer of its existence.

For all our prayers of peace, we are a nation at war this Independence Day. Our military is fighting in Afghanistan and Iraq, of course, but that's not what I mean—or at least, not all that I mean. We are also at war with ourselves, with the very idea and ideal of the United States of America.

We are fighting about immigration, a necessary conversation about securing our borders that nevertheless sinks often into mud holes of xenophobia and racism. We are fighting about diversity, and the Southern Poverty Law Center warns that the number of hate groups in this country has risen 40 percent since 2000. We are fighting about the abridgement of civil liberties, the conduct of war, the idea that torture should be a tool of interrogation.

We are fighting about identity, about who we are and who we are willing to be.

Is America great?

I told him Yes, of course. Hedged it with disclaimers so he would not get too rosy an impression. But I told him Yes.

Not that he needed my affirmation. The beatific smile on his face suggested he had already made up his mind beyond my ability to change or subtract. That smile bespoke a conviction: Hope lives in the United States. In so many places, hope lies strangled or stillborn, abandoned or forgot. But hope has a home in America.

Lately, I have been hearing more and more a term I like: "American exceptionalism," as in the abiding conviction that this is a nation set apart, a nation unique among all the nations of the world.

And it seems to me that it is not the people who make America great, but America that has made the people great. Meaning that we are blessed to have been shaped by revolutionary ideals. Equality before the law. The freedom of speech. The freedom of assembly. The freedom from unreasonable search and seizure. The inalienable right to pursue one's own happiness.

Is America great?

Not always, no. And when we are not great, it has usually been because the people have been unable or unwilling or scared to be as large as the nation's ideals. History tells us it has happened too often: with the Alien and Sedition Acts of 1798, with slavery, with government censorship of periodicals and songs during World War I, with the internment of Americans of Japanese heritage during World War II, with segregation, with McCarthyism, with government surveillance of civil rights workers and anti-war activists in the 1960s.

One can only wonder what history will someday say about this era where torture is defended, the rule of law is flouted, civil liberties are abridged, hate groups are rising, people are frightened and the very idea of American exceptionalism, that there are some risks you take, some things you don't do, some challenges you just have to meet, because this is, after all, America, seems frayed and worn and spent.

And you might say, well, who cares? It's just an ideal. Can ideals save this country?

Actually, ideals are the only things that ever have.

JULY 18, 2007

EXPEDIENCE NO REASON TO KILL A MAN

You don't know what it's like, and neither do I. But we can imagine.

I've always thought it must feel like being buried alive. Lungs starving, lying in blackness, pounding on the coffin lid with dirt showering down, no one hearing your cries.

Or maybe it's like locked-in syndrome, a condition where you lose muscle control—can't move a finger, turn your head, speak. Your body entombs you. You scream within, but no one hears.

Something like that, I think. Something where you're trapped, claustrophobic, unable to believe what is happening, unable to make anyone hear you. That's how it must feel to be an innocent person on Death Row as execution day draws close.

Tuesday was Troy Anthony Davis' scheduled execution day, though I have no idea if he is an innocent person. I do know that he was convicted of the 1989 killing of a police officer, Mark Allen MacPhail, in Savannah, Ga. And I know that he was on the scene, a Burger King parking lot, that fateful night.

But I also know that Davis has always his maintained his innocence. And that no physical evidence—no gun, no fingerprint, no DNA—ever tied him to the crime. And that he was convicted on the testimony of nine key witnesses. And that seven of them have now recanted. They lied, they say. They were scared, they were bullied and threatened, and they said what the cops wanted to hear. Of the two witnesses who have not recanted, one is a fellow named Sylvester "Red" Coles; some witnesses claim he's the one who actually shot MacPhail when the officer tried to break up a parking lot altercation.

Monday, one day before Davis was scheduled to die, the state parole board issued a 90-day stay of execution.

You and I have no idea how that must feel, either, but we can imagine. The buried man gets a sip of air. The paralyzed man moves his toe.

And then back down into the coffin, back down into the tomb of your own skin, back in line to die.

Surely Davis' lawyers have explained to him the 1996 federal law, signed by President Clinton, that is throwing roadblocks in his way. Designed to streamline capital cases, it prohibits the introduction of exculpatory evidence once the state appeals process is done.

But just as surely Davis, if he is innocent, must wonder how he could have presented evidence he didn't yet have. And he must wonder, too, how there can be a time limit on truth—especially when a human life is at stake. How can you execute a man when there remain serious questions about his guilt?

That's barbarism, not justice.

What's fascinating is that, though 67 percent of those polled by Gallup pollsters approve of capital punishment in murder cases (and 51 percent say it's not imposed often enough), 64 percent admit it does not deter murder and 63 percent believe an innocent person has probably been executed since 2001.

In other words, the system doesn't work, we *know* it doesn't work, yet we want it to continue—and indeed, expand. What kind of madness is that? It's an intellectual disconnect, a refusal to follow logic to its logical end.

It is, of course, easier to countenance that madness, ignore that refusal, when the issue is abstract, when Death Row is distant, theoretical and does not involve you.

But what must it feel like when it is not abstract, when it is *you* sitting there in the cell watching the calendar move inexorably toward the day the state will kill you for something you absolutely did not do? Is there a suspension of belief? Do you tell yourself that surely people will come to their senses any minute now? Does the air close on you like a coffin lid? Does darkness sit on your chest like a weight?

You and I can only imagine. Some men have no need to try.

SEPTEMBER 2, 2007

I KNOW HE'S OUT THERE—SOMEWHERE

I was sitting on the deck in a chaise lounge. God was floating on His back in the pool.

I pointed to the night sky, a white disk of moon rising magisterially into an infinity of black. "Nice work," I said. God didn't answer.

"And hey, thanks for the weather today," I said. "75 degrees, low humidity, a nice breeze. Well done."

Still no answer. He gets in these quiet moods sometimes.

"Now I know how Mother Teresa felt," I groused, laughing to show Him I was just kidding. Might as well have been laughing at the moon.

I picked up the copy of *Time* magazine from where it had fallen during my nap, held it up so He could see the Mother's portrait on the cover. "You should read this," I said. "It's fascinating."

The article was about a new book, *Mother Teresa: Come Be My Light*, based on 66 years of her correspondence. The letters reveal a startling fact: For the last 50 years of her life, this iconic, holy woman felt spiritually abandoned, cut off from God. She felt no Presence. She felt alone.

"... [T]he silence and emptiness is so great," she wrote in 1979, "that I look and do not see—Listen and do not hear ..."

"... I am told that God loves me," she wrote in an undated letter, "—and yet the reality of darkness & coldness & emptiness is so great that nothing touches my soul."

"You know," I said, "you could have given her a sign. Would that have killed you?"

Nothing.

"Answer me when I'm talking to you!" I was mortified to hear myself yelling at Him, but I couldn't make myself stop. "Do you have any idea how much easier you make it for atheists when you act like this? It makes their argument so much simpler. If a woman who had given her very life over to this 'God' couldn't get a word out of Him for years, isn't the logical conclusion that He does not exist? Is that really what you want people to think?" God drifted in the pool, silent.

"Is this a faith thing?" I asked. "Is that it? Even though she had doubt, she continued to minister to people in one of the poorest places on Earth. Is that your point? Have faith?"

The sound of a breeze playing among the trees drew me around sharply. "Was that You?" I said.

Silence. I said, "You know you're making me crazy here, right? I feel like the conflicted priest from that TV show, *Nothing Sacred*. There was this one episode where he gave a homily and asked, 'Which man is crazy, the one who hears thunder and thinks it's the voice of God, or the one who hears the voice of God and thinks it's only thunder?'"

I sighed my frustration. For a moment, the only sound was the water lapping in the pool. Then I said softly, "You know, sometimes, I think atheists have a point. When you see nothing, when you feel nothing, isn't it logical to conclude it's because there is nothing?" I couldn't bear to look at Him as I said this.

"I think the only reason I don't go with them," I whispered, "is because of all those other times when you do see ... something. When you feel connected to something so vast it defies comprehension. It fills you. It settles you. It gives you peace. And you say to yourself, 'Lord, where did that come from? It couldn't be my imagination, because I couldn't imagine anything so ... perfect.'"

Still He was silent.

I looked up.

"You know, this mysterious ways thing gets a little ... "

I froze. God wasn't there. God was gone. Sitting alone under the blind white cataract of the moon, I shivered. Then I saw Him. He had climbed out of the pool and was drying himself with a towel. He had been there all along.

"Thank God," I breathed.

"I used to like that show," He said thoughtfully.

"Huh? What show?"

"That *Nothing Sacred*. That was a good show. I hated when they canceled it."

God finished drying Himself and went into the house. It started to rain.

JANUARY 13, 2008

FORGET ABOUT SPEARS MINUTIAE

I've got nothing against fame. I'm famous myself. Sort of.

OK, not Will Smith famous. Or Ellen DeGeneres famous. All right, not even Marilu Henner famous.

I'm the kind of famous where you fly into some town to give a speech before that shrinking subset of Americans who still read newspapers and, for that hour, they treat you like a rock star, applauding, crowding around, asking for autographs.

Then it's over. You walk through the airport the next day and no one gives a second glance. You are nobody again.

Dave Barry told me this story once about Mark Russell, the political satirist. It seems Russell gave this performance where he packed the hall, got a standing O. He was The Man. Later, at the hotel, The

Man gets hungry, but the only place to eat is a McDonald's across the road. The front door is locked, but the drive-through is still open. So he stands in it. A car pulls in behind him. The driver honks and yells, "Great show, Mark!"

The moral of the story is that a certain level of fame—call it the level of minor celebrity—comes with a built-in reality check. One minute, you're the toast of Milwaukee. The next, you're standing behind a Buick waiting to order a Big Mac.

That level of fame might stroke your ego from time to time, but it won't isolate or imprison you. And it will leave you your dignity. Which is more than Britney Spears has right now.

I will leave it to others to talk about the child (the noun is appropriate) and her latest public meltdown, as captured on a jittery video showing her in the back of an ambulance after a three-hour standoff that began when she refused to surrender her kids to an emissary from her ex-husband. What gets me is that the jittery video exists. And that an army of photographers pressed against the ambulance so that it was forced to wade slowly through them. And that all this was captured from a helicopter overhead.

Friends and neighbors, that is not news coverage. It's a stakeout. It's harassment. It's stalking. And there ought to be—I'm in earnest about this—a law. Call it the Get A Life Act of 2008.

Look, I understand that fascination with celebrity deeds and misdeeds is nothing new. It's older than James Brown leading a police chase, older than Lana Turner's daughter killing her mom's gangster lover, even older than Fatty Arbuckle on trial for rape. I also understand that the relationship between celebrities and cameras is symbiotic. And yes, I know it's difficult to work up empathy or outrage over something that affects a small class of people richer and better looking than the rest of us.

But see, I also know something has gone wrong, some essential perspective has been lost, when a Julia Roberts feels compelled—as she did a few weeks back—to chase down a photographer who had reportedly been staking out her children at school.

I'm embarrassed as a journalist that these members of my professional family—distant cousins, granted—have found no level to which they will not stoop to feed the public fixation on celebrity gossip. But I am also appalled, just as a person, that we the people provide the demand that drives the suppliers, that we support this voyeuristic intrusion, all-access trespass, 24/7 surveillance, of other people's lives.

For criminy sake, America: Do you really need pictures of Britney in an ambulance so badly? Go read a book. Play with your kids. Make love. Something. Anything.

One is reminded of how photographers stood snapping away over the wreck of Princess Diana's car, like vultures feeding on carrion. And one is sickened.

If that's what it means to be truly famous, keep it. I'd rather stand in line behind a Buick.

APRIL 9, 2008

ARROGANCE, INDISCIPLINE COME DOWN FROM THE TOP

Return with me to Abu Ghraib. You remember it. You may not want to, but you do.

The Iraqi prison was the epicenter of an international scandal in 2004 when it was revealed that U.S. soldiers were mistreating detainees, forcing them to stand in stress positions, sexually humiliating them, menacing them with dogs, denying them clothes, dragging them on leashes, threatening them with electrocution.

All of it was captured in photos that shocked the world. One of the most memorable showed then–21-year-old Army private Lynndie England, cigarette poking from a idiotic grin, index fingers cocked like guns as she pointed to the genitals of a naked Iraqi man.

We stared at those images and asked how this could have happened, how American soldiers could have become so degraded and undisciplined, could have wandered so far afield from the moorings of simple, human decency. Many answers were proffered. Mob mentality. Dehumanizing conditions. Lack of oversight.

But as the years have passed, a truer answer has coalesced. Where did these young soldiers get the idea that the rules were suspended, that free rein was given, that they could do whatever they wanted to the men in their custody?

It came from the top.

The latest proof: A recently declassified 2003 memo from John Yoo, then a Justice Department lawyer. The memo, eventually rescinded by Justice, authorized torture as a means of interrogation, a finding that carried the force of law.

Much of the media coverage of the 81-page document has focused on the—and this word is unavoidably ironic—bloodless legalese in which Yoo contemplates the permissibility of putting a prisoner's eyes out, slitting his tongue, scalding him with water, dosing him with mind-altering drugs, disfiguring him with acid.

But what is also appalling is Yoo's contention—repeatedly restated in the memo—that in time of war the president enjoys virtually unfettered authority over, and is accountable to no one for, the treatment of prisoners.

Legal scholars have accused Yoo of sloppy reasoning. Eugene Fidell, who teaches military justice at Yale and American universities, told the *International Herald Tribune* the document was a monument to the "imperial presidency." Yoo disagrees. He calls the memo a "boilerplate" defense of presidential authority.

Your humble correspondent doesn't know from legal scholarship. He does know this: Seven years ago when the nation was attacked and Americans wanted to pitch in, wanted to help, wanted to sacrifice, our leaders told us to go shopping. Prop the economy up, they said. Don't worry about the war. Let us handle it. Go shopping.

And we did. Nor, scared as we were, eager for the illusion of security as we were, did we look too closely or examine too intently the things that were being done in our names. We became, many of us, expert at ignoring the screams from behind the curtain, discounting the growing mountain of evidence that things were not as we had been told, brushing off nagging questions about what we have become and how that does not square with what we are supposed to be.

We shopped, and did not fret overmuch about the price of our moral laxity.

Maybe that's because the price is paid in tiny increments of our national honor yet somehow, never by those who most deserve to foot the bill. So that, seven years later, George W. Bush is still president of the United States, Donald Rumsfeld is working on his memoirs, John Yoo is a law professor at UC Berkeley.

But Lynndie England is a single mother, on parole and looking for work, living in a trailer with her folks.

SEPTEMBER 7, 2008

I MEAN, BAFFLE GRAB ON THE FREAK FLAKE

"We need change, all right. Change from a liberal Washington to a conservative Washington. We have a prescription for every American who wants change in Washington—throw out the big-government liberals."—Mitt Romney, Sept. 3, 2008

And then the gorilla run knee socks paint porno on the Cadillac. But school laughed and didn't we sing hats?

Ahem.

Maybe you wonder what the preceding gobbledygook means. I would ask which gobbledygook you mean: mine or Mitt Romney's? If he's allowed to spew nonsense and people act as if he's spoken intelligently, why can't I? If he gets to behave as if words no longer have objective meaning, why can't I?

I mean, baffle grab on the freak flake. Really.

And again, ahem.

If you're a regular here, you've heard me rant from time to time about intellectual dishonesty. By this, I mean more than just your garden variety lie. No, to be intellectually dishonest means to argue that which you know to be untrue and to substitute ideology for intellect to the degree that you'll do violence to language and logic rather than cross the party line.

Yes, we're all intellectually dishonest on occasion. But no one does it like Republican conservatives. They are to intellectual dishonesty what Michael Jordan was to basketball or the Temptations to harmony: the avatar, the exemplar, the paradigm. They have elevated it beyond hypocrisy and political expedience. They have made it ... art.

Which returns us to the astonishing thing Mitt Romney said while addressing the party faithful in St. Paul. You want to walk around it the way you would Michelangelo's *David*, admiring the elegance of the workmanship. You hesitate to touch it, much less pull it apart. To do so seems almost an act of desecration.

Unfortunately, some of us are too plodding and earthbound, too blind to the seductions of art, too stubbornly wedded to some vestigial notion that intellectual honesty matters, to walk past a steaming pile of bovine excreta without calling it a steaming pile of bovine excreta.

So excuse me, beg pardon, so sorry, but I have to ask: What liberal Washington is he talking about? The federal government has three branches. The legislative, i.e., Congress, was under conservative control from 1995 until 2007. The judicial, i.e., the Supreme Court, consists of nine justices, seven of whom were nominated by conservative presidents. The executive, i.e., the president, is George W. Bush. Enough said.

Washington is already what Romney wants to make it. Our current state of affairs, love it or loathe it, is indisputably a product of conservative governance. I wish that mattered more than it does.

That it doesn't matter much at all you can credit to conservative politicians who have, over the years, trained their followers to respond with Pavlovian faithfulness to certain terms. Say "conservative" and they wag their tails. Say "liberal" and they bare their fangs. More to the point, say either and all thinking ceases, so much so that a representative of the ideology that has controlled most of Washington most of the last 12 years can say with a straight face that his ideology needs to seize control of Washington to fix what is broken there. And people hear this Orwellian doublespeak ... and cheer. Why not? They have been taught that words mean what you need them to in a given moment.

Sadly, it has proved an easy lesson to impart. Turns out, all it requires is a limitless supply of gall and the inherent belief that people are dumber than a bag of hammers.

And all it costs us is language, the ability to have reasoned and intelligent political discourse, the idea that words do, and should, have weight, dimension and intrinsic meaning. Maybe you disagree. In which case, let me just say this:

Piffle crack eat monkey snow. Really.

MARCH 11, 2009

WHEN A MAN HITS A WOMAN

Dear Robyn Rihanna Fenty:

I was maybe 7 years old when this happened.

My old man had been kicked out of the house for being an abuser and a cheat. Now, here he came a few days later, begging forgiveness. Mom wouldn't open the door, so he pleaded his case through the mail slot, promising to do better, promising to change. Mom stood firm. I, on the other hand, stood bawling like, well ... a kid who missed his Dad. He saw that, and he worked me like a 9-to-5 job.

"Dad, I want you to come home," I wailed.

"I want to," he said, "but your mother won't let me."

So naturally, I turned on her. "Mom, why won't you let Dad come home?"

Still she held out. Finally, he left our door. We knelt on the couch and watched him walk toward the car. Halfway to the curb, though, he was seized by some dark impulse that wheeled him around and sent him hurtling toward the window. I ducked before he kicked it in. Mom didn't.

She took him back not long afterward. And he beat her on a regular basis until the day, about eight years later, terminal cancer rendered him too sick and weak to do so. I've always regretted whatever part my caterwauling played in influencing her to let him come back home.

Ms. Fenty, I know you've got a lot of people in your business right now, all with an opinion about how you should run your life.

I would not be surprised if you are fed up with it. I would only beg you to put that emotion aside and try to hear what you are being told: If this guy did what you say he did, you need to drop him like a hot rock.

"This guy," of course, being your boyfriend, singer Chris Brown. Last week, court papers were released detailing the alleged Feb. 8 altercation between the two of you. They tell how you and Brown, 19, were in a Lamborghini, leaving a music industry party in Beverly Hills, when you confronted him about a text message on his phone from his old girlfriend. How he allegedly told you he was going to beat the expletive deleted out of you when he got you home. How he allegedly pushed your head against the window, punched you with his right fist while steering with his left. How you pretended to be on the phone with your assistant and asked her to call the police. How he said, "You just did the stupidest thing ever! Now I'm really going to kill you!" How he allegedly choked you, threw your phone out the window, put you in a headlock, bit you.

You can understand, perhaps, why many of us find it incomprehensible that you were reportedly spotted with him, apparently reconciled, just days later. Incomprehensible and yet, not surprising at all. On the contrary, it is the classic behavior of the battered woman. They tell themselves it was their fault. They tell themselves it was a one-time thing. They tell themselves he really is a good guy at heart. They tell themselves their love will change him.

They tell themselves lies, Ms. Fenty—lies, evasions and rationalizations. They tell themselves everything but the truth: that the man they love is damaged and dysfunctional. And that, absent some intense and committed therapy, he will do it again.

Repeating for emphasis: He will do it again. And again.

Yes, you're right. I've got a lot of nerve. I don't know you. Indeed, before this incident, I barely knew of you. You are a 21-year-old singer my youngest son has a crush on. My last crush was Gladys Knight.

But this issue strikes a resonant chord with me for obvious reasons. You deserve—every man and woman deserves—to be with someone you don't have to fear, someone who will not abuse, someone who will not resolve quarrels with his fists. Please think about it, Ms. Fenty.

I understand if you love him. But it's OK to love yourself some, too.

MARCH 18, 2009

DON'T EXPECT SYMPATHY CARDS FROM CROOKS, CORRUPT POLITICIANS

On the day the last newspaper is published, I expect no sympathy card from Kwame Kilpatrick. Were it not for a newspaper—the

Detroit Free Press—his use of public funds to cover up his affair with one of his aides would be unrevealed and, he might still be mayor of Detroit.

Nor will I expect flowers from Larry Craig. Were it not for a newspaper—the *Idaho Statesman*—we would not know of his propensity for taking a "wide stance" in airport men's rooms and he might still be serving in the U.S. Senate. And I doubt there will be a toast of commiseration from Reynaldo Diaz and Oscar Rivero. Were it not for a newspaper—the *Miami Herald*—they would still be living large on money scammed from an agency that builds housing for the poor.

In short, the day the last newspaper is published—a day that seems to be rushing at us like a brick wall in an old Warner Bros. cartoon—I will not be surprised if the nation's various crooks, crumbs and corruptors fail to shed a tear. But the unkindest cut of all, the *"Et tu, Brute?"* dagger in the back, is the fact that, according to a new survey from the Pew Project for Excellence in Journalism, most other Americans won't, either. Pew found 63 percent of respondents saying that if their local paper went down, they would miss it very little or not at all.

It is the insult that compounds the injury, by which I mean the growing sense that we are working on the last major story of our lives, and it is an obituary. Ours.

There remain pockets of optimism—Pew's new State of the News Media report says "We still do not subscribe to the theory that the death of the industry is imminent. The industry over all in 2008 remained profitable."—but it is hard to find much reflection of that sunny outlook in the newsroom, as colleagues are shoved unceremoniously into the unemployment line, media giants declare bankruptcy, and century-old papers shut down.

And yes, I know some putative conservatives, displaying their usual delusions of potency, are gloating over all that. These hard times, they feel, are due to people turning against an industry they regard as biased against their ideology. But if that were true, the only papers in trouble would be those that endorsed Kerry over Bush and Obama over McCain.

That is not the case. We are *all* suffering. That's because the industry's decline is not due to ideology but to the fact that it was slow to recognize and react to the threat the Internet represented. So if we die, it will not be at the hands of righteous conservatives, but because we failed to anticipate and strategize.

Which is small comfort. Dead is dead.

And too many of us fail to understand what that death would mean, believe newspapers provide no service they can't get elsewhere. But there is a reason Craig and Kilpatrick were not taken down by CNN or the local TV news. Local TV news specializes in crime, weather and sports. CNN has a national purview. Even the Internet primarily synthesizes reporting done in other media.

No, only the local paper performs the critical function of holding accountable the mayor, the governor, the local magnates and potentates for how they spend your money, run your institutions, validate or violate your trust. If newspapers go, no other entity will have the wherewithal to do that. Which means the next Craig gets away with it. The next Kilpatrick is never caught. The next Diaz and Rivero laugh all the way to the bank. And the next Freddie Pitts and Wilbert Lee, two innocent men saved from Death Row by the indefatigable reporting of the *Miami Herald*'s Gene Miller, are executed.

Sixty-three percent of all Americans think they won't miss the daily paper? I think 63 percent of all Americans are wrong.

ABOUT THE AUTHOR

LEONARD PITTS, JR. won the 2004 Pulitzer Prize for commentary for his syndicated column, which appears in more than 200 newspapers, and has won numerous other journalism awards. Born and raised in Southern California, he now lives in suburban Washington, DC, with his wife and children. He is the author of the nonfiction title *Becoming Dad* (Agate, 2006) and the novel *Before I Forget* (Agate Bolden, 2009).

Before I Forget

An Agate Bolden Trade Paperback Original • $16 • 978-1-932841-43-5

Praise for Leonard Pitts, Jr. and *Before I Forget*

"A powerful novel about regrets, second chances, forgiveness and responsibility....This is a beautiful, tragic and riveting work."
Marilyn Dahl, *Shelf Awareness*

"An unsettling, compelling first novel about secrets, illness, and the role of African-American men in society and family life. ...Bold in spirit and scope, this is a rare, memorable debut that should net Pitts a wide new expanse of fans."
Publishers Weekly

Printed in the USA
CPSIA information can be obtained
at www.ICGtesting.com
JSHW011942151223
53808JS00002B/2